T0273778

Polygon Mesh Processing

Polygon Mesh Processing

Mario Botsch
Leif Kobbelt
Mark Pauly
Pierre Alliez
Bruno Lévy

CRC Press
Taylor & Francis Group
Boca Raton London New York

CRC Press is an imprint of the
Taylor & Francis Group, an **informa** business

AN A K PETERS BOOK

CRC Press
Taylor & Francis Group
6000 Broken Sound Parkway NW, Suite 300
Boca Raton, FL 33487-2742

© 2010 by Taylor & Francis Group, LLC
CRC Press is an imprint of Taylor & Francis Group, an Informa business

No claim to original U.S. Government works

Visit the Taylor & Francis Web site at
http://www.taylorandfrancis.com

and the CRC Press Web site at
http://www.crcpress.com

CONTENTS

Preface   ix

1 Surface Representations   1

1.1 Surface Definition and Properties   3
1.2 Approximation Power   5
1.3 Parametric Surface Representations   7
1.4 Implicit Surface Representations 13
1.5 Conversion Methods 15
1.6 Summary and Further Reading 20

2 Mesh Data Structures   21

2.1 Face-Based Data Structures 22
2.2 Edge-Based Data Structures 24
2.3 Halfedge-Based Data Structure 25
2.4 Directed-Edge Data Structure 27
2.5 Summary and Further Reading 28

3 Differential Geometry   29

3.1 Curves 29
3.2 Surfaces 31
3.3 Discrete Differential Operators 40
3.4 Summary and Further Reading 48

4 Smoothing   49
4.1   Fourier Transform and Manifold Harmonics   50
4.2   Diffusion Flow   54
4.3   Fairing   57
4.4   Summary and Further Reading   61

5 Parameterization   63
5.1   General Goals   64
5.2   Parameterization of a Triangulated Surface   66
5.3   Barycentric Mapping   67
5.4   Conformal Mapping   71
5.5   Methods Based on Distortion Analysis   78
5.6   Summary and Further Reading   82

6 Remeshing   85
6.1   Local Structure   86
6.2   Global Structure   87
6.3   Correspondences   89
6.4   Voronoi Diagrams and Delaunay Triangulations   89
6.5   Triangle-Based Remeshing   92
6.6   Quad-dominant Remeshing   104
6.7   Summary and Further Reading   110

7 Simplification & Approximation   111
7.1   Vertex Clustering   113
7.2   Incremental Decimation   115
7.3   Shape Approximation   122
7.4   Out-of-Core Methods   127
7.5   Summary and Further Reading   130

8 Model Repair   131
8.1   Types of Artifacts: The "Freak Show"   132
8.2   Types of Repair Algorithms   132
8.3   Types of Input   135
8.4   Surface-Oriented Algorithms   139
8.5   Volumetric Repair Algorithms   144
8.6   Summary and Further Reading   150

9 Deformation   151
9.1   Transformation Propagation   153
9.2   Shell-Based Deformation   155
9.3   Multi-Scale Deformation   157
9.4   Differential Coordinates   164

9.5   Freeform Deformation   169
9.6   Radial Basis Functions   173
9.7   Limitations of Linear Methods   175
9.8   Summary and Further Reading   177

A Numerics   181
A.1   Discretizing Poisson and Laplace Equations   181
A.2   Data Structures for Sparse Matrices   184
A.3   Iterative Solvers   187
A.4   Sparse Direct Cholesky Solver   193
A.5   Non-Symmetric Indefinite Systems   196
A.6   Comparison   197

Bibliography   203

Index   226

PREFACE

Recent innovation in 3D acquisition technology, such as computer tomography, magnetic resonance imaging, 3D laser scanning, ultrasound, radar, and microscopy has enabled highly accurate digitization of complex 3D objects. Numerous scientific disciplines, such as neuroscience, mechanical engineering, and astrophysics, rely on the analysis and processing of such geometric data to understand intricate geometric structures and facilitate new scientific discoveries. A similar abundance of digital 3D content can be observed in other fields and industries, including entertainment, cultural heritage, geo-exploration, architecture, and urban modeling. Concurrent to these advances in 3D sensing technology, we are experiencing a revolution in digital manufacturing technology (e.g., in bio-medicine, commodity product design, and architecture). Novel materials and robotic production will soon allow the automated creation of complex, fully functional physical artifacts from a digital design plan.

Between acquisition and production lies the discipline of *digital geometry processing*, a relatively new field of computer science that is concerned with mathematical models and algorithms for analyzing and manipulating geometric data. Typical operations include surface reconstruction from point samples, filtering operations for noise removal, geometry analysis, shape simplification, and geometric modeling and interactive design. The abundance of data sources, processing operations, and manufacturing technologies has resulted in a great wealth of mathematical representations for geometric data. In this context, polygon meshes have become increasingly popular in recent years and are nowadays used intensively in many different areas of computer graphics and geometry processing. In computer-aided geometric design (CAGD), triangle and polygon meshes have developed into a valuable alternative to traditional spline surfaces since their conceptual simplicity allows for flexible and highly efficient processing. Moreover, the consequent use of polygon meshes as a surface representation avoids error-prone conversions (e.g., from CAD surfaces to mesh-based input data of numerical simulations). Besides classical geometric modeling, other major areas frequently employing polygon meshes are computer games and movie production. In this context, geometric models acquired by 3D scanning techniques typically have to undergo postprocessing and shape optimization techniques before being used in production.

This book discusses the main components of the geometry processing pipeline based on polygon meshes, as illustrated on the right. For the instructive purposes of this book, the order in which topics are described deviates somewhat from the typical processing order shown in the figure. We first discuss general concepts of surface representations in Chapter 1 and highlight the advantageous properties of polygon meshes for digital geometry processing. Chapter 2 presents efficient data structures for the implementation of polygon meshes. Chapter 3 introduces fundamental concepts of differential geometry and gives derivations for their discrete analogs. These form the basis of algorithms for mesh smoothing (Chapter 4) to reduce noise in scanned surfaces by generalizing signal processing techniques to irregular polygon meshes. Chapter 5 introduces different methods for computing surface parameterizations that are essential in many geometry processing tasks. General

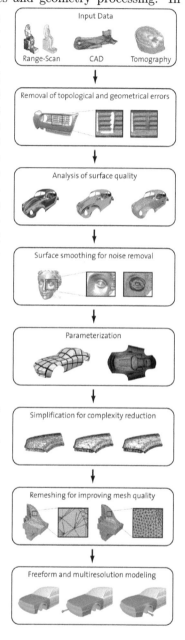

Figure 1. Geometry processing pipeline. (Image from [Botsch et al. 06b].)

remeshing methods (Chapter 6) allow optimizing the shape of triangle or polygon elements, which is important for the robustness of numerical simulations and further processing operations. Mesh simplification and approximation techniques (Chapter 7) are commonly required for error-controlled simplification of highly complex meshes acquired by 3D scanning or automatically generated along the processing pipeline. Chapter 8 describes the different sources of input data and introduces different types of geometric and topological degeneracies and inconsistencies. We discuss methods for removing these artifacts, resulting in defect-free 2-manifold meshes suitable for further processing. Chapter 9 presents techniques for intuitive and interactive shape deformation. Since linear systems appear in many of the presented mesh processing algorithms, in the appendix we describe efficient algorithms for solving linear systems and compare several existing libraries.

The idea for this book originated from a series of tutorials and courses on mesh processing and geometric modeling. In 2006, Mario and Mark organized and taught a course on polygon mesh processing for industry practitioners at ETH Zurich. The same year, Leif, as well as Christian Rössl and Stephan Bischoff, joined them for two full-day tutorials at ACM SIGGRAPH and Eurographics, respectively. The syllabus was restructured for courses at SIGGRAPH 2007 and Eurographics 2008, with Pierre and Bruno replacing Christian and Stephan as presenters.

Our thanks go to Christian Rössl and Stephan Bischoff for their contributions to the early versions of the course, to Henrik Zimmer for help with the book cover model, and to Silke Kölsch for proofreading the text. We are immensely grateful to Alice Peters of A K Peters for her encouragement, advice, and patience, to Sarah Cutler for the excellent editing, and the entire A K Peters team for their support. This book would not have been possible without the contributions of our numerous scientific collaborators and colleagues who helped shape the field of polygon mesh processing. Last but not least, a big thanks to our students. Their questions and feedback have been immensely valuable for refining the material of the book, and their enthusiasm has been the ultimate source of motivation for this project.

SURFACE REPRESENTATIONS

Geometry processing is mostly about applying algorithms to geometric models. If the algorithms represent the *action*, then the geometry is the *object*. In this section we are going to discuss various mathematical representations for geometric objects. While these representations can be 2D or 3D, the actual geometry that we are dealing with will always be the 2D surface of a 3D solid object. As we will see throughout this book, for each specific problem in geometry processing, we can identify a characteristic set of operations by which the computation is dominated, and hence we have to choose an appropriate representation that supports the efficient implementation of these operations.

From a high-level point of view, there are two major classes of surface representations: *parametric* representations and *implicit* representations. Parametric surfaces are defined by a vector-valued parameterization function $\mathbf{f} \colon \Omega \to \mathcal{S}$ that maps a 2D parameter domain $\Omega \subset \mathbb{R}^2$ to the surface $\mathcal{S} = \mathbf{f}(\Omega) \subset \mathbb{R}^3$. In contrast, an implicit (or volumetric) surface representation is defined to be the zero set of a scalar-valued function $F \colon \mathbb{R}^3 \to \mathbb{R}$, i.e., $\mathcal{S} = \{\mathbf{x} \in \mathbb{R}^3 \mid F(\mathbf{x}) = 0\}$.

For illustration, we can define curves analogously in a parametric fashion by functions $\mathbf{f} \colon \Omega \to \mathcal{C}$ with $\Omega = [a, b] \subset \mathbb{R}$. A corresponding implicit definition is only available for *planar* curves, i.e., $\mathcal{C} = \{\mathbf{x} \in \mathbb{R}^2 \mid F(\mathbf{x}) = 0\}$ with $F \colon \mathbb{R}^2 \to \mathbb{R}$. A simple 2D example is the unit circle, which can be defined by the range of a parametric function

$$\mathbf{f}\colon [0, 2\pi] \to \mathbb{R}^2, \quad t \mapsto \begin{pmatrix} \cos t \\ \sin t \end{pmatrix},$$

as well as by the kernel of the implicit function

$$F\colon \mathbb{R}^2 \to \mathbb{R}, \quad (x, y) \mapsto \sqrt{x^2 + y^2} - 1.$$

Similarly, in 3D, a sphere can be represented by a parametric or an implicit equation (see Section 3.2 for more details).

For more complex shapes, it is often not feasible to find an explicit formulation with a single function that approximates a given shape with sufficient accuracy. Hence, the function domain is usually split into smaller sub-regions and an individual function (*surface patch*) is defined for each segment. In this *piecewise* definition, each function needs to approximate the given shape only locally, while the global approximation tolerance is controlled by the size and number of the segments. The mathematical challenge is to guarantee a consistent transition from each patch to its neighboring ones. The most common piecewise surface definition in the parametric case is the segmentation of Ω into triangles or quadrangles. For implicit surface definitions, the embedding space is usually split into hexahedral (*voxels*) or tetrahedral cells.

Both parametric and implicit representations have their particular strengths and weaknesses, such that for each geometric problem the better suited one should be chosen. In order to analyze geometric operations and their requirements on the surface representation, one can classify them into the following three categories [Kobbelt 03]:

▶ Evaluation. This entails the sampling of the surface geometry or of other surface attributes, e.g., the surface normal field. A typical application example is surface rendering.

▶ Query. Spatial queries are used to determine whether or not a given point $\mathbf{p} \in \mathbb{R}^3$ is inside or outside of the solid bounded by a surface $\mathcal{S}$, which is a key component for solid modeling operations. Another typical query is the computation of a point's distance to a surface.

▶ Modification. A surface can be modified either in terms of *geometry* (surface deformation) or in terms of *topology* (e.g., when different parts of the surface are to be merged, cut, or deleted).

We will see that parametric and implicit surface representations have complementary advantages with respect to these three types of geometric operations, i.e., the strengths in terms of efficiency or robustness of the one are often the drawbacks of the other. Hence, for each specific geometric problem, the more suitable representation should be chosen, which, in turn, requires efficient conversion routines between the two representations (see Section 1.5). In Section 1.6 we present an outlook to approaches that combine both representations in order to design algorithms that are both efficient and robust.

1.1   Surface Definition and Properties

The common definition of a *surface* in the context of computer graphics applications is "an orientable continuous 2D manifold embedded in $\mathbb{R}^3$." Intuitively, this can be understood as the boundary surface of a non-degenerate 3D solid where *non-degenerate* means that the solid does not have any infinitely thin parts or features such that the surface properly separates the "interior" and "exterior" of the solid (see Figure 1.1). A surface with boundaries is one that can be extended into a proper manifold surface by filling the holes.

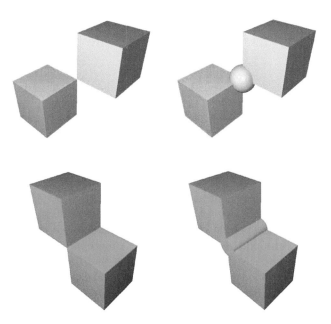

Figure 1.1. An orientable continuous 2-manifold describes the surface of a non-degenerate solid. A degenerate/non-manifold vertex (top left), which is fixed in (top right). A solid with a degenerate/non-manifold edge (bottom left), fixed in (bottom right).

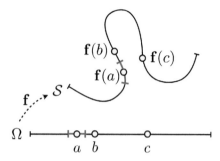

Figure 1.2.   A manifold curve. While the points $\mathbf{f}(a)$, $\mathbf{f}(b)$, and $\mathbf{f}(c)$ are all in close *spatial* proximity, only $\mathbf{f}(a)$ and $\mathbf{f}(b)$ are *geodesic* neighbors since their pre-images a and b are neighbors, too. In red: The pre-image of a sufficiently small δ neighborhood around $\mathbf{f}(a)$ in $\mathbb{R}^2$ lies in an ε neighborhood of a in $\mathbb{R}$.

Since in most applications the raw information about the input surface is obtained by discrete sampling (i.e., by *evaluation* if there already exists a digital representation, or by *probing* if the input comes from a real object), the first step in generating a mathematical surface representation is to establish *continuity*. This requires building a consistent neighborhood relation between the samples. In this context, *consistency* refers to the existence of a manifold surface from which the samples are drawn.

While this so-called *geodesic* neighborhood relation (in contrast to a *spatial* neighborhood relation) is difficult to access in implicit representations, it is quite easy to extract from parametric representations in which two points on the surface are in geodesic proximity, if the corresponding pre-images in Ω are close to each other (see Figure 1.2). From this observation we can derive an alternative characterization of *local manifoldness*: a continuous parametric surface is locally manifold at a surface point $\mathbf{p}$ if, for every other surface point $\mathbf{q}$ within a sufficiently small sphere of radius δ around $\mathbf{p}$, the corresponding pre-image is contained in a circle of some radius $\varepsilon = O(\delta)$ around the pre-image of $\mathbf{p}$. A more intuitive way to express this condition is to say that the surface patch that lies within a sufficiently small δ-sphere around $\mathbf{p}$ is topologically equivalent (homeomorphic) to a disk. Since this second definition does not require a parameterization, it applies to implicit representations as well.

When generating a continuous surface from a set of discrete samples, we can either require this surface to *interpolate* the samples or to *approximate* them subject to a certain prescribed tolerance. The latter case is considered more relevant in practical applications, since samples are usually affected by position noise and the surface in between the samples is an approximation

Figure 1.3. Three examples of fair surfaces, which define a blend between two cylinders: a membrane surface that minimizes the surface area (left), a thin-plate surface that minimizes total curvature (center), and a surface that minimizes the variation of mean curvature (right). (Image taken from [Botsch and Kobbelt 04a]. ©2004 ACM, Inc. Included here by permission.)

anyway. In the next section we will consider the issue of approximation in more detail.

Except for a well-defined set of sharp feature-curves and -corners, a surface should be *smooth* in general. Mathematically this is measured by the number k of continuous derivatives that the functions $\mathbf{f}$ or F have. Notice that this analytical definition of C^k smoothness coincides with the intuitive geometrical understanding of smoothness only if the partial derivatives of $\mathbf{f}$ or the gradient of F, respectively, do not vanish locally (*regularity*).

An even stricter requirement for surfaces is *fairness*, where not only the continuity of the derivatives but also their magnitude and variation is considered. There is no general formal definition for the aesthetic concept of fairness, but a surface is usually considered fair if, e.g., the curvature or its variation is globally minimized (see Figure 1.3).

In Chapter 3 we will explain how the notion of curvature can be generalized to polygon meshes such that properties like smoothness and fairness can be applied to meshes as well (see Chapter 4).

1.2   Approximation Power

The exact mathematical modeling of a real object or its boundary is usually intractable. Hence, a digital surface representation can only be an approximation in general. As mentioned in the introduction, in order to simplify the approximation tasks, the domain of the representation is often split into small segments, and for each segment a function (a patch) is defined that locally approximates the part of the input that belongs to the segment.

Since our surface representations are supposed to support efficient processing, a natural choice is to restrict functions to the class of *polynomials* because those can be evaluated by elementary arithmetic operations. Another justification for the restriction to polynomials is the well-known *Weierstrass theorem* that guarantees that each smooth function can be approximated by a polynomial up to any desired precision [Ross 80].

From calculus we know that a C^∞ function g with bounded derivatives can be approximated over an interval of length h by a polynomial of degree p such that the approximation error behaves like $O(h^{p+1})$ (e.g., Taylor's theorem or generalized mean value theorem) [Rudin 02]. As a consequence there are, in principle, two possibilities to improve the accuracy of an approximation with piecewise polynomials. We can either raise the degree of the polynomial (*p-refinement*) or we can reduce the size of the individual segments and use more segments for the approximation (*h-refinement*).

In geometry processing applications, h-refinement is usually preferred over p-refinement since, for a discretely sampled input surface, we cannot make reasonable assumptions about the boundedness of higher-order derivatives. Moreover, for piecewise polynomials with higher degree, the C^k smoothness conditions between segments are sometimes quite difficult to satisfy. Finally, with today's computer architectures, processing a large number of very simple objects is often much more efficient than processing a smaller number of more complex ones. This is why the somewhat extremal choice of C^0 piecewise linear surface representations, i.e., *polygonal meshes*, have become the widely established standard in geometry processing.

While, for parametric surfaces, the $O(h^{p+1})$ approximation error estimate follows from the mean value theorem in a straightforward manner, a more careful consideration is necessary for implicit representations. The generalized mean value theorem states that if a sufficiently smooth function g over an interval $[a, a+h]$ is interpolated at the abscissae $t_0, \ldots, t_p$ by a polynomial f of degree p, then the approximation error is bounded by

$$|f(t) - g(t)| \leq \frac{1}{(p+1)!} \max f^{(p+1)} \prod_{i=0}^{p} (t_i - t) = O(h^{p+1}).$$

For an implicit representation $G \colon \mathbb{R}^3 \to \mathbb{R}$ and the corresponding polynomial approximant F, this theorem is still valid; however, here the actual surface geometry is not defined by the function values $G(\mathbf{x})$, for which this theorem gives an error estimate, but by the zero level set of G, i.e., by $\mathcal{S} = \{\mathbf{x} \in \mathbb{R}^3 \mid G(\mathbf{x}) = 0\}$.

Consider a point $\mathbf{x}$ on the implicit surface defined by the approximating polynomial F, i.e., $F(\mathbf{x}) = 0$ within some voxel. We can find a corresponding point $\mathbf{x} + \mathbf{d}$ on the implicit surface defined by G, i.e., $G(\mathbf{x} + \mathbf{d}) = 0$ by shooting a ray in normal direction to F, i.e., $\mathbf{d} = d\,\nabla F/\|\nabla F\|$. For a sufficiently small voxel size h, we obtain

$$|F(\mathbf{x} + \mathbf{d})| \ \approx \ |d| \ \|\nabla F(\mathbf{x})\| \quad \Rightarrow \quad |d| \ \approx \ \frac{|F(\mathbf{x} + \mathbf{d})|}{\|\nabla F(\mathbf{x})\|},$$

and from the mean value theorem we get

$$|F(\mathbf{x} + \mathbf{d}) - G(\mathbf{x} + \mathbf{d})| \ = \ |F(\mathbf{x} + \mathbf{d})| \ = \ O(h^{p+1}),$$

which yields $|d| = O(h^{p+1})$ if the magnitude of the gradient $\|\nabla F\|$ is bounded from below by some $\varepsilon > 0$. In practice one tries to find an approximating polynomial F with low variation of the gradient magnitude in order to have a uniform distribution of the approximation error.

1.3 Parametric Surface Representations

Parametric surface representations have the advantage that the function $\mathbf{f} : \Omega \to \mathcal{S}$ enables the reduction of many 3D problems on the surface $\mathcal{S}$ to 2D problems in the parameter domain Ω. For instance, sample points on the surface can easily be generated by sampling the domain Ω and evaluating the function $\mathbf{f}$. In a similar manner, geodesic neighborhoods, i.e., neighborhoods on the surface $\mathcal{S}$, can easily be found by considering neighboring points in the parameter domain Ω. A simple composition of $\mathbf{f}$ with a deformation function $\mathbf{d} : \mathbb{R}^3 \to \mathbb{R}^3$ results in an efficient modification of the surface geometry.

On the other hand, generating a parametric surface parameterization $\mathbf{f}$ can be very complex, since the parameter domain Ω has to match the topological and metric structure of the surface $\mathcal{S}$ (Chapter 5). When changing the shape of $\mathcal{S}$, it might be necessary to update the parameterization accordingly in order to reflect the respective changes of the underlying geometry: a low-distortion parameterization requires the metrics in $\mathcal{S}$ and Ω to be similar, and hence we have to avoid or adapt to excessive stretching.

Since the manifold surface $\mathcal{S}$ is defined as the range of the parameterization $\mathbf{f}$, its topology is equivalent to that of Ω if $\mathbf{f}$ is continuous and injective. This implies that changing the topology of a parametric surface $\mathcal{S}$ can be extremely complicated because not only the parameterization but also the domain Ω has to be adjusted accordingly. The typical inside/outside or signed distance queries are, in general, also very expensive on parametric surfaces since they usually require finding the closest point on $\mathcal{S}$ to the query point (*foot point*). The same applies to the detection of self-collisions (i.e., non-injectivities). Hence, topological modification and spatial queries are the weak points of parametric surfaces.

1.3.1 Spline Surfaces

Tensor-product spline surfaces—often called NURBS—are the standard surface representation in today's CAD systems. They are used for constructing high-quality surfaces ("class A") as well as for freeform surface editing tasks. Spline surfaces can be described conveniently by piecewise polynomial or rational B-spline basis functions $N_i^n(\cdot)$. For more detail, see e.g., [Farin 97, Piegl and Tiller 97, Prautzsch et al. 02].

A tensor product spline surface $\mathbf{f}$ of bi-degree n is a piecewise polynomial surface that is built by connecting several polynomial patches in a smooth C^{n-1} manner. The rectangular segments are defined by two knot vectors $\{u_0, \ldots, u_{m+n}\}$ and $\{v_0, \ldots, v_{k+n}\}$ and the overall surface is then obtained by

$$\mathbf{f} \colon [u_n, u_m] \times [v_n, v_k] \quad \to \quad \mathbb{R}^3 \tag{1.1}$$

$$(u, v) \quad \mapsto \quad \sum_{i=0}^{m} \sum_{j=0}^{k} \mathbf{c}_{ij} N_i^n(u) N_j^n(v). \tag{1.2}$$

The *control points* $\mathbf{c}_{ij} \in \mathbb{R}^3$ define the so-called *control mesh* of the spline surface. Because $N_i^n(u) \geq 0$ and $\sum_i N_i^n \equiv 1$, each surface point $\mathbf{f}(u, v)$ is a convex combination of the control points $\mathbf{c}_{ij}$; i.e., the surface lies within the convex hull of the control mesh. Due to the minimal support of the basis functions, each control point has local influence only. These two properties cause spline surfaces to closely follow the control mesh, thereby providing a geometrically intuitive metaphor for modeling the shape of surfaces by adjusting their control points.

A tensor-product surface—as the image of a rectangular domain under the parameterization $\mathbf{f}$—always represents a rectangular surface patch embedded in $\mathbb{R}^3$. If shapes of more complicated topological structure are to be represented by spline surfaces, the model has to be decomposed into a number of (possibly trimmed) tensor-product patches.

As a consequence of these *topological constraints*, typical CAD models often consist of a huge collection of surface patches. In order to represent a high-quality, globally smooth surface, these patches have to be connected in a smooth manner, leading to additional *geometric constraints* that have to be taken care of throughout all surface processing phases. The large number of surface patches and the resulting topological and geometric constraints significantly complicate surface construction, and in particular the later surface modeling tasks.

Another drawback of classical tensor-product spline representations is that adding more control vertices (*refinement*) is only possible by splitting parameter intervals $[u_i, u_{i+1}]$ or $[v_j, v_{j+1}]$, which affects an entire row or column of the control mesh, respectively. Here, the alternative representation by *T-splines* can improve the situation since they enable the local refinement of the control mesh [Sederberg et al. 03].

1.3.2 Subdivision Surfaces

Subdivision surfaces [Zorin et al. 00] can be considered a generalization of spline surfaces since they are also controlled by a coarse *control mesh*, but in contrast to spline surfaces, they can represent surfaces of arbitrary topology. Subdivision surfaces are generated by repeated refinement of control meshes: after each topological refinement step, the positions of the (old and new) vertices are adjusted based on a set of local averaging rules (see Figure 1.4). A careful analysis of these rules reveals that in the limit this process results in a surface of provable smoothness [Peters and Reif 08].

As a consequence, subdivision surfaces are restricted neither by topological (other than manifoldness) nor by geometric constraints as spline surfaces are, and their inherent hierarchical structure allows for highly efficient algorithms. However, subdivision techniques are limited to producing meshes with so-called semiregular *subdivision connectivity*, i.e., surface meshes whose triangulations are the result of repeated uniform refinement of a coarse control mesh. As this constraint is not met by arbitrary meshes, those would have to be *remeshed* to subdivision connectivity in a

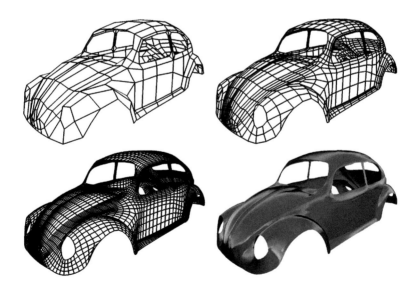

Figure 1.4. Subdivision surfaces are generated by iterative uniform refinement of a coarse control mesh. (Image taken from [Botsch 05].)

preprocessing step [Eck et al. 95, Lee et al. 98, Kobbelt et al. 99a, Guskov et al. 00]. But, since this remeshing corresponds to a resampling of the surface, it usually leads to sampling artifacts and loss of information. In order to avoid the restrictions caused by these *connectivity constraints*, our goal is to work on arbitrary triangle meshes, as they provide higher flexibility and still allow for efficient surface processing.

1.3.3 Triangle Meshes

In many geometry processing algorithms, *triangle meshes* are considered a collection of triangles without any particular mathematical structure. In principle, however, each triangle defines, via its barycentric parameterization, a segment of a piecewise linear surface representation.

Every point $\mathbf{p}$ in the interior of a triangle $[\mathbf{a}, \mathbf{b}, \mathbf{c}]$ can be written in a unique fashion as a barycentric combination of the corner points:

$$\mathbf{p} = \alpha\,\mathbf{a} + \beta\,\mathbf{b} + \gamma\,\mathbf{c}, \tag{1.3}$$

with

$$\alpha + \beta + \gamma = 1, \quad \alpha, \beta, \gamma \geq 0.$$

By choosing an arbitrary triangle $[\mathbf{u}, \mathbf{v}, \mathbf{w}]$ in the parameter domain, we can define a linear mapping $\mathbf{f} : \mathbb{R}^2 \to \mathbb{R}^3$ with

$$\alpha\,\mathbf{u} + \beta\,\mathbf{v} + \gamma\,\mathbf{w} \quad \mapsto \quad \alpha\,\mathbf{a} + \beta\,\mathbf{b} + \gamma\,\mathbf{c}. \tag{1.4}$$

Based on this per-triangle mapping, it is sufficient to define a 2D position for each vertex in order to derive a global parameterization for an entire triangle mesh. In Chapter 5 we will discuss sophisticated methods for choosing this triangulation in the parameter domain such that the distortion caused by the piecewise linear mapping from $\mathbb{R}^2$ to $\mathbb{R}^3$ is minimized.

A triangle mesh $\mathcal{M}$ consists of a geometric and a topological component, where the latter can be represented by a graph structure (simplicial complex) with a set of vertices

$$\mathcal{V} = \{v_1, \ldots, v_V\}$$

and a set of triangular faces connecting them

$$\mathcal{F} = \{f_1, \ldots, f_F\}, \quad f_i \in \mathcal{V} \times \mathcal{V} \times \mathcal{V}.$$

However, as we will see in Chapter 2, it is sometimes more efficient to represent the connectivity of a triangle mesh in terms of the edges of the respective graph,

$$\mathcal{E} = \{e_1, \ldots, e_E\}, \quad e_i \in \mathcal{V} \times \mathcal{V}.$$

The geometric embedding of a triangle mesh into $\mathbb{R}^3$ is specified by associating a 3D position $\mathbf{p}_i$ to each vertex $v_i \in \mathcal{V}$:

$$\mathcal{P} = \{\mathbf{p}_1, \ldots, \mathbf{p}_V\}, \quad \mathbf{p}_i := \mathbf{p}(v_i) = \begin{pmatrix} x(v_i) \\ y(v_i) \\ z(v_i) \end{pmatrix} \in \mathbb{R}^3,$$

such that each face $f \in \mathcal{F}$ actually corresponds to a triangle in 3-space specified by its three vertex positions. Notice that even if the geometric embedding is defined by assigning 3D positions to the *discrete* vertices, the resulting polygonal surface is still a *continuous* surface consisting of triangular pieces with linear parameterization functions (Equation (1.4)).

If a sufficiently smooth surface is approximated by such a piecewise linear function, the approximation error is of the order $O(h^2)$, with h denoting the maximum edge length. Due to this quadratic approximation power, the error is reduced by a factor of about $1/4$ when halving the edge lengths. As this refinement splits each triangle into four sub-triangles, it increases the number of triangles from F to $4F$ (see Figure 1.5). Hence, the approximation error of a triangle mesh is inversely proportional to its number of faces. The actual magnitude of the approximation error depends on the second-order terms of the Taylor expansion, i.e., on the curvature of the underlying smooth surface. From this we can conclude that a sufficient approximation is possible with just a moderate mesh complexity: the vertex density has to be locally adapted to the surface curvature, such that flat areas are sparsely sampled, while in curved regions the sampling density is higher.

As stated before, an important topological quality of a surface is whether or not it is *2-manifold* (short for *two-dimensional manifold*), which is the case if, for each point, the surface is locally homeomorphic to a disk (or a half-disk at boundaries). A triangle mesh is a 2-manifold if it contains neither non-manifold edges nor non-manifold vertices nor self-intersections. A *non-manifold edge* has more than two incident triangles and a *non-manifold*

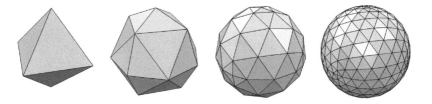

Figure 1.5. Each subdivision step halves the edge lengths, increases the number of faces by a factor of 4, and reduces the approximation error by a factor of about $\frac{1}{4}$. (Image taken from [Botsch et al. 06b].)

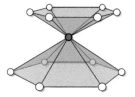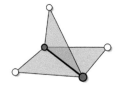

Figure 1.6. Two surface sheets meet at a non-manifold vertex (left). A non-manifold edge has more than two incident faces (center). The right configuration, although being non-manifold in the strict sense, can be handled by most data structures (see Chapter 2). (Image taken from [Botsch 05].)

vertex is generated by pinching two surface sheets together at that vertex such that the vertex is incident to more than one fan of triangles (see Figure 1.6). Non-manifold meshes are problematic for most algorithms, since around non-manifold configurations there exists no well-defined local geodesic neighborhood.

The famous *Euler formula* [Coxeter 89] states an interesting relation between the numbers of vertices V, edges E, and faces F in a closed and connected (but otherwise unstructured) mesh:

$$V - E + F = 2(1 - g), \tag{1.5}$$

where g is the *genus* of the surface and intuitively counts the number of handles of an object (see Figure 1.7). Since for most practical applications the genus is small compared to the number of elements, the righthand side of Equation (1.5) can be assumed to be negligible. Given this and the fact that each triangle is bounded by three edges and that each interior manifold edge is incident to two triangles, one can derive the following interesting mesh statistics:

Figure 1.7. A sphere of genus 0 (left), a torus of genus 1 (center), and a double-torus of genus 2 (right). (Image taken from [Botsch et al. 06b].)

▶ The number of triangles is twice the number of vertices: $F \approx 2V$.

▶ The number of edges is three times the number of vertices: $E \approx 3V$.

▶ The average vertex valence (number of incident edges) is 6.

These relations will become important when estimating the runtime complexity of mesh processing algorithms and when analyzing data structures or file formats for triangle meshes in Chapter 2.

1.4   Implicit Surface Representations

The basic concept of *implicit* or *volumetric* representations for geometric models is to characterize the whole embedding space of an object by classifying each 3D point to lie either inside, outside, or exactly on the surface $\mathcal{S}$ that bounds a solid object.

There are different representations for implicit functions, such as algebraic surfaces, radial basis functions, or discrete voxelizations. In any case, the surface $\mathcal{S}$ is defined to be the zero-level isosurface of a scalar-valued function $F \colon \mathbb{R}^3 \to \mathbb{R}$. By convention, negative function values of F designate points inside the object and positive value points outside the object. The zero-level isosurface $\mathcal{S}$ contains the points exactly *on* the surface, separating the inside from the outside. An implicit surface does not have any holes as long as the defining function F is continuous. Moreover, since an implicit surface is a level set of a potential function, geometric self-intersections cannot occur. This will later be exploited for mesh repair (Chapter 8).

As a consequence, geometric inside/outside queries simplify to function evaluations of F and checking the sign of the resulting value. This makes implicit representations well suited for constructive solid geometry (CSG), where complex objects are constructed by Boolean operations applied to geometric primitives (see Figure 1.8). The different Boolean operations

Figure 1.8. A complex object constructed by Boolean operations. (Image taken from [Botsch et al. 06b].)

can easily be computed by *min* and *max* combinations of the individual primitives' implicit functions.

Implicit surfaces can be deformed by decreasing (= growing) or increasing (= shrinking) the function values of F locally. Since the structure of F (e.g., the voxel grid) is independent from the topology of the level-set surface, we can easily change the surface topology and connectivity.

The implicit function F for a given surface $\mathcal{S}$ is not uniquely determined since, e.g., any scalar multiple λF yields the same zero-set. However, the most common and most natural representation is the so-called *signed distance function*, which maps each 3D point $\mathbf{x}$ to its signed distance $d(\mathbf{x})$ from the surface $\mathcal{S}$: the absolute value $|d(\mathbf{x})|$ measures the distance of $\mathbf{x}$ to $\mathcal{S}$; the sign indicates whether the point $\mathbf{x}$ is inside or outside of the solid bounded by $\mathcal{S}$. In addition to inside/outside queries, this representation also simplifies distance computations to simple function evaluations, which can be used to compute and control the global error for mesh processing algorithms [Wu and Kobbelt 03, Botsch et al. 04] or for collision detection computations.

On the other hand, generating sample points on an implicit surface, finding geodesic neighborhoods, and even just rendering the surface is relatively difficult. Moreover, implicit surfaces do not provide any means of parameterization, which is why it is very difficult to consistently paste textures onto evolving implicit surfaces.

The most common spatial data structures for implicit surface representations are regular grids and adaptive data structures (discussed below).

1.4.1   Regular Grids

In order to efficiently process implicit representations, the continuous scalar field F is typically discretized in some bounding box around the object using a sufficiently dense grid with nodes $\mathbf{g}_{ijk} \in \mathbb{R}^3$. The most basic representation, therefore, is a uniform scalar grid of sampled values $F_{ijk} := F(\mathbf{g}_{ijk})$, and function values within voxels are derived by trilinear interpolation, thus providing quadratic approximation order. However, the memory consumption of this naive data structure grows cubically if the precision is increased by reducing the edge length of grid voxels.

1.4.2   Adaptive Data Structures

For better memory efficiency, the sampling density is often adapted to the local geometric significance in the scalar field F: since precise signed distance values are most important in the vicinity of the surface, a higher sampling rate has to be used in these regions only. Instead of a uniform 3D grid, a hierarchical octree is then used to store the sampled values [Samet 94]. The further refinement of an octree cell lying completely inside

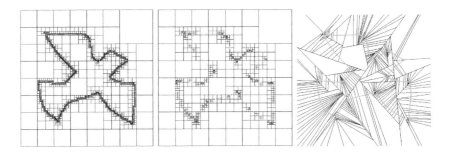

Figure 1.9. Different adaptive approximations of a signed distance field with the same accuracy: three-color quadtree (left, 12040 cells), adaptively sampled distance fields (ADF) [Frisken et al. 00] (center, 895 cells), and binary space partitioning (BSP) tree [Wu and Kobbelt 03] (right, 254 cells). (Image taken from [Wu and Kobbelt 03].)

(black) or outside (white) the object does not improve the approximation of the surface $\mathcal{S}$. Adaptively refining only those cells that are intersected by the surface (grey) yields a uniformly refined crust of leaf cells around the surface and reduces the storage complexity from cubic to quadratic (see Figure 1.9 (left)). This structure is called *three-color octree* because it consists of black, white, and grey cells.

If the local refinement is additionally restricted to those cells where the trilinear interpolant deviates more than a prescribed tolerance from the actual distance field, the resulting approximation adapts to the locality of the surface as well as to its local shape complexity [Frisken et al. 00] (see Figure 1.9 (center)). Since extreme refinement is only necessary in regions of high surface curvature, this approach reduces the storage complexity even further and results in a memory consumption comparable to that of mesh representations.

Similarly, an adaptive binary space-decomposition with linear (instead of trilinear) interpolants at the leaves can be used [Wu and Kobbelt 03]. Although the asymptotic complexity as well as the approximation power are the same, the latter method provides slightly better memory efficiency at the cost of less compact cells (see Figure 1.9 (right)).

1.5 Conversion Methods

In order to exploit the specific advantages of parametric and implicit surface representations, efficient conversion methods between the two are necessary. However, notice that both kinds of representations are usually finite samplings (e.g., triangle meshes in the parametric case, uniform/adaptive grids in the implicit case) and that each conversion corresponds to a re-sampling step. Hence, special care has to be taken in order to minimize loss of information during these conversion routines.

1.5.1   Parametric to Implicit

The conversion of a parametric surface representation to an implicit one amounts to the computation or approximation of its signed distance field. This can be done very efficiently by voxelization or 3D scan-conversion tech-niques [Kaufman 87], but the resulting approximation is piecewise constant only. As a surface's distance field is, in general, not smooth everywhere, a piecewise linear or piecewise trilinear approximation seems to be the best compromise between approximation accuracy and computational efficiency.

Since we focus on polygonal meshes as parametric representation in this book, the conversion to an implicit representation basically requires the computation of signed distances to the triangle mesh at the nodes of a (uniform or adaptive) 3D grid.

Computing the exact distance of a grid node to a given mesh requires to calculate the distance to the closest triangle, which can be found efficiently by using spatial data structures, e.g., kd-trees [Samet 94]. Notice that, in order to compute a *signed* distance field, one additionally has to determine whether a grid node lies inside or outside the object. If $\mathbf{g}$ denotes the grid node and $\mathbf{c}$ its closest point on the surface, then the sign can be derived from the angle between the vector $\mathbf{g} - \mathbf{c}$ and the outer normal $\mathbf{n}(\mathbf{c})$: The point $\mathbf{g}$ is defined to be inside if $(\mathbf{g} - \mathbf{c})^T \mathbf{n}(\mathbf{c}) < 0$. The robustness and reliability of this test strongly depends on the way the normal $\mathbf{n}(\mathbf{c})$ is computed. Using angle-weighted pseudo-normals for faces, edges, and vertices can be shown to yield correct results [Bærentzen and Aanæs 05].

Computing the distances on the entire grid can be accelerated by *fast marching* methods [Sethian 96]. In a first step, the exact signed distance values are computed for all grid nodes in the immediate vicinity of the tri-angle mesh. After this initialization, the fast marching method propagates distances to the remaining grid nodes with unknown distance value in a breadth-first manner.

1.5.2   Implicit to Parametric

The conversion from an implicit or volumetric representation to a trian-gle mesh, the so-called *isosurface extraction*, occurs for instance in CSG modeling (see Figure 1.8) and in medical applications, e.g., to extract the skull surface from a CT head scan. The de-facto standard algorithm for isosurface extraction is *marching cubes* [Lorensen and Cline 87]. This grid-based method samples the implicit function on a regular grid and processes

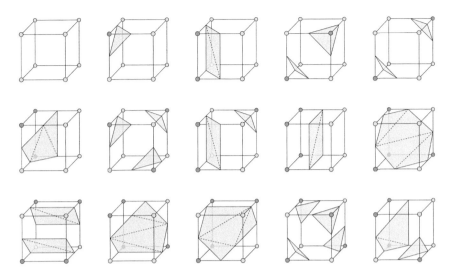

Figure 1.10. The 15 base configurations of the marching cubes triangulation table. The other 241 cases can be found by rotation, reflection, or inversion. (Image taken from [Botsch 05].)

each cell of the discrete distance field separately, thereby allowing for trivial parallelization. For each cell that is intersected by the isosurface $\mathcal{S}$, a surface patch is generated based on local criteria. The collection of all these small pieces eventually yields a triangle mesh approximation of the complete isosurface $\mathcal{S}$.

For each grid edge intersecting the surface $\mathcal{S}$, the marching cubes algorithm computes a sample point that approximates this intersection. In terms of the scalar field F, this means that the sign of F differs at the grid edge's endpoints $\mathbf{p}_1$ and $\mathbf{p}_2$. Since the trilinear approximation F is actually linear along the grid edges, the intersection point $\mathbf{s}$ can be found by linear interpolation of the distance values $d_1 := F(\mathbf{p}_1)$ and $d_2 := F(\mathbf{p}_2)$ at the edge's endpoints:

$$\mathbf{s} = \frac{|d_2|}{|d_1| + |d_2|}\,\mathbf{p}_1 + \frac{|d_1|}{|d_1| + |d_2|}\,\mathbf{p}_2.$$

The resulting sample points of each cell are then connected to a triangulated surface patch based on a triangulation look-up table holding all possible configurations of edge intersections (see Figure 1.10). Since the possible combinatorial configurations are determined by the signs at a cell's corners, their number, and hence the size of the table, is $2^8 = 256$.

Notice that a few cell configurations are ambiguous, which might lead to cracks in the extracted surface. A properly modified look-up table yields a simple and efficient solution, however, at the price of sacrificing the symmetry with regard to sign inversion of F [Montani et al. 94]. The resulting isosurfaces then are watertight 2-manifolds, which is exploited by many mesh repair techniques (Chapter 8).

Marching cubes computes intersection points on the edges of a regular grid only, which causes sharp edges or corners to be "chopped off." A faithful reconstruction of sharp features requires additional sample points within the cells containing them. The Extended Marching Cubes algorithm [Kobbelt et al. 01] therefore examines the distance function's gradient ∇F to detect those cells that contain a sharp feature and to find additional sample points by intersecting the estimated tangent planes at the edge intersection points of the voxel.

This principle is depicted in 2D in Figure 1.11, and a 3D example of the well-known *fandisk* dataset is shown in Figure 1.12. An example implementation of extended marching cubes based on the OpenMesh data structure [Botsch et al. 02] can be downloaded from [Kobbelt et al. 05].

The high triangle complexity of the extracted isosurfaces remains a major problem for marching cubes-like approaches. Instead of decimating the resulting meshes (see Chapter 7) in a post-process, the algorithm can be modified to work directly on adaptively refined octrees [Westermann et al. 99].

Ju et al. [Ju et al. 02] proposed the *dual contouring* approach, which also extracts meshes from adaptive octrees directly. In contrast to marching cubes, dual contouring generates the vertices in the interior of the voxels and constructs a polygon for every voxel edge that intersects the isosurface. A drawback, however, is that the dual approach yields non-manifold meshes for cell configurations containing multiple surface sheets. This can be fixed by the technique described in [Bischoff et al. 05]. Another promising approach is the cubical marching squares algorithm [Ho et al. 05], which also provides adaptive and feature-sensitive isosurface extraction.

Finally, an alternative to marching cubes and its variants consists of refining and filtering a 3D Delaunay triangulation [Boissonnat and Oudot 05]. The resulting surface mesh is shown to contain only well-shaped triangles and faithfully approximates the input surface in terms of both topology and geometry. An example implementation of a Delaunay refinement approach can be downloaded from the website of the Computational Geometry Algorithms Library (CGAL) [CGAL 09].

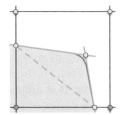 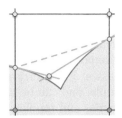

Figure 1.11. By using point and normal information on both sides of the sharp feature, one can find a good estimate for the feature point at the intersection of the tangent elements. The dashed lines are the result the standard marching cubes algorithm would produce, and the bold lines are the tangents used in the extended algorithm. (Image taken from [Botsch 05].)

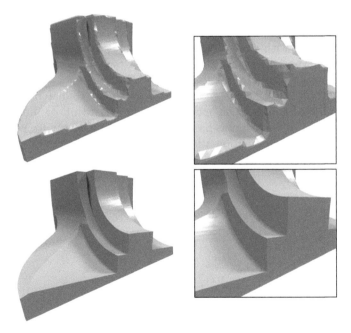

Figure 1.12. Two reconstructions of the fandisk dataset from a $65 \times 65 \times 65$ sampling of its signed distance field. The standard marching cubes algorithm leads to severe alias artifacts near sharp features (top), whereas the feature-sensitive isosurface extraction faithfully reconstructs them (bottom).

1.6   Summary and Further Reading

In this chapter we discussed the advantages and disadvantages of various mathematical geometry representations. The two major concepts of *parametric* vs. *implicit* representations have almost complementary strengths and weaknesses. Parametric surfaces can capture even the finest detail, are easy to sample, and can be modified intuitively but it is difficult to answer distance queries and topological changes require a major restructuring. On the other hand, topological changes and distance queries are easy for implicit surfaces but sampling and shape editing is not straightforward and the geometric detail resolution depends on the voxel size.

There is the approach of *hybrid representations* [Bischoff and Kobbelt 05, Bischoff et al. 05], which merges the two concepts such that the advantages of both can be combined. For example, an adaptive octree with a set of triangles stored in each voxel cell supports efficient distance queries as well as a high detail resolution.

There are many other conversion techniques for further reading. Shen et al. [Shen et al. 04], e.g., have proposed an approach which converts a polygon soup into implicit surfaces, which can range from interpolating to approximating with adjustable smoothness and tolerance.

Besides the approaches described here, which are most relevant for the techniques presented in this book, there are many other representations suitable for efficient geometry processing. Radial basis functions [Light 92] are a prominent example, as are partition of unity implicits [Ohtake et al. 03] and point-based representations [Pauly 03, Kobbelt and Botsch 04]—just to mention a few.

MESH DATA STRUCTURES

The efficiency and memory consumption of the geometric modeling algorithms presented in this book largely depend on the underlying surface mesh data structures. This chapter provides a brief overview of the most common data structures of the wide variety described in the literature.

Choosing a mesh data structure requires taking into account topological as well as algorithmic considerations:

▶ Topological requirements. Which kinds of meshes need to be represented by the data structure? Can we rely on 2-manifold meshes, or do we need to represent complex edges and singular vertices (see Section 1.3.3)? Can we restrict ourselves to pure triangle meshes, or do we need to represent arbitrary polygonal meshes? Are the meshes regular, semi-regular, irregular (see Chapter 6)? Do we want to build up a hierarchy of increasingly refined meshes (see Section 1.3.2)?

▶ Algorithmic requirements. Which kinds of algorithms will be operating on the data structure? Do we simply want to render the mesh, or do we need efficient access to local neighborhoods of vertices, edges, and faces? Will the mesh be static or will its geometry and/or connectivity change over time? Do we need to associate additional data with vertices, edges, and faces of the mesh? Do we have special requirements in terms of memory consumption (i.e., are the data sets massive)?

Evaluating a data structure requires measuring various criteria such as (a) time to construct it during preprocessing, (b) time to answer a specific query, (c) time to perform a specific operation, and (d) memory consumption and redundancy. While it is not uncommon to design a data structure specialized to a particular algorithm, there are a number of data structures common to several algorithms in geometry processing, which we review in this chapter.

2.1 Face-Based Data Structures

The simplest way to represent a surface mesh consists of storing a set of *individual* polygonal faces represented by their vertex positions (the so-called *face-set*). For the simpler case of triangular meshes this requires storing three vertex positions per face (see Figure 2.1 (left)). Using 32-bit single precision numbers to represent vertex coordinates, this requires $3 \cdot 3 \cdot 4 = 36$ bytes per triangle. Since due to Euler's formula (Equation (1.5)) the number of faces F is about twice the number of vertices V, this data structure consumes on average 72 bytes/vertex. As it does not represent the mesh connectivity, it is commonly referred to as *triangle soup* or polygon soup. Some data exchange formats, such as stereolithography (STL), use this representation as a common denominator.

However, this representation is not sufficient for most applications: connectivity information cannot be accessed explicitly, and vertices and associated data are replicated as many times as the degree of the vertices. The latter redundancy can be avoided by a so-called *indexed face set* or *shared-vertex* data structure, which stores an array of vertices and encodes polygons as sets of indices into this array (see Figure 2.1 (right)). For the case of triangle meshes, and using 32 bits to store vertex coordinates and face indices, this representation requires 12 bytes for each vertex and for each triangle, i.e., it consumes on average 12 bytes/vertex + 12 bytes/face = 36 bytes/vertex, which is only half of the face-set structure.

Triangles		
x_{11} y_{11} z_{11}	x_{12} y_{12} z_{12}	x_{13} y_{13} z_{13}
x_{21} y_{21} z_{21}	x_{22} y_{22} z_{22}	x_{23} y_{23} z_{23}
$\cdots$	$\cdots$	$\cdots$
$\cdots$	$\cdots$	$\cdots$
$\cdots$	$\cdots$	$\cdots$
x_{F1} y_{F1} z_{F1}	x_{F2} y_{F2} z_{F2}	x_{F3} y_{F3} z_{F3}

Vertices	Triangles
x_1 y_1 z_1	i_{11} i_{12} i_{13}
$\cdots$	$\cdots$
x_v y_v z_v	$\cdots$
	$\cdots$
	i_{F1} i_{F2} i_{F3}

Figure 2.1. Face-set data structure (left) and indexed face-set data structure (right) for triangle meshes.

Because it is simple and efficient in storage, this representation is used in many file formats such as OFF, OBJ, and VRML. Similarly, it is relevant for a class of efficient rendering algorithms that assume static data (OpenGL vertex arrays; see [Shreiner and Khronos OpenGL ARB Working Group 09]).

However, without additional connectivity information, this data structure requires expensive searches to recover the local adjacency information of a vertex and hence is not efficient enough for most algorithms.

This is a minimal set of operations frequently used by most algorithms:

▶ Access to individual vertices, edges, and faces. This includes the enumeration of all elements in unspecified order.

▶ Oriented traversal of the edges of a face, which refers to finding the next edge (or previous edge) in a face. With additional access to vertices, for example, the rendering of faces is enabled.

▶ Access to the incident faces of an edge. Depending on the orientation, this is either the left or right face in the manifold case. This enables access to neighboring faces.

▶ Given an edge, access to its two endpoint vertices.

▶ Given a vertex, at least one incident face or edge must be accessible. Then for manifold meshes all other elements in the so-called *one-ring neighborhood* of a vertex can be enumerated (i.e., all incident faces or edges and neighboring vertices).

These operations, which enable both local and global traversal of the mesh, relate vertices, edges, and faces of the mesh by connectivity information (and orientation).

We now review several data structures devised for fast traversal of surface meshes.

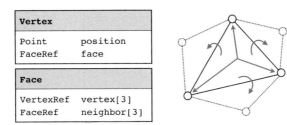

Figure 2.2. Connectivity information stored in a face-based data structure.

A standard face-based data structure for triangle meshes that includes connectivity information consists of storing, for each face, references to its three vertices as well as references to its neighboring triangles. Each vertex stores a reference to one of its incident faces in addition to its 3D position (see Figure 2.2). Based on this connectivity information one can circulate around a vertex in order to enumerate its one-ring neighborhood, and perform all other operations listed above. This representation is used, for instance, for the 2D triangulation data structures of CGAL [CGAL 09] and consumes only 24 bytes/face + 16 bytes/vertex = 64 bytes/vertex.

However, this data structure also has some drawbacks. First, it does not explicitly store edges, so, for example, no data can be attached to edges. Second, enumerating the one-ring of a center vertex requires a large number of case distinctions (is the center vertex the first, second, or third vertex of the current triangle?). Finally, if this data structure is to be used for general polygonal meshes, the data type for faces no longer has constant size, which makes the implementation more complex and less efficient.

2.2   Edge-Based Data Structures

Data structures for general polygon meshes are logically edge-based, since the connectivity primarily relates to the mesh edges. Well-known edge-based data structures are the *winged-edge* [Baumgart 72] and *quad-edge* [Guibas and Stolfi 85] data structures in different variants (see, for instance, [O'Rourke 94]).

The winged-edge structure is depicted in Figure 2.3. Each edge stores references to its endpoint vertices, to its two incident faces, and to the next and previous edge within the left and right face, respectively. Vertices and faces store a reference to one of its incident edges. In total, this leads to a memory consumption of 16 bytes/vertex + 32 bytes/edge + 4 bytes/face = 120 bytes/vertex (since $F \approx 2V$ and $E \approx 3V$ due to the Euler formula in Equation (1.5)).

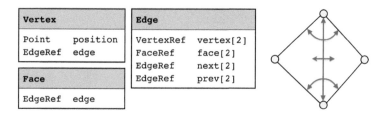

Figure 2.3. Connectivity information stored in an edge-based data structure.

While an edge-based data structure can represent arbitrary polygonal meshes, traversing the one-ring still requires case distinctions (is the center vertex the first or second vertex of an edge?). This issue is finally addressed by halfedge data structures, as described in the next section.

2.3 Halfedge-Based Data Structure

Halfedge data structures [Mantyla 88, Kettner 99] avoid the case distinctions of edge-based data structures by splitting each (unoriented) edge into two oriented *halfedges*, as depicted in Figure 2.4. This data structure is able to represent arbitrary polygonal meshes that are subsets of orientable (combinatorial) 2-manifolds (no complex edges and vertices, see Figure 1.6).

In a halfedge data structure, halfedges are oriented consistently in counterclockwise order around each face and along each boundary. Each boundary may therefore be seen here as an empty face of potentially high degree. As a by-product, each halfedge designates a unique corner (a non-shared vertex in a face) and hence attributes such as texture coordinates or normals can be stored per corner.

For each halfedge we store a reference to

▶ the vertex it points to,

▶ its adjacent face (a zero pointer if it is a boundary halfedge),

▶ the next halfedge of the face or boundary (in counterclockwise direction),

▶ the previous halfedge in the face, and

▶ its opposite (or inverse) halfedge.

Note that the opposite halfedge does not have to be stored if two opposing halfedges are always grouped in pairs and stored in subsequent array

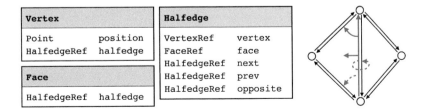

Figure 2.4. Connectivity information stored in an halfedge-based data structure.

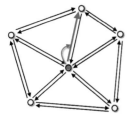 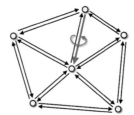 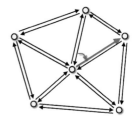

Figure 2.5. The one-ring neighbors of the center vertex can be enumerated by starting with an outgoing halfedge of the center (left), and then repeatedly rotating clockwise by stepping to the opposite halfedge (center) and next halfedge (right) until the first halfedge is reached again.

locations halfedges[i] and halfedges[i+1]. The opposite halfedge is then given implicitly by addition modulo 2. Moreover, we obtain an explicit representation for "full" edges as a pair of two halfedges, which is important when we want to associate data with edges rather than with halfedges. The reference to the previous halfedge in a face may also be omitted, since it can be found by stepping along the next halfedge references.

Additionally, each face stores a reference to one of its halfedges, and each vertex stores an outgoing halfedge. Since the number of halfedges H is about six times the number of vertices V, the total memory consumption is 16 bytes/vertex + 20 bytes/halfedge + 4 bytes/face = 144 bytes/veretx. Not explicitly storing the previous and opposite halfedge reduces the memory costs to 96 bytes/vertex.

A halfedge data structure enables us to enumerate for each element (i.e., vertex, edge, halfedge, or face) all of its adjacent elements. In particular, the one-ring neighborhood of a given vertex can now be enumerated without inefficient case distinctions, as shown in Figure 2.5 and in the pseudocode below.

```
void enumerate\_one\_ring(VertexRef center, Function func)
{
HalfedgeRef h = outgoing\_halfedge(center);
HalfedgeRef hstop = h;
  do {
    VertexRef v = vertex(h);
    func(v); // process vertex v
    h = next\_halfedge( opposite\_halfedge(h) );
  } while (h != hstop);
}
```

The implementation of the references (e.g., HalfedgeRef) can be realized, for instance, by using pointers or indices. In practice, index representations (see, e.g., Section 2.4) are more flexible even though memory access is indirect: using indices into data arrays enables efficient memory relocation (and simpler and more compact memory management) and *all* attributes of a vertex (edge, halfedge, face) can be identified by the same index.

2.4 Directed-Edge Data Structure

The directed-edge data structure [Campagna et al. 98] is a memory-efficient variant of the halfedge data structure that is particularly designed for triangle meshes. It is based on indices that reference each element in the mesh (vertex, face, or halfedge). The indexing follows certain rules that *implicitly* encode some of the connectivity information of the triangle mesh. Instead of pairing opposite halfedges (as proposed in the previous section), this data structure groups the three halfedges belonging to a common triangle.

To be more precise, let f be the index of a face. Then, the indices of its three halfedges are given as

$$\text{halfedge}(f, i) = 3f + i, \quad i = 0, 1, 2.$$

Now let h be the index of a halfedge. Then, the index of its adjacent face and its index within that face are simply given by

$$\text{face}(h) = h/3, \qquad \text{face\_index}(h) = h \bmod 3.$$

The index of h's next halfedge can be computed as $(h + 1) \bmod 3$. The remaining parts of the connectivity have to be stored explicitly: each vertex stores its position and the index to an outgoing halfedge; each halfedge stores the index of its opposite halfedge and the index of its vertex. This leads to a memory consumption of only 16 bytes/vertex + 8 bytes/halfedge = 64 bytes/vertex, which is just as much as the simple face-based structure of Section 2.1, although the directed edges data structure offers much more functionality.

Directed edges can represent all triangle meshes that can be represented by a general halfedge data structure. Note, however, that the boundaries are handled by special (e.g., negative) indices indicating that the opposite halfedge is invalid. Traversing boundary loops is more expensive, since there is no atomic operation to enumerate the next boundary edge. For a general halfedge structure, this can efficiently be accessed by the **next** halfedge along the boundary.

Although we have here described the directed-edge data structure for pure triangle meshes, an adaption to pure quad meshes is straightforward. However, it is not possible to mix triangles and quads, or to represent general polygonal meshes. The main benefit of directed edges is its memory efficiency. Its drawbacks are (a) the restriction to pure triangle/quad meshes and (b) the lack of an explicit representation of edges.

2.5   Summary and Further Reading

Carefully designed data structures are central for geometry processing algorithms based on polygonal meshes. For most algorithms presented in this book we recommend halfedge data structures, or directed-edge data structures as a special case for triangle meshes. While implementing such data structures may look like a simple programming exercise at a first glance, it is actually much harder to achieve a good balance between versatility, memory consumption, and computational efficiency. For those reasons we recommend using existing implementations that provide a number of generic features and that have been matured over time. Some of the publicly available implementations include CGAL,[1] OpenMesh,[2] and MeshLab.[3]

For a detailed overview and comparison of different mesh data structures we refer the reader to [Kettner 99], and to [Floriani and Hui 03, Floriani and Hui 05] for data structures for *non-manifold* meshes. For further reading there are a number of data structures that are specialized for a variety of tasks and size of data, such as processing massive meshes [Isenburg and Lindstrom 05] and view-dependent rendering of massive meshes [Cignoni et al. 04]. Finally, we point the reader to data structures that offer a trade-off between low memory consumption and full access [Kallmann and Thalmann 01, Aleardi et al. 08].

---

[1]CGAL: http://www.cgal.org
[2]OpenMesh: http://www.openmesh.org
[3]MeshLab: http://www.meshlab.org

DIFFERENTIAL GEOMETRY 3

This chapter introduces some of the fundamental concepts of differential geometry. We focus on properties that are relevant for the geometry processing algorithms described in subsequent chapters and refer to standard textbooks such as [do Carmo 76] for proofs and an in-depth discussion. Differential geometry employs methods of differential calculus to describe local properties of smooth curves and surfaces. We will start our discussion with planar curves to provide some geometric intuition, before reviewing fundamental differential geometry concepts of smooth 2-manifold surfaces. The remainder of the chapter will be concerned with the extension to polygonal surfaces. In particular, we will present discrete curvature measures and give a derivation of the standard discrete approximation of the Laplace-Beltrami operator for triangle meshes.

3.1 Curves

We consider smooth planar curves, that is, differentiable 1-manifolds embedded in $\mathbb{R}^2$. Such a curve can be represented in parametric form by a vector-valued function $\mathbf{x} \colon [a, b] \to \mathbb{R}^2$ with $\mathbf{x}(u) = (x(u), y(u))^T$ for $u \in [a, b] \subset \mathbb{R}$ (see Chapter 1). The coordinates x and y are assumed to be differentiable functions of u. The *tangent vector* $\mathbf{x}'(u)$ to the curve at a point $\mathbf{x}(u)$ is defined as the first derivative of the coordinate function, that is $\mathbf{x}'(u) = (x'(u), y'(u))^T$. For instance, in point mechanics, the trajectory of a point is a curve parameterized by time ($u = t$) and the tangent vector $\mathbf{x}'(t)$ corresponds to the velocity vector at time t. We assume the parameterization to be *regular* such that $\mathbf{x}'(u) \neq \mathbf{0}$ for all $u \in [a, b]$. A *normal vector* $\mathbf{n}(u)$ at $\mathbf{x}(u)$ can be computed as $\mathbf{n}(u) = \mathbf{x}'(u)^{\perp}/\|\mathbf{x}'(u)^{\perp}\|$, where $^{\perp}$ denotes rotation by $90°$.

Since a curve is defined as the image of a function $\mathbf{x}$, the same curve can be obtained with a different parameterization. For example, both $\mathbf{x}_1(u) = (u, u)^T$ and $\mathbf{x}_2(u) = (u^2, u^2)^T$ describe the same curve for $u \in [0, 1]$, namely the straight line segment connecting the points $(0, 0)^T$ and $(1, 1)^T$. However, their parameterization is different and thus in general $\mathbf{x}_1(u) \neq \mathbf{x}_2(u)$ for a fixed u. As this example illustrates, we can change the parameterization without changing the shape of the curve. Using the *reparameterization* $v(u) = u^2$, we obtain $\mathbf{x}_1(v(u)) = \mathbf{x}_1(u^2) = \mathbf{x}_2(u)$. Differential geometry of curves is concerned with properties of a curve that are independent of a specific parameterization, such as length or curvature.

3.1.1 Arc Length

The length $l(c, d)$ of any curve segment defined on an interval $[c, d] \subseteq [a, b]$ can be computed as the integral of the tangent vector, i.e., $l(c, d) = \int_c^d \|\mathbf{x}'(u)\| du$. The tangent vector $\mathbf{x}'$ thus encodes the *metric* of the curve. Parametric curves allow for a unique parameterization that can be defined as a length-preserving mapping, i.e., an *isometry*, between the parameter interval and the curve using the reparameterization

$$s = s(u) = \int_a^u \|\mathbf{x}'(t)\| dt. \tag{3.1}$$

This *arc length parameterization* is independent of the specific representation of the curve and maps the parameter interval $[a, b]$ to $[0, L]$, where $L = l(a, b) = \int_a^b \|\mathbf{x}'(u)\| du$ is the total length of the curve. The name stems from the important property that for any point $\mathbf{x}(s)$ on the curve, the length of the curve from $\mathbf{x}(0)$ to $\mathbf{x}(s)$ is equal to s. While any regular curve can be parameterized with respect to arc length, we will see in Chapter 5 that such a canonical parameterization cannot in general be defined for surfaces.

3.1.2 Curvature

Assuming a regular curve is parameterized with respect to arc length, we can define the curvature at a point $\mathbf{x}(s)$ as

$$\kappa(s) := \|\mathbf{x}''(s)\|.$$

For an arbitrary regular curve with parameterization u, we can define curvature using the reparameterization according to arc length $s(u)$. Intuitively, curvature measures how strongly a curve deviates from a straight line. In other words, curvature relates the derivative of the tangent vector of a curve and the curve normal vector and can also be defined using the relation $\mathbf{x}''(s) = \kappa(s)\mathbf{n}(s)$. Note that in this definition curvature is signed and thus changes sign when the orientation of the normal is reversed. It can easily be seen that the curvature of a straight line vanishes and that any curve with zero curvature everywhere must be a line segment. Planar curves of constant curvature are circular arcs. Curvature can also be defined as the inverse of the radius of the *osculating circle*. This circle best approximates the curve locally at a point $\mathbf{x}(u)$ and can be constructed as follows: Let $c(u_-, u, u_+)$ be the circle that passes through three curve points $\mathbf{x}(u_-)$, $\mathbf{x}(u)$, and $\mathbf{x}(u_+)$ with $u_- < u < u_+$. Then the osculating circle $c(u)$ at $\mathbf{x}(u)$ is defined as $c = \lim_{u_-, u_+ \to u} c(u_-, u, u_+)$. The osculating circle has radius $1/\kappa(u)$ and is tangent to the curve at $\mathbf{x}(u)$.

3.2 Surfaces

Length and curvature are Euclidean invariants of a curve; that is, they do not change under rigid motions. We will now look at similar metric and curvature properties for smooth surfaces embedded in $\mathbb{R}^3$. These properties are easier to define using a parametric representation of the surface, explained below. Then, metric properties will be derived from this parametric representation. The discretization of these differential properties to triangle meshes will be described in Section 3.3.

3.2.1 Parametric Representation of Surfaces

To give an example of a parametric surface representation, we consider the problem of drawing a map of the world. As shown in Figure 3.1, the problem is to find a way to "unfold" the surface of the world, in order to obtain a flat 2D surface. Since the surface of the world is closed, a cut is necessary to unfold it. For instance, it can be cut along a meridian, i.e., a curve joining the two poles. In the unfolding process, note that the two poles are stretched and become two curves. The North Pole is transformed into the segment **AC**, and the South Pole into the segment **BD**. It can also be noticed that the meridian along which the sphere has been cut corresponds to two different curves: the segments **AB** and the **CD**. In other words, if a city is located exactly on this meridian, it appears on the map twice.

As shown in Figure 3.2, it is possible to provide each point of the map with two coordinates (θ, ϕ). In the mapping shown in Figure 3.1, the

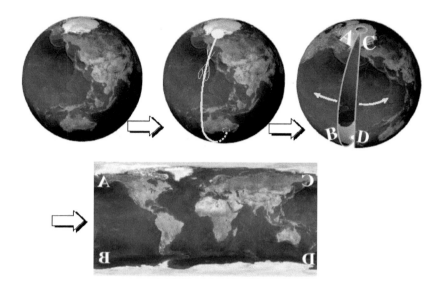

Figure 3.1. Cut me a meridian, and I will unfold the world! (Image taken from [Hormann et al. 07]. ©2007 ACM, Inc. Included here by permission.)

(x, y, z) coordinates in 3D space and the (θ, ϕ) coordinates in the map are linked by the following equation, referred to as a *parametric* equation of a sphere:

$$\mathbf{x}(\theta, \phi) = \begin{pmatrix} x(\theta, \phi) \\ y(\theta, \phi) \\ z(\theta, \phi) \end{pmatrix} = \begin{pmatrix} R \cos(\theta) \cos(\phi) \\ R \sin(\theta) \cos(\phi) \\ R \sin(\phi) \end{pmatrix},$$

where $\theta \in [0, 2\pi]$, $\phi \in [-\pi/2, \pi/2]$, and R denotes the radius of the

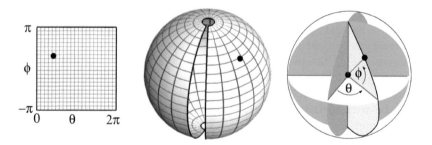

Figure 3.2. Spherical coordinates. (Image taken from [Hormann et al. 07]. ©2007 ACM, Inc. Included here by permission.)

sphere. For a general surface we will later denote this mapping by $\mathbf{x}(u,v) = (x(u,v),\, y(u,v),\, z(u,v))^T$.

Note that this equation is different from the *implicit* equation of the sphere, $x^2 + y^2 + z^2 = R^2$. The implicit equation provides a means of testing whether a given point is on the sphere, whereas the parametric equation describes a way of transforming the rectangle $[0, 2\pi] \times [-\pi/2, \pi/2]$ into a sphere (see also Chapter 1).

For the parametric equation, the following definitions can be given:

▶ The coordinates (θ, ϕ) at a point $\mathbf{p} = (x, y, z)$ are referred to as the *spherical coordinates* of $\mathbf{p}$.

▶ Each vertical line in the map, defined by $\theta = $ constant, corresponds to a curve on the 3D surface, referred to as an *iso-θ curve*. In our case, the iso-θ curves are circles traversing the two poles of the sphere (the *meridians* of the globe).

▶ Each horizontal line in the map, defined by $\phi = $ constant, corresponds to an *iso-ϕ curve*. In our case, the iso-ϕ curves are the *parallels* of the globe, and the iso-ϕ corresponding to $\phi = 0$ is the *equator*.

As can be seen in Figure 3.2, drawing the iso-θ and the iso-ϕ curves helps understanding how the map is *distorted* when applied onto the surface. In the map, the iso-θ and iso-ϕ curves are respectively vertical and horizontal lines, forming a regular grid. Visualizing what this grid becomes when the map is applied onto the surface makes it possible to see the distortion occurring near the poles. In these zones, the squares of the grid are highly distorted. The next subsection presents a way of measuring and quantifying the corresponding distortions, before we generalize the notion of curvature from curves to surfaces.

3.2.2   Metric Properties

Let a continuous surface $\mathcal{S} \subset \mathbb{R}^3$ be given in parametric form as

$$\mathbf{x}(u,v) = \begin{pmatrix} x(u,v) \\ y(u,v) \\ z(u,v) \end{pmatrix}, \quad (u,v) \in \Omega \subset \mathbb{R}^2,$$

where x, y, and z are differentiable functions in u and v, and Ω is the parameter domain. The scalars (u,v) are the coordinates in parameter space.

Similar to the curve case, the metric of the surface is determined by the first derivatives of the function $\mathbf{x}$. As shown in Figure 3.3, the two partial

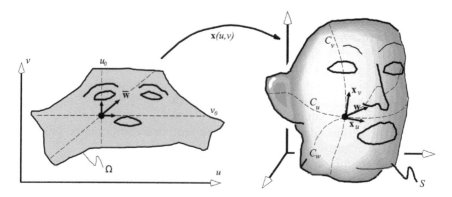

Figure 3.3. Transforming a vector $\bar{\mathbf{w}}$ from parametric space into a tangent vector $\mathbf{w}$ of a surface $\mathcal{S}$ described by a parameterization $\mathbf{x}$. (Image taken from [Hormann et al. 07]. ©2007 ACM, Inc. Included here by permission.)

derivatives

$$\mathbf{x}_u(u_0, v_0) := \frac{\partial \mathbf{x}}{\partial u}(u_0, v_0) \quad \text{and} \quad \mathbf{x}_v(u_0, v_0) := \frac{\partial \mathbf{x}}{\partial v}(u_0, v_0)$$

are, respectively, the tangent vectors of the two *iso-parameter curves*

$$\mathbf{C_u}(t) = \mathbf{x}(u_0 + t, v_0) \quad \text{and} \quad \mathbf{C_v}(t) = \mathbf{x}(u_0, v_0 + t)$$

at the point $\mathbf{x}(u_0, v_0) \in \mathcal{S}$. In the following we drop the parameters (u_0, v_0) or (u, v) for notational brevity. It is important to remember, however, that all quantities are defined point-wise and will typically vary across the surface.

Assuming a *regular parameterization*, i.e., $\mathbf{x}_u \times \mathbf{x}_v \neq \mathbf{0}$, the tangent plane to $\mathcal{S}$ is spanned by the two tangent vectors $\mathbf{x}_u$ and $\mathbf{x}_v$. The surface *normal vector* is orthogonal to both tangent vectors and can thus be computed as

$$\mathbf{n} = \frac{\mathbf{x}_u \times \mathbf{x}_v}{\|\mathbf{x}_u \times \mathbf{x}_v\|}.$$

In addition, we can define arbitrary *directional derivatives* of $\mathbf{x}$. Given a direction vector $\bar{\mathbf{w}} = (u_w, v_w)^T$ defined in parameter space, we consider the straight line parameterized by t passing through (u_0, v_0) and oriented by $\bar{\mathbf{w}}$ given by $(u, v) = (u_0, v_0) + t\bar{\mathbf{w}}$. The image of this straight line through $\mathbf{x}$ is the curve

$$\mathbf{C_w}(t) = \mathbf{x}(u_0 + tu_w, v_0 + tv_w).$$

The directional derivative $\mathbf{w}$ of $\mathbf{x}$ at (u_0, v_0) relative to the direction $\bar{\mathbf{w}}$ is defined to be the tangent to $\mathbf{C_w}$ at $t = 0$, given by $\mathbf{w} = \partial \mathbf{C_w}(t)/\partial t$. By applying the chain rule, it follows that $\mathbf{w} = \mathbf{J}\bar{\mathbf{w}}$, where $\mathbf{J}$ is the *Jacobian matrix* of $\mathbf{x}$ defined as

$$\mathbf{J} = \begin{bmatrix} \frac{\partial x}{\partial u} & \frac{\partial x}{\partial v} \\ \frac{\partial y}{\partial u} & \frac{\partial y}{\partial v} \\ \frac{\partial z}{\partial u} & \frac{\partial z}{\partial v} \end{bmatrix} = \begin{bmatrix} \mathbf{x}_u, & \mathbf{x}_v \end{bmatrix}.$$

First fundamental form. The Jacobian matrix of the parameterization function $\mathbf{x}$ corresponds to the linear map that transforms a vector $\bar{\mathbf{w}}$ in parameter space into a tangent vector $\mathbf{w}$ on the surface. More generally, the Jacobian matrix encodes the metric of the surface in the sense that it allows measuring how angles, distances, and areas are transformed by the mapping from the parameter domain to the surface. Let $\bar{\mathbf{w}}_1$ and $\bar{\mathbf{w}}_2$ be two unit direction vectors in the parameter space. The cosine of the angle between these two vectors is given by the scalar product $\bar{\mathbf{w}}_1^T \bar{\mathbf{w}}_2$. The scalar product between the corresponding tangent vectors on the surface is then given as

$$\mathbf{w}_1^T \mathbf{w}_2 = (\mathbf{J}\bar{\mathbf{w}}_1)^T (\mathbf{J}\bar{\mathbf{w}}_2) = \bar{\mathbf{w}}_1^T \left(\mathbf{J}^T \mathbf{J} \right) \bar{\mathbf{w}}_2.$$

The matrix product $\mathbf{J}^T \mathbf{J}$ is also known as the *first fundamental form* of $\mathbf{x}$ and typically written as

$$\mathbf{I} = \mathbf{J}^T \mathbf{J} = \begin{bmatrix} E & F \\ F & G \end{bmatrix} := \begin{bmatrix} \mathbf{x}_u^T \mathbf{x}_u & \mathbf{x}_u^T \mathbf{x}_v \\ \mathbf{x}_u^T \mathbf{x}_v & \mathbf{x}_v^T \mathbf{x}_v \end{bmatrix}. \tag{3.2}$$

The first fundamental form $\mathbf{I}$ defines an inner product on the tangent space of $\mathcal{S}$. Besides measuring angles, we can use this inner product to determine the squared length of a tangent vector $\mathbf{w}$ as $||\mathbf{w}||^2 = \bar{\mathbf{w}}^T \mathbf{I} \bar{\mathbf{w}}$.

This allows measuring the *length* of a curve $\mathbf{x}(t) = \mathbf{x}(\mathbf{u}(t))$, defined as the image of a regular curve $\mathbf{u}(t) = (u(t), v(t))$ in the parameter domain. The tangent vector of the curve is given by the chain rule as

$$\frac{d\mathbf{x}(\mathbf{u}(t))}{dt} = \frac{\partial \mathbf{x}}{\partial u}\frac{du}{dt} + \frac{\partial \mathbf{x}}{\partial v}\frac{dv}{dt} = \mathbf{x}_u u_t + \mathbf{x}_v v_t.$$

Hence, we can determine the length $l(a,b)$ of $\mathbf{x}(\mathbf{u}(t))$ for a parameter interval $[a,b]$ using Equation (3.1) as

$$l(a,b) = \int_a^b \sqrt{(u_t, v_t)\mathbf{I}(u_t, v_t)^T} dt$$

$$= \int_a^b \sqrt{E u_t^2 + 2F u_t v_t + G v_t^2} dt.$$

Similarly, we can measure the *surface area* A corresponding to a certain parameter region $U \subseteq \Omega$ as

$$A = \iint_U \sqrt{\det(\mathbf{I})} \, du \, dv = \iint_U \sqrt{EG - F^2} \, du \, dv. \qquad (3.3)$$

Since it allows measuring angles, distances and areas, the first fundamental form $\mathbf{I}$ can be considered as a *geometric tool*, sometimes also denoted by the letter $\mathbf{G}$ and called the *metric tensor*.

Anisotropy. Using the Jacobian matrix, a direction $\bar{\mathbf{w}}$ emanating from a parameter-space location (u_0, v_0) can be transformed through the parameterization into a tangent vector $\mathbf{w}$. As shown in Figure 3.4, it is also possible to transform a small circle through the parameterization $\mathbf{x}$, and show that it becomes a small ellipse, called the *anisotropy ellipse*. Considering the eigenvectors $\bar{\mathbf{e}}_1$ and $\bar{\mathbf{e}}_2$ of the first fundamental form $\mathbf{I}$ and the associated eigenvalues λ_1 and λ_2, the anisotropy ellipse is characterized as follows:

▶ the axes of the anisotropy ellipse are $\mathbf{e}_1 = \mathbf{J}\bar{\mathbf{e}}_1$ and $\mathbf{e}_2 = \mathbf{J}\bar{\mathbf{e}}_2$;

▶ the lengths of the axes are $\sigma_1 = \sqrt{\lambda_1}$ and $\sigma_2 = \sqrt{\lambda_2}$.

Note that the lengths of the axes σ_1 and σ_2 also correspond to the singular values of the Jacobian matrix $\mathbf{J}$.

   Their expression can be found by computing the square roots of the zeros of the characteristic polynomial $p(\sigma) = \det(\mathbf{I} - \sigma \, \mathbf{Id})$, where $\mathbf{Id}$ denotes

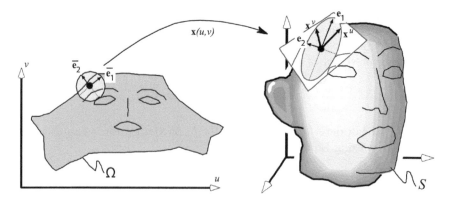

Figure 3.4. Anisotropy: a small circle is transformed into a small ellipse. (Image taken from [Hormann et al. 07]. ©2007 ACM, Inc. Included here by permission.)

the identity matrix:

$$\sigma_1 = \sqrt{1/2(E+G) + \sqrt{(E-G)^2 + 4F^2}},$$

$$\sigma_2 = \sqrt{1/2(E+G) - \sqrt{(E-G)^2 + 4F^2}},$$

where E, F, G denote the coefficients of the first fundamental form $\mathbf{I}$ (Equation (3.2)).

3.2.3 Surface Curvature

To extend the notion of curvature from curves to surfaces, we look at the curvature of curves embedded in the surface. Let $\mathbf{t} = u_t \mathbf{x}_u + v_t \mathbf{x}_v$ be a tangent vector at a surface point $\mathbf{p} \in \mathcal{S}$ represented as $\bar{\mathbf{t}} = (u_t, v_t)^T$ in parameter space. The *normal curvature* $\kappa_n(\bar{\mathbf{t}})$ at $\mathbf{p}$ is the curvature of the planar curve created by intersecting the surface at $\mathbf{p}$ with the plane spanned by $\mathbf{t}$ and the surface normal $\mathbf{n}$ (see Figure 3.5). We can express normal curvature in direction $\bar{\mathbf{t}}$ as

$$\kappa_n(\bar{\mathbf{t}}) \;=\; \frac{\bar{\mathbf{t}}^T \mathbf{II}\, \bar{\mathbf{t}}}{\bar{\mathbf{t}}^T \mathbf{I}\bar{\mathbf{t}}} \;=\; \frac{e u_t^2 + 2f u_t v_t + g v_t^2}{E u_t^2 + 2F u_t v_t + G v_t^2}, \tag{3.4}$$

where $\mathbf{II}$ denotes the *second fundamental form* defined as

$$\mathbf{II} = \begin{bmatrix} e & f \\ f & g \end{bmatrix} := \begin{bmatrix} \mathbf{x}_{uu}^T \mathbf{n} & \mathbf{x}_{uv}^T \mathbf{n} \\ \mathbf{x}_{uv}^T \mathbf{n} & \mathbf{x}_{vv}^T \mathbf{n} \end{bmatrix}.$$

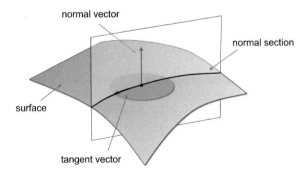

Figure 3.5. The intersection of the surface with a plane spanned by a tangent vector and the normal vector defines a normal section: a planar curve embedded in the surface. By analyzing the curvature of such curves, we can define the curvature of the surface.

Here, second-order partial derivatives of $\mathbf{x}$ are denoted as

$$\mathbf{x}_{uu} := \frac{\partial^2 \mathbf{x}}{\partial u^2}, \quad \mathbf{x}_{uv} := \frac{\partial^2 \mathbf{x}}{\partial u\,\partial v}, \quad \mathbf{x}_{vv} := \frac{\partial^2 \mathbf{x}}{\partial v^2}.$$

The curvature properties of the surface can be characterized by considering the curvature of all normal sections at $\mathbf{p}$, i.e., by rotating the tangent vector $\mathbf{t}$ around the surface normal. Assuming $\kappa_n(\bar{\mathbf{t}})$ varies with $\bar{\mathbf{t}}$, it can be shown that the rational quadratic function of Equation (3.4) has two distinct extremal values, called the *principal curvatures*. We denote with κ_1 the *maximum curvature* and with κ_2 the *minimum curvature*.

If $\kappa_1 \neq \kappa_2$, we can identify two unique unit tangent vectors $\mathbf{t}_1$ and $\mathbf{t}_2$, called the *principal directions*, that are associated with the two principal curvatures κ_1 and κ_2, respectively. Surface points with $\kappa_1 = \kappa_2$ are called *umbilical* or *locally spherical*. For such points, all tangent vectors can be considered principal directions and the curvature profile is isotropic. For example, every point on a sphere or plane is umbilical, and every connected surface that consists of umbilical points only must be either contained in a sphere or a plane.

Euler theorem. An important theorem by Euler relates the normal curvature to the principal curvatures:

$$\kappa_n(\bar{\mathbf{t}}) \;=\; \kappa_1 \cos^2 \psi + \kappa_2 \sin^2 \psi,$$

where ψ is the angle between $\mathbf{t}$ and $\mathbf{t}_1$. This relation shows that the curvature of a surface is entirely determined by the two principal curvatures; any normal curvature is a convex combination of the minimum and maximum curvature. Euler's theorem also states that principal directions are always orthogonal to each other. This property can be exploited, for example, in quad-dominant remeshing (as described in Chapter 6), where a network of *lines of curvature* is computed. For all non-umbilical points, these curves are tangent to the two unique principal directions and thus intersect at right angles on the surface.

Curvature tensor. The local properties of a surface can be described compactly using the *curvature tensor* $\mathbf{C}$, a symmetric 3×3 matrix with eigenvalues κ_1, κ_2, 0, and corresponding eigenvectors $\mathbf{t}_1$, $\mathbf{t}_2$, $\mathbf{n}$. The curvature tensor can be constructed as $\mathbf{C} = \mathbf{P}\mathbf{D}\mathbf{P}^{-1}$, with $\mathbf{P} = [\mathbf{t}_1, \mathbf{t}_2, \mathbf{n}]$ and $\mathbf{D} = \operatorname{diag}(\kappa_1, \kappa_2, 0)$.

Two other curvature measures will be used extensively throughout the book:

▶ The *mean curvature* H is defined as the average of the principal curvatures:

$$H = \frac{\kappa_1 + \kappa_2}{2}. \tag{3.5}$$

Figure 3.6. Color-coded curvature values, mean curvature (left) and Gaussian curvature (right). (Image taken from [Botsch et al. 06b]. ©2006 ACM, Inc. Included here by permission.)

▶ The *Gaussian curvature* K is defined as the product of the principal curvatures, i.e.,

$$K = \kappa_1 \kappa_2. \tag{3.6}$$

Gaussian curvature can be used to classify surface points into three distinct categories: *elliptical* points ($K > 0$), *hyperbolic* points ($K < 0$), and *parabolic* points ($K = 0$). At hyperbolic points the surface is locally saddle-shaped, while elliptical points indicate local convexity. Parabolic points typically lie on curves separating elliptical and hyperbolic regions. Gaussian and mean curvature are often used for visual inspection of surfaces, as shown in Figure 3.6.

Intrinsic geometry. In differential geometry, properties that only depend on the first fundamental form (Equation (3.2)) are called *intrinsic*. Intuitively, the intrinsic geometry of a surface can be perceived by 2D creatures that live on the surface without knowledge of the third dimension. Examples include length and angles of curves on the surface. Gauss' famous *Theorema Egregium* states that the Gaussian curvature is invariant under local isometries and as such also intrinsic to the surface [do Carmo 76]. Thus Gaussian curvature can be determined directly from the first fundamental form. In contrast, mean curvature is not invariant under isometries but depends on the embedding. Note that the term *intrinsic* is often also used to denote independence of a particular parameterization.

Laplace operator. The following chapters will make extensive use of the *Laplace operator* Δ and the *Laplace-Beltrami operator* Δ_S. In general, the Laplace operator is defined as the divergence of the gradient, i.e., $\Delta = \nabla^2 = \nabla \cdot \nabla$. For a 2-parameter function $f(u, v)$ in Euclidean space this second-order differential operator can be written as the sum of second partial derivatives

$$\Delta f \;=\; \mathrm{div}\nabla f \;=\; \mathrm{div}\begin{pmatrix} f_u \\ f_v \end{pmatrix} \;=\; f_{uu} + f_{vv}.$$

The *Laplace-Beltrami operator* extends this concept to functions defined on surfaces. For a given function f defined on a manifold surface $\mathcal{S}$, the Laplace-Beltrami is defined as

$$\Delta_{\mathcal{S}} f = \mathrm{div}_{\mathcal{S}} \, \nabla_{\mathcal{S}} f,$$

which requires a suitable definition of the divergence and gradient operators on manifolds (see [do Carmo 76] for details). Applied to the coordinate function $\mathbf{x}$ of the surface, the Laplace-Beltrami operator evaluates to the *mean curvature normal*:

$$\Delta_{\mathcal{S}}\,\mathbf{x} = -2H\mathbf{n}. \tag{3.7}$$

Note that even though this equation relates the Laplace-Beltrami operator to the (non-intrinsic) mean curvature of the surface, the operator itself is an intrinsic property that only depends on the metric of the surface, i.e., the first fundamental form. For simplicity, we often drop the subscript and simply use the symbol Δ to denote the Laplace-Beltrami operator when clear from the context.

3.3   Discrete Differential Operators

The differential properties defined in the previous section require a surface to be sufficiently often differentiable, e.g., the definition of curvature requires the existence of second derivatives. Since polygonal meshes are piecewise linear surfaces, the concepts introduced above cannot be applied directly. The following definitions of discrete differential operators are thus based on the assumption that meshes can be interpreted as piecewise linear approximations of smooth surfaces. The goal is then to compute approximations of the differential properties of this underlying surface directly from the mesh data. Different approaches have been proposed in recent years. We will focus on the de-facto standard discretization of the Laplace-Beltrami operator and provide a brief derivation of the resulting formula, closely following [Meyer et al. 03]. Alternative derivations of the same result have been presented in [Pinkall and Polthier 93, Desbrun et al. 99]. For more details we refer to the references provided in Section 3.4 and the survey [Petitjean 02].

3.3.1   Local Averaging Region

The general idea is to compute discrete differential properties as spatial averages over a local neighborhood $\mathcal{N}(\mathbf{x})$ of a point $\mathbf{x}$ on the mesh. Often

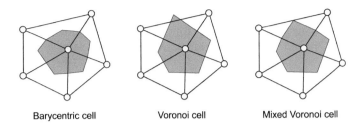

Barycentric cell   Voronoi cell   Mixed Voronoi cell

Figure 3.7. Blue color indicates the local averaging regions used for computing discrete differential operators associated with the center vertex of the one-ring neighborhood.

$\mathbf{x}$ coincides with a mesh vertex v_i, and n-ring neighborhoods $\mathcal{N}_n(v_i)$ or local geodesic balls are used as the averaging domain. The size of the local neighborhood critically affects the stability and accuracy of the discrete operators. The bigger the neighborhoods, the more smoothing is introduced by the averaging operation, which makes the computations more stable in the presence of noise. For clean data sets, small neighborhoods are typically preferable, as they more accurately capture fine-scale variations of differential properties. Figure 3.7 illustrates three variants of averaging regions defined on vertex one-ring neighborhoods. The *barycentric cell* connects the triangle barycenters with the edge midpoints. Alternatively, we can define a local *Voronoi cell* by replacing the triangle barycenters with triangle circumcenters. The tightness of the Voronoi cell leads to tight error bounds for the discrete operators as shown in [Meyer et al. 03]. However, as the figure illustrates, the circumcenter can be outside of the triangle. While this does not invalidate the discretizations presented below, slightly better approximation properties can be obtained by ensuring that the local averaging regions build a perfect tiling of the mesh surface. This can be achieved by replacing the circumcenter for obtuse triangles with the midpoint of the edge opposing the center vertex. The resulting averaging area is denoted as *mixed Voronoi cell*.

3.3.2 Normal Vectors

Many operations in geometry processing and computer graphics require normal vectors, either per face or per vertex; for example, in Phong shading. Normal vectors for individual triangles $T = (\mathbf{x}_i, \mathbf{x}_j, \mathbf{x}_j)$ can be computed as the normalized cross-product of two triangle edges:

$$\mathbf{n}(T) = \frac{(\mathbf{x}_j - \mathbf{x}_i) \times (\mathbf{x}_k - \mathbf{x}_i)}{\|(\mathbf{x}_j - \mathbf{x}_i) \times (\mathbf{x}_k - \mathbf{x}_i)\|}.$$

Computing vertex normals as spatial averages of normal vectors in a local one-ring neighborhood leads to a normalized weighted average of the (constant) normal vectors of incident triangles:

$$\mathbf{n}(v) \;=\; \frac{\sum_{T \in \mathcal{N}_1(v)} \alpha_T \, \mathbf{n}(T)}{\left\| \sum_{T \in \mathcal{N}_1(v)} \alpha_T \, \mathbf{n}(T) \right\|}.$$

There are numerous alternatives for the weights α_T. We describe the most frequently used ones below and compare them in Figure 3.8:

▶ Constant weights $\alpha_T = 1$ are efficient to compute but do not consider edge lengths, triangle areas, or angles, and hence can give counterintuitive results for irregular meshes.

▶ The local averaging regions shown in Figure 3.7 suggest a weighting based on triangle area, i.e., $\alpha_T = |T|$. This method is particularly efficient to compute, since the area-weighted face normals are just the (un-normalized) cross-product of two triangle edges. However, counterintuitive results can occur, too.

▶ Averaging over sufficiently small geodesic disks corresponds to weighting by incident triangle angles $\alpha_T = \theta_T$ (see Figure 3.10). The involved trigonometric functions make this method computationally more expensive, but it gives superior results in general.

For most applications, angle-weighted face normals provide a good trade-off between computational efficiency and accuracy. More details and a comparison of different methods can be found in [Max 99, Jin et al. 05].

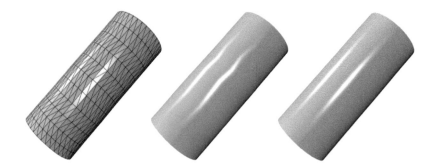

Figure 3.8. Different methods for computing per-vertex normals on a regularly tessellated cylinder: constant weights and area weights yield the result in the center; angle weights, the result on the right.

3.3.3 Gradients

Since the Laplace-Beltrami operator is defined as the divergence of the gradient, we will first look at a suitable definition of the gradient of a function on a piecewise linear triangle mesh. These gradients also play an important role in mesh parameterization (Chapter 5) and deformation (Chapter 9).

We assume a piecewise linear function f that is given at each mesh vertex as $f(v_i) = f(\mathbf{x}_i) = f(\mathbf{u}_i) = f_i$ and interpolated linearly within each triangle $(\mathbf{x}_i, \mathbf{x}_j, \mathbf{x}_k)$:

$$f(\mathbf{u}) = f_i B_i(\mathbf{u}) + f_j B_j(\mathbf{u}) + f_k B_k(\mathbf{u}),$$

where $\mathbf{u} = (u, v)$ is the parameter pair corresponding to the surface point $\mathbf{x}$ in a 2D conformal parameterization induced by the triangle (see also Chapter 5). Figure 3.9 shows the linear barycentric basis functions used for the interpolation.

The gradient of f is given as

$$\nabla f(\mathbf{u}) = f_i \nabla B_i(\mathbf{u}) + f_j \nabla B_j(\mathbf{u}) + f_k \nabla B_k(\mathbf{u}).$$

Since the basis functions satisfy the barycentric condition of partition of unity, i.e., $B_i(\mathbf{u}) + B_j(\mathbf{u}) + B_k(\mathbf{u}) = 1$ for all $\mathbf{u}$, the gradients of the basis functions sum to zero, i.e., $\nabla B_i(\mathbf{u}) + \nabla B_j(\mathbf{u}) + \nabla B_k(\mathbf{u}) = 0$. Hence the above equation can be written as

$$\nabla f(\mathbf{u}) = (f_j - f_i) \nabla B_j(\mathbf{u}) + (f_k - f_i) \nabla B_k(\mathbf{u}).$$

As Figure 3.9 illustrates, the steepest ascent direction of the basis functions is orthogonal to the opposite edge of the corresponding vertex. With appropriate normalization, the gradient of B_i is therefore given as

$$\nabla B_i(\mathbf{u}) = \frac{(\mathbf{x}_k - \mathbf{x}_j)^\perp}{2 A_T}, \qquad (3.8)$$

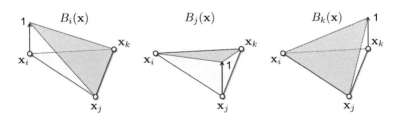

Figure 3.9. The linear basis functions for barycentric interpolation on a triangle.

where $\perp$ denotes a counterclockwise rotation by $90°$ in the triangle plane and A_T is the area of triangle T. Consequently, the gradient of the piecewise linear function f within a triangle T evaluates to the constant

$$\nabla f(\mathbf{u}) \;=\; (f_j - f_i)\frac{(\mathbf{x}_i - \mathbf{x}_k)^{\perp}}{2A_T} \;+\; (f_k - f_i)\frac{(\mathbf{x}_j - \mathbf{x}_i)^{\perp}}{2A_T}. \qquad (3.9)$$

3.3.4   Discrete Laplace-Beltrami Operator

We discuss two discretizations of the Laplace-Beltrami operator: the uniform graph Laplacian and the widely used cotangent formula.

Uniform Laplacian. Taubin [Taubin 95] proposed the uniform discretization of the Laplace-Beltrami operator

$$\Delta f(v_i) \;=\; \frac{1}{|\mathcal{N}_1(v_i)|} \sum_{v_j \in \mathcal{N}_1(v_i)} (f_j - f_i), \qquad (3.10)$$

where the sum is taken over all one-ring neighbors $v_j \in \mathcal{N}_1(v_i)$. Applied to the coordinate function $\mathbf{x}$, the uniform graph Laplacian $\Delta \mathbf{x}_i$ evaluates to the vector pointing from the center vertex $\mathbf{x}_i$ to the average of the one-ring vertices $\mathbf{x}_j$. While simple and efficient to compute, the resulting vector can be non-zero even for a planar configuration of vertices. However, in such a setting we would expect a zero Laplacian since the mean curvature over the entire mesh region is zero (c.f. Equation (3.7)). This indicates that the uniform Laplacian is not an appropriate discretization for non-uniform meshes. Indeed, since the definition only depends on the connectivity of the mesh, the uniform Laplacian does not adapt at all to the spatial distribution of vertices. While disadvantageous in many applications, we discuss in Chapters 4 and 6 how this invariance to the embedding can be exploited to improve the local distribution of vertices in isotropic remeshing.

Cotangent formula. A more accurate discretization of the Laplace-Beltrami operator can be derived using a mixed finite element/finite volume method [Meyer et al. 03]. The goal is to integrate the divergence of the gradient of a piecewise linear function over a local averaging domain $A_i = A(v_i)$. To simplify the integration we make use of the divergence theorem for a vector-valued function $\mathbf{F}$:

$$\int_{A_i} \operatorname{div} \mathbf{F}(\mathbf{u})\, dA \;=\; \int_{\partial A_i} \mathbf{F}(\mathbf{u}) \cdot \mathbf{n}(\mathbf{u})\, ds.$$

This equation relates the integration over the averaging area A_i to an integration along the boundary ∂A_i of A_i, where $\mathbf{n}$ is the outward pointing

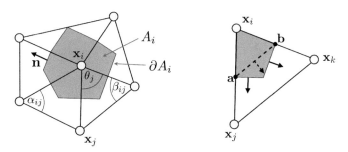

Figure 3.10. Illustration of the quantities used in the derivation of the discrete Laplace-Beltrami operator and discrete Gaussian curvature operator.

unit normal of the boundary (see Figure 3.10). Applied to the Laplacian, this evaluates to

$$\int_{A_i} \Delta f(\mathbf{u})\,\mathrm{d}A \;=\; \int_{A_i} \mathrm{div}\nabla f(\mathbf{u})\,\mathrm{d}A \;=\; \int_{\partial A_i} \nabla f(\mathbf{u})\cdot\mathbf{n}(\mathbf{u})\,\mathrm{d}s.$$

We split this integral by considering the integration separately for each triangle. Since the boundary of the local Voronoi region passes through the midpoints $\mathbf{a}$ and $\mathbf{b}$ of the two triangle edges (see Figure 3.10 (right)), and $\nabla f(\mathbf{x})$ is constant within each triangle, the integral for a triangle T evaluates to

$$\int_{\partial A_i \cap T} \nabla f(\mathbf{u})\cdot\mathbf{n}(\mathbf{u})\mathrm{d}s \;=\; \nabla f(\mathbf{u})\cdot(\mathbf{a}-\mathbf{b})^{\perp}$$

$$\;=\; \frac{1}{2}\nabla f(\mathbf{u})\cdot(\mathbf{x}_j-\mathbf{x}_k)^{\perp}.$$

Plugging in Equation (3.9) yields

$$\int_{\partial A_i \cap T} \nabla f(\mathbf{u})\cdot\mathbf{n}(\mathbf{u})\mathrm{d}s \;=\; (f_j-f_i)\frac{(\mathbf{x}_i-\mathbf{x}_k)^{\perp}\cdot(\mathbf{x}_j-\mathbf{x}_k)^{\perp}}{4A_T}$$

$$+\; (f_k-f_i)\frac{(\mathbf{x}_j-\mathbf{x}_i)^{\perp}\cdot(\mathbf{x}_j-\mathbf{x}_k)^{\perp}}{4A_T}.$$

Let γ_j,γ_k denote the inner triangle angles at vertices v_j, v_k, respectively. Since $A_T = \frac{1}{2}\sin\gamma_j\,\|\mathbf{x}_j-\mathbf{x}_i\|\,\|\mathbf{x}_j-\mathbf{x}_k\| = \frac{1}{2}\sin\gamma_k\,\|\mathbf{x}_i-\mathbf{x}_k\|\,\|\mathbf{x}_j-\mathbf{x}_k\|$, and $\cos\gamma_j = \frac{(\mathbf{x}_j-\mathbf{x}_i)\cdot(\mathbf{x}_j-\mathbf{x}_k)}{\|\mathbf{x}_j-\mathbf{x}_i\|\|\mathbf{x}_j-\mathbf{x}_k\|}$ and $\cos\gamma_k = \frac{(\mathbf{x}_i-\mathbf{x}_k)\cdot(\mathbf{x}_j-\mathbf{x}_k)}{\|\mathbf{x}_i-\mathbf{x}_k\|\|\mathbf{x}_j-\mathbf{x}_k\|}$, this expression simplifies to

$$\int_{\partial A_i \cap T} \nabla f(\mathbf{u})\cdot\mathbf{n}(\mathbf{u})\mathrm{d}s \;=\; \frac{1}{2}\left(\cot\gamma_k(f_j-f_i)+\cot\gamma_j(f_k-f_i)\right).$$

Thus when integrating over the entire averaging region A_i we obtain

$$\int_{A_i} \Delta f(\mathbf{u}) \mathrm{d}A \;=\; \frac{1}{2} \sum_{v_j \in \mathcal{N}_1(v_i)} (\cot \alpha_{i,j} + \cot \beta_{i,j})(f_j - f_i),$$

where we re-labeled the angles as shown in Figure 3.10. Thus the discrete average of the Laplace-Beltrami operator of a function f at vertex v_i is given as

$$\Delta f(v_i) \;:=\; \frac{1}{2A_i} \sum_{v_j \in \mathcal{N}_1(v_i)} (\cot \alpha_{i,j} + \cot \beta_{i,j}) \, (f_j - f_i). \qquad (3.11)$$

Equation (3.11) is probably the most widely used discretization of the Laplace-Beltrami operator for triangle meshes in computer graphics and is typically applied for various geometry processing tasks, such as surface smoothing (Chapter 4), parameterization (Chapter 5), and shape modeling (Chapter 9).

However, there are also some disadvantages of the cotangent discretization. The cotangent weights $(\cot \alpha_{i,j} + \cot \beta_{i,j})$ become negative if $\alpha_{i,j} + \beta_{i,j} > \pi$. This can lead to flipped triangles in certain applications, e.g., when computing a parameterization (see Chapter 5). In addition, the discrete Laplace-Beltrami of Equation (3.11) is not purely intrinsic, i.e., its evaluation can lead to different results, even for two isometric surfaces with different triangulations. We refer to the references of Section 3.4 for some alternative discrete definitions of the Laplace-Beltrami that address some of these shortcomings.

Since the Laplacian is defined as the divergence of the gradient, for completeness we briefly describe the *divergence operator* [Tong et al. 03]. Consider a vector field $\mathbf{w} \colon \mathcal{S} \to \mathbb{R}^3$ defined by a constant vector $\mathbf{w}_T$ per triangle T (e.g., the gradient of a piecewise linear function f). The discrete divergence computes a scalar value $\mathrm{div}\,\mathbf{w}(v_i)$ per vertex v_i from the vector field at its incident triangles $T \in \mathcal{N}(v_i)$:

$$\mathrm{div}\,\mathbf{w}(v_i) \;=\; \frac{1}{A_i} \sum_{T \in \mathcal{N}_1(v_i)} \nabla B_i|_T \cdot \mathbf{w}_T \, A_T, \qquad (3.12)$$

where $\nabla B_i|_T$ is the (constant) gradient vector of the basis function of vertex v_i in triangle T (see Equation (3.8)). Note that the discretizations of divergence (3.12), gradient (3.9), and Laplacian (3.11) are consistent in the sense that $\Delta f = \mathrm{div}\,\nabla f$ holds also in the discrete case.

3.3.5 Discrete Curvature

When applied to the coordinate function $\mathbf{x}$, the Laplace-Beltrami operator provides a discrete approximation of the mean curvature normal (see

Equation (3.7)). Thus we can define the absolute discrete mean curvature at vertex v_i as

$$H(v_i) = \frac{1}{2} \|\Delta \mathbf{x}_i\|. \tag{3.13}$$

Meyer and colleagues [Meyer et al. 03] also present a derivation of a discrete operator for Gaussian curvature:

$$K(v_i) = \frac{1}{A_i} \left(2\pi - \sum_{v_j \in \mathcal{N}_1(v_i)} \theta_j \right), \tag{3.14}$$

where the θ_js denote the angles of the incident triangles at vertex v_i (see Figure 3.10). This formula is a direct consequence of the Gauss-Bonnet theorem [do Carmo 76]. Given the discrete approximations of mean curvature (Equation (3.13)) and Gaussian curvature (Equation (3.14)), the principal curvatures can be computed from Equations (3.6) and (3.5) as

$$\kappa_{1,2}(v_i) = H(v_i) \pm \sqrt{H(v_i)^2 - K(v_i)}.$$

3.3.6 Discrete Curvature Tensor

Similar to the plenitude of discrete versions of the Laplace-Beltrami operator, numerous methods have been proposed for directly estimating the curvature tensor on polygonal surfaces (see references in Section 3.4). We briefly describe the method introduced by Cohen-Steiner and Morvan [Cohen-Steiner and Morvan 03], which has been successfully applied for surface remeshing [Alliez et al. 03a] and curvature-domain shape processing [Eigensatz et al. 08]. A similar definition has been presented in [Hildebrandt and Polthier 04].

The basic idea is to define a curvature tensor for each edge by assigning a minimum curvature of zero along the edge and a maximum curvature according to the dihedral angle across the edge. Averaging over the local neighborhood region $A(v)$ yields a simple summation formula over the edges intersecting $A(v)$:

$$\mathbf{C}(v) = \frac{1}{A(v)} \sum_{\mathbf{e} \in A(v)} \beta(\mathbf{e}) \, \|\mathbf{e} \cap A(v)\| \, \bar{\mathbf{e}} \, \bar{\mathbf{e}}^T,$$

where $\beta(\mathbf{e})$ is the signed dihedral angle between the normals of the two incident faces of edge $\mathbf{e}$, $\|\mathbf{e} \cap A(v)\|$ is the length of the part of $\mathbf{e}$ that is contained in $A(v)$, and $\bar{\mathbf{e}} = \mathbf{e}/\|\mathbf{e}\|$. The local neighborhood $A(v)$ is typically chosen to be the one- or two-ring of the vertex v, but can also be computed as a local geodesic disk, i.e., all points on the mesh that are within a certain (geodesic) distance from v. This can be more appropriate for non-uniformly tessellated surfaces, where the size of n-ring neighborhoods $\mathcal{N}_n(v)$ can vary significantly over the mesh. As noted in [Rusinkiewicz 04], tensor averaging can yield inaccurate results for low-valence vertices and small (e.g., one-ring) neighborhoods.

3.4   Summary and Further Reading

The derivation of discrete analogs to differential properties of smooth surfaces has been an active area of research for many years. Pinkall and Polthier discuss discrete minimal surfaces and present a derivation of Equation (3.11) using a minimization of the Dirichlet energy on the mesh [Pinkall and Polthier 93]. Bobenko and Springborn [Bobenko and Springborn 07] evaluate Equation (3.11) on an intrinsic Delaunay triangulation of the simplicial surface, which makes the evaluation independent of the specific tessellation of the mesh. Zayer and co-workers [Zayer et al. 05b] replace the cotangent weights with the positive mean value coordinates [Floater 03] and integrate over circle areas instead of Voronoi areas. While this leads to a less accurate discretization of the Laplace-Beltrami, negative weights are avoided. A systematic study of convergence conditions for discrete geometry properties is given in [Hildebrandt et al. 06].

An alternative approach to estimating local surface properties uses a local higher-order reconstruction of the surface, followed by analytic evaluation of the desired properties on the reconstructed surface patch. Local surface patches, typically bivariate polynomials of low degree, are fitted to sample points [Cazals and Pouget 03, Petitjean 02, Welch and Witkin 94] and possibly normals [Goldfeather and Interrante 04] within a local neighborhood.

Rusinkiewicz proposed a scheme that approximates the curvature tensor using finite differences of vertex normals [Rusinkiewicz 04]. A related approach by Theisel and co-workers [Theisel et al. 04] considers the piecewise linear surface together with a piecewise linear normal field.

Grinspun and colleagues provide an extensive overview of different concepts and applications of discrete differential geometry. In particular, they present an alternative approach to define discrete differential operators based on discrete exterior calculus [Grinspun et al. 08]. Wardetzky and colleagues classify the most common discrete Laplace operators according to a set of desirable properties derived from the smooth setting [Wardetzky et al. 07]. They show that the discrete operators cannot simultaneously satisfy all of the identified properties of symmetry, locality, linear precision, and positivity. For example, the cotangent formula of Equation (3.11) satisfies the first three properties, but not the fourth, since edge weights can assume negative values. The choice of discretization thus depends on the specific application.

SMOOTHING

Building on the concepts of differential geometry and the discrete counterparts introduced in Chapter 3, in this chapter we present *mesh smoothing*. On an abstract level, mesh smoothing is concerned with the design and computation of smooth functions $\mathbf{f}\colon \mathcal{S} \to \mathbb{R}^d$ on a triangle mesh. Due to this very general formulation, mesh smoothing is a fundamental tool in geometry processing. The function $\mathbf{f}$ can flexibly be chosen to describe, for instance, vertex positions, texture coordinates, or vertex displacements, such that the techniques introduced in this chapter can be used for mesh parameterization (Chapter 5), isotropic remeshing (Chapter 6), hole filling (Chapter 8), and mesh deformation (Chapter 9).

We will discuss two aspects of mesh smoothing: *denoising* and *fairing*. Denoising is used to remove high-frequency noise from the function $\mathbf{f}$. In most cases, $\mathbf{f}$ denotes the vertex positions, which might be corrupted by high frequency noise due to a physical scanning process (see Figure 4.1). Removing the noise (the high frequencies) and keeping the overall shape (the low frequencies) requires generalizing the concepts of frequencies and low-pass filters to functions living on discrete triangle meshes. We will present the "mesh version" of Fourier transform and diffusion filters in Sections 4.1 and 4.2, respectively.

Mesh fairing, discussed in Section 4.3, does not just slightly smooth the function $\mathbf{f}$ in order to remove the high frequency noise. It also smooths the function as much as possible in order to obtain, e.g., an as-smooth-as-possible surface patch or an as-smooth-as-possible shape deformation. "As smooth as possible" means that certain fairness energies have to be

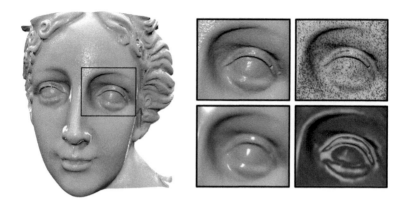

Figure 4.1. A 3D laser scan of a statue's face on the left is corrupted by typical measurement noise, which can be removed by low-pass filtering of the surface geometry. On the right, the top row shows a close-up of the original mesh and a color-coded visualization of its mean curvature. The bottom row depicts the denoising result around the eye region.

minimized, typically involving curvatures or higher-order derivatives. We will show that mesh fairing directly computes the limit surfaces of iterative denoising processes, which illustrates the connection between these two approaches.

4.1   Fourier Transform and Manifold Harmonics

The Fourier transform is the classic tool for analyzing a signal's frequency spectrum. It allows for efficient implementations of low-pass filters and more general convolution filters. We will first consider low-pass filtering of simple univariate functions $f(x)$ based on the Fourier transform, and then generalize these concepts to signal processing on triangle meshes.

4.1.1   1D Fourier Transform

The Fourier transform maps a univariate function $f\colon \mathbb{R} \to \mathbb{C}$ from its representation $f(x)$ in the *spatial domain* to its representation $F(\omega)$ in the *frequency domain*. This transformation and its inverse can be written as

$$F(\omega) = \int_{-\infty}^{\infty} f(x)\, e^{-2\pi i \omega x}\, dx, \tag{4.1}$$

$$f(x) = \int_{-\infty}^{\infty} F(\omega)\, e^{2\pi i \omega x}\, d\omega. \tag{4.2}$$

These equations have an intuitive geometric interpretation: the function $f(x)$ can be considered an element of a certain vector space (integrable complex-valued functions), which is equipped with the inner product

$$\langle f, g \rangle = \int_{-\infty}^{\infty} f(x)\, \overline{g(x)}\, dx,$$

where $\overline{(a + ib)} = (a - ib)$ denotes complex conjugation. The complex exponential functions

$$e_\omega(x) := e^{2\pi i \omega x} = \cos(2\pi\omega x) - i\sin(2\pi\omega x)$$

consist of sine and cosine functions of frequency ω and hence are considered as *complex waves* of frequency ω. They build a frequency-related orthogonal basis of our vector space—the *frequency domain*.

In this context the Fourier transform is simply a change of basis by orthogonal projection of the "vector" f onto the "basis vectors" e_ω:

$$f(x) = \sum_{\omega=-\infty}^{\infty} \langle f, e_\omega \rangle\, e_\omega.$$

The scalar coefficient $\langle f, e_\omega \rangle$ is nothing other than $F(\omega)$ in Equation (4.1). It describes how much of the basis function e_ω is contained in f, i.e., what amplitude of the frequency ω is contained in the signal $f(x)$. Since the frequencies ω are real values and not just integers, the sum in the above equation turns into an integral, which reproduces Equation (4.2).

Since the coordinates $F(\omega)$ with respect to the basis e_ω directly correspond to frequencies, we can implement an ideal *low-pass filter* by simply cutting off all frequencies above a user-defined threshold ω_{max}. This is equivalent to reconstructing the filtered function $\tilde{f}$ from the lower frequencies $|\omega| < \omega_{max}$ only:

$$\tilde{f}(x) = \int_{-\omega_{max}}^{\omega_{max}} \langle f, e_\omega \rangle\, e_\omega\, d\omega. \tag{4.3}$$

4.1.2 Manifold Harmonics

The 1D Fourier framework is now to be generalized to functions $f : \mathcal{S} \rightarrow \mathbb{R}$ on a (discrete) 2-manifold surface. The Fourier transform of Equation (4.1) cannot be translated directly to functions on manifolds. The missing link is provided by the following observation: sine and cosine functions, and therefore also the complex waves e_ω, are eigenfunctions of the Laplace operator, i.e.,

$$\Delta\left(e^{2\pi i \omega x}\right) = \frac{d^2}{dx^2} e^{2\pi i \omega x} = -(2\pi\omega)^2\, e^{2\pi i \omega x}.$$

A function e_i is an eigenfunction of the Laplacian with eigenvalue λ_i if $\Delta e_i = \lambda_i e_i$, similar to an eigenvector of a matrix $\mathbf{A} \mathbf{e}_i = \lambda_i \mathbf{e}_i$.

Hence, the basis functions of the 1D Fourier transform are eigenfunctions of the Laplacian. It therefore seems natural to choose eigenfunctions of the Laplace-Beltrami operator on 2-manifold surfaces as generalized basis functions. Because we know how to discretize the Laplace-Beltrami, this will also provide the generalization of the Fourier transform to discrete triangle meshes.

This idea is also consistent with other frequency-related basis functions on bivariate surfaces: for a 2D square, the eigenfunctions of the Laplace-Beltrami operator correspond to the basis functions of the discrete cosine transform (used by the JPEG format) and, for a sphere, they correspond to spherical harmonics. Thus, the eigenfunctions of the Laplace-Beltrami generalize these notions to arbitrary 2-manifold surfaces. Therefore, they are called *manifold harmonics*.

For a discretization on a triangle mesh, we replace the continuous function $f(\mathbf{x})$ by the vector of sample values at the n mesh vertices

$$f \colon \mathcal{S} \to \mathbb{R} \quad \longrightarrow \quad (f(v_1), \ldots, f(v_n))^T. \tag{4.4}$$

The Laplace-Beltrami operator Δ then becomes the Laplace-Beltrami matrix $\mathbf{L}$ that computes the Laplacian for each vertex:

$$\begin{pmatrix} \Delta f(v_1) \\ \vdots \\ \Delta f(v_n) \end{pmatrix} = \mathbf{L} \begin{pmatrix} f(v_1) \\ \vdots \\ f(v_n) \end{pmatrix}.$$

This matrix contains in each row i the weights w_{ij} for discretizing the Laplacian at vertex v_i (see Section 3.3 and Section A.1):

$$\Delta f(v_i) = \sum_{v_j \in \mathcal{N}_1(v_i)} w_{ij} \left(f(v_j) - f(v_i) \right).$$

Here we assume that the weights are not normalized by vertex valence or Voronoi area, but instead are chosen such that the matrix $\mathbf{L}$ is symmetric, e.g., as $w_{ij} = 1$ for the uniform Laplacian, or $w_{ij} = (\cot \alpha_{i,j} + \cot \beta_{i,j})$ for the cotangent discretization (see [Vallet and Lévy 08] for a more detailed analysis of discretization and symmetrization).

The eigenfunctions $e_\omega(x)$ of the Laplace-Beltrami operator in the continuous setting now become the eigenvectors $\mathbf{e}_1, \ldots, \mathbf{e}_n$ of the Laplace matrix: an n-dimensional eigenvector $\mathbf{e}_i$ can be considered a discrete sampling $(\mathbf{e}_i(v_1), \ldots, \mathbf{e}_i(v_n))^T$ of a continuous eigenfunction $\mathbf{e}_i(\mathbf{x})$, just as in Equation (4.4). The kth entry of $\mathbf{e}_i$ corresponds to the amplitude of the wave $\mathbf{e}_i$

Figure 4.2. Some elements of manifold harmonic basis functions. The color values can be thought of as the amplitude of a standing wave on the mesh geometry. (Image taken from [Vallet and Lévy 08]. Model courtesy of Pisa Visual Computing Lab.)

at vertex v_k; the frequency of the wave is determined by the corresponding eigenvalue λ_i. The eigenvectors of **L** are therefore called the *natural vibrations* of the triangle mesh, and the eigenvalues the *natural frequencies* [Taubin 95, Taubin 00]. Some basis functions of this so-called *manifold harmonic basis* [Vallet and Lévy 08] are shown in Figure 4.2, with color values denoting the per-vertex amplitudes.

Since the matrix **L** is symmetric and positive semi-definite (see Section A.1), its eigenvectors build an orthogonal basis of $\mathbb{R}^n$, such that we can exactly represent each vector $\mathbf{f} = (f_1, \ldots, f_n)^{\mathrm{T}}$ in this basis:

$$\mathbf{f} = \sum_{i=1}^{n} \langle \mathbf{e}_i, \mathbf{f} \rangle \, \mathbf{e}_i,$$

with $\langle \mathbf{e}_i, \mathbf{f} \rangle = \mathbf{e}_i^T \mathbf{f}$. The discrete analog of the low-pass filter of Equation (4.3) is to reconstruct the filtered function $\tilde{\mathbf{f}}$ from the low-frequency basis functions only, i.e., from the first $m < n$ eigenvectors:

$$\tilde{\mathbf{f}} = \sum_{i=1}^{m} \langle \mathbf{e}_i, \mathbf{f} \rangle \, \mathbf{e}_i.$$

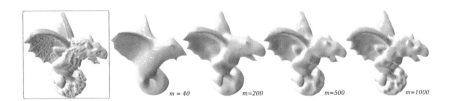

Figure 4.3. Reconstructions obtained using an increasing number of manifold harmonic basis functions. (Image taken from [Vallet and Lévy 08]. Model courtesy of Pisa Visual Computing Lab.)

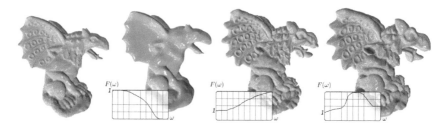

Figure 4.4. Once the manifold harmonic basis and transform have been computed, general convolution filtering with a user-defined transfer function can be performed: low-pass filter (left), high-pass filter (center), and enhancement (right). (Image taken from [Vallet and Lévy 08]. Model courtesy of Pisa Visual Computing Lab.)

A filtering or smoothing of the mesh *geometry* can now be achieved by replacing $\mathbf{f}$ in the above equation by the n-dimensional vectors of all x, y, and z vertex coordinates. Figure 4.3 shows meshes reconstructed from an increasing number of manifold harmonic bases, thereby containing more and more geometric details. Finally, as with the Fourier transform, it is easy to perform general convolution filtering by individually damping or boosting frequencies $F(\omega)$ based on a user-defined transfer function, as shown in Figure 4.4.

The manifold harmonics provide a natural generalization of the Fourier transform to continuous and discrete 2-manifold surfaces of arbitrary geometry and topology. They allow for ideal low-pass filtering using exact cut-off frequencies $\omega_{\max}$ and also for flexible convolution filtering. Unfortunately, this approach is too expensive for many applications, since the required eigenvector decomposition of the potentially very large Laplace matrix $\mathbf{L}$ is numerically difficult to compute [Vallet and Lévy 08].

A cheaper and therefore more practical approach is diffusion flow, discussed in the next section. It corresponds to a damping of high frequencies by multiplying them with a Gaussian kernel instead of strictly cutting off all frequencies above a threshold $\omega_{\max}$. Since the inverse Fourier transform of a Gaussian in the frequency domain yields a Gaussian in the spatial domain, the Fourier transform is not necessary in this approach and the smoothing can be computed directly in the spatial domain, i.e., on the triangle mesh [Taubin 95].

4.2   Diffusion Flow

Diffusion flow is a mathematically well-understood model for the time-dependent process of smoothing a given signal $f(\mathbf{x}, t)$. Many physical processes can be described by diffusion flow (e.g., heat diffusion and Brownian motion). Diffusion flow is modeled by the *diffusion equation*

$$\frac{\partial f(\mathbf{x}, t)}{\partial t} = \lambda \Delta f(\mathbf{x}, t). \tag{4.5}$$

This equation is a second-order linear partial differential equation (PDE), which states that the function f changes over time by a scalar diffusion coefficient λ times its spatial Laplacian Δf. As an example, if $f(\mathbf{x}, t)$ denotes the temperature at time t of a material point $\mathbf{x}$, the equation describes the temporal heat diffusion in an object, and is therefore also called the *heat equation*.

We can employ the diffusion equation to smooth an arbitrary function $f\colon \mathcal{S} \to \mathbb{R}$ on a manifold surface $\mathcal{S}$, simply by replacing the regular Laplace operator by the manifold Laplace-Beltrami. Since Equation (4.5) is a continuous time-dependent PDE, we have to discretize it both in space and in time.

For the spatial discretization we again replace the function f by its sample values at the mesh vertices $(f(v_1, t), \ldots, f(v_n, t))^T$ and compute the discrete Laplace-Beltrami using either the uniform or cotangent discretizations (Section 3.3). This yields an equation for the evolution of the function value of each vertex,

$$\frac{\partial}{\partial t} f(v_i, t) = \lambda \Delta f(v_i, t), \quad i = 1, \ldots, n, \tag{4.6}$$

which can be written in matrix notation as $\partial \mathbf{f}(t)/\partial t = \lambda \mathbf{L} \mathbf{f}(t)$ using the Laplace matrix discussed in Section A.1.

For the temporal discretization we divide the time axis into regular intervals of size h, yielding time steps $\{t, t+h, t+2h, \ldots\}$. Approximating the time derivative by finite differences

$$\frac{\partial \mathbf{f}(t)}{\partial t} \approx \frac{\mathbf{f}(t+h) - \mathbf{f}(t)}{h}$$

and solving for $\mathbf{f}(t+h)$ yields the *explicit Euler integration*:

$$\mathbf{f}(t+h) = \mathbf{f}(t) + h\,\frac{\partial \mathbf{f}(t)}{\partial t} = \mathbf{f}(t) + h\,\lambda \mathbf{L} \mathbf{f}(t).$$

Note that for numerically robust integration a sufficiently small time step h has to be chosen. In order to guarantee unconditional robustness even for large time steps, implicit time integration should be used [Desbrun et al. 99]. Evaluating the Laplace $\Delta \mathbf{f}$ at the *next* time step $(t+h)$ instead of the current time t leads to the *implicit Euler integration*:

$$\mathbf{f}(t+h) = \mathbf{f}(t) + h\,\lambda \mathbf{L} \mathbf{f}(t+h) \quad \Leftrightarrow \quad (\mathbf{Id} - h\lambda\mathbf{L})\,\mathbf{f}(t+h) = \mathbf{f}(t).$$

Note that now a sparse $(n \times n)$ linear system has to be solved for the function values $\mathbf{f}(t+h)$. The appendix gives more details on the construction of the linear system and possible solution methods. Even with highly efficient solvers, implicit integration is considerably more complex than explicit integration, but in turn guarantees numerical stability.

In order to smooth the mesh geometry $\mathbf{x}$ instead of an arbitrary function $\mathbf{f}$, we simply apply the above update rules to the vertex positions $(\mathbf{x}_1, \ldots, \mathbf{x}_n)^T$. The explicit per-vertex update of the resulting so-called *Laplacian smoothing* is

$$\mathbf{x}_i \ \leftarrow \ \mathbf{x}_i + h\,\lambda\,\Delta\mathbf{x}_i.$$

Since the Laplace-Beltrami of vertex positions corresponds to the mean curvature normal ($\Delta\mathbf{x} = -2H\mathbf{n}$, Equation (3.7)), all vertices move in the normal direction by an amount determined by the mean curvature H. The above flow equation is therefore is also called the *mean curvature flow* [Desbrun et al. 99]. Some examples are depicted in Figure 4.1 and Figure 4.5.

However, the movement in the normal direction is only (approximately) true for the cotangent Laplacian. It does not hold for the uniform Laplacian (see Equation (3.10)), since the latter does not take the mesh geometry into account and therefore is a rather inaccurate discretization of the true Laplace-Beltrami. Laplacian smoothing with the *uniform* Laplacian tries to move each vertex to the barycenter of its one-ring neighbors. This smooths the mesh geometry and at the same time also leads to a tangential relaxation of the triangulation (see Figure 4.6). Depending on the application, this can be a desired feature (e.g., in isotropic remeshing, Chapter 6) or a disadvantage.

Finally, note that higher-order Laplacian flows $\partial\mathbf{f}/\partial t = \lambda\Delta^k\mathbf{f}$ can also be used where discretizations of higher-order Laplacians are computed

Figure 4.5. Curvature flow smoothing of the bunny mesh (left), showing the result after ten iterations (center) and 100 iterations (right). The color coding shows the mean curvature. (Model courtesy of the Stanford Computer Graphics Laboratory.)

Figure 4.6. Smoothing the object on the left (ten iterations) using the uniform Laplacian also regularizes the triangulation (center), whereas the cotangent Laplacian preserves the triangle shapes (right).

recursively as $\Delta^k f = \Delta(\Delta^{k-1} f)$ (see Section A.1). Higher-order flows are more expensive to compute since they depend on a larger stencil of vertices, but they provide better low-pass filtering properties [Desbrun et al. 99]. In practice, bi-Laplacian smoothing ($k = 2$) is a good trade-off between computational efficiency and smoothing quality. When the smoothing is applied only locally, the bi-Laplacian smoothing leads to a C^1 smooth blend between the smoothed and the fixed region, whereas the Laplacian smoothing achieves C^0 boundary smoothness only.

4.3 Fairing

The primary application of diffusion flow is to remove high frequency noise from a signal while preserving its low frequencies. In contrast, the goal of surface fairing is to compute shapes that are as smooth as possible. How to actually measure smoothness or fairness obviously depends on the application, but in general fair surfaces should follow the *principle of simplest shape*: the surface should be free of any unnecessary details or oscillations [Moreton and Séquin 92, Welch and Witkin 92].

This can be modeled by a suitable energy that penalizes unaesthetic behavior of the surface. A minimization of this fairness energy—subject to user-defined constraints—eventually yields the desired shape. Example applications include the construction of smooth blend surfaces and hole filling by smooth patches, as illustrated in Figure 4.7.

Let us do the following derivations for a smooth parametric surface $\mathbf{x} \colon \Omega \to \mathcal{S}$ and discuss the case of discrete triangle meshes afterward. A frequently used fairness functional is the membrane energy

$$E_{\mathrm{M}}(\mathbf{x}) \;=\; \iint_{\Omega} \sqrt{\det(\mathbf{I})} \, du \, dv, \tag{4.7}$$

which measures the area of the surface $\mathcal{S}$ (see Equation (3.3)). This energy is to be minimized under user-defined constraints, which typically fix the positions $\mathbf{x}(u, v)$ on the surface boundary $\partial\Omega$. The resulting surface of minimal area corresponds to a clamped soap bubble and is called a *membrane surface* or *minimal surface*.

Unfortunately, the energy of Equation (4.7) is highly nonlinear, containing the square root of the determinant of the (already nonlinear) first fundamental form. This makes the efficient and robust minimization of this energy a numerically very difficult task. We therefore linearize the membrane energy by replacing the first fundamental form by first-order partial derivatives, leading to the *Dirichlet energy*

$$\tilde{E}_M(\mathbf{x}) = \iint_\Omega \|\mathbf{x}_u\|^2 + \|\mathbf{x}_v\|^2 \, du \, dv, \qquad (4.8)$$

where we use the shorthand notation $\mathbf{x}_u = \partial\mathbf{x}/\partial u$ and $\mathbf{x}_v = \partial\mathbf{x}/\partial v$. Since partial derivation is a linear operator, this energy is quadratic in $\mathbf{x}$.

In order to minimize the above linearized energy we employ *calculus of variations* [Gelfand and Fomin 00, Kobbelt 97], which we introduce on a 1D version of Equation (4.8). We are looking for a function $f\colon [a, b] \to \mathbb{R}$ that minimizes the 1D membrane energy

$$E(f) = \int_a^b (f_x)^2 \, dx,$$

subject to boundary constraints that fix $f(a)$ and $f(b)$. Let us assume that f actually *is* the minimizer of $E(f)$. If we then pick an arbitrary function $u(x)$ with $u(a) = u(b) = 0$, we get $E(f) < E(f + u)$. If we furthermore consider $E(f + \lambda u)$ as a function of the scalar parameter λ, then this function has a minimum at $\lambda = 0$. Consequently, its derivative with respect to λ has to vanish at $\lambda = 0$:

$$\left.\frac{\partial E(f + \lambda u)}{\partial \lambda}\right|_{\lambda=0} = \int_a^b 2f_x u_x = 0.$$

Figure 4.7. Applications of surface fairing include constructing smooth blends between given surface parts (left) and filling holes with smooth patches (right).

Integrating by parts and exploiting $u(a) = u(b) = 0$ transforms this into $-\int_a^b f_{xx} u = 0$. Note that this means that $\int_a^b f_{xx} u$ has to vanish for *any arbitrary* u with $u(a) = u(b) = 0$. This, however, is only possible if

$$f_{xx} = \Delta f = 0.$$

This is the so-called *Euler-Lagrange equation* of the minimization problem $E(f) \to \min$. Intuitively it states that at the minimum f the first derivative of $E(f)$ with respect to f has to vanish. Since $E(f)$ is a functional (a function of a function), the resulting equation is a PDE. Based on this observation, we can solve the Euler-Lagrange PDE to find the minimizer f instead of numerically minimizing $E(f)$.

The same mechanism can be applied to the minimization of Equation (4.8), but it requires using more complex boundary constraints and exploiting the divergence theorem instead of partial integration. As the result we get the Euler-Lagrange equation

$$\tilde{E}_M(\mathbf{x}) \to \min \qquad \Leftrightarrow \qquad \Delta\mathbf{x}(u,v) = 0 \text{ for } (u,v) \in \Omega,$$

again subject to boundary constraints on $\partial\Omega$.

We can finally transfer this continuous formulation to discrete triangle meshes by (1) replacing the continuous coordinate function $\mathbf{x}(u,v)$ with the vector of vertex coordinates $\mathbf{x} = (\mathbf{x}_1, \ldots, \mathbf{x}_n)^T$, and (2) using the discrete Laplace-Beltrami operator. This leads to a linear Laplace system

$$\mathbf{Lx} = \mathbf{0}$$

that is solved for the optimal vertex positions $\mathbf{x}$ (see the Appendix for details on the numerical solution). Figure 4.8 (left) shows an example of a discrete membrane surface.

Figure 4.8. The blue region is determined by minimizing a fairness functional: membrane surface ($\Delta\mathbf{x} = 0$, left), thin-plate surface ($\Delta^2\mathbf{x} = 0$, center), and minimum variation surface ($\Delta^3\mathbf{x} = 0$, right). The order k of the Euler-Lagrange equation $\Delta^k\mathbf{x} = 0$ determines the maximum smoothness C^{k-1} at the boundary. (Image taken from [Botsch and Kobbelt 04a]. ©2004 ACM, Inc. Included here by permission.)

If the goal is to minimize curvature instead of surface area, we start from the nonlinear *thin-plate energy*

$$E_{TP}(\mathbf{x}) = \iint_\Omega \kappa_1^2 + \kappa_2^2 \; du\, dv,$$

where κ_1 and κ_2 denote the principal curvatures. Linearization replaces curvatures by second derivatives, leading to

$$\tilde{E}_{TP}(\mathbf{x}) = \iint_\Omega \|\mathbf{x}_{uu}\|^2 + 2\,\|\mathbf{x}_{uv}\|^2 + \|\mathbf{x}_{vv}\|^2 \; du\, dv.$$

The corresponding Euler-Lagrange equation is $\Delta^2 \mathbf{x}(u, v) = 0$ in Ω, with suitable C^1 boundary constraints prescribing positions $\mathbf{x}(u, v)$ and normals $\mathbf{n}(u, v)$ on $\partial\Omega$. Translated to a discrete triangle mesh, we get the linear bi-Laplacian system

$$\mathbf{L}^2\mathbf{x} = \mathbf{0}.$$

In the discrete case, it is typically easier to fix the positions of two rings of boundary vertices instead of prescribing positions and normals for one ring of boundary vertices [Kobbelt et al. 98b]. Both kinds of boundary constraints lead to (approximate) C^1 boundary smoothness, as shown in Figure 4.8 (center).

Even higher-order fairness can be achieved by minimizing not curvature, but the variation of curvature

$$\iint_\Omega \left(\frac{\partial \kappa_1}{\partial \mathbf{t}_1}\right)^2 + \left(\frac{\partial \kappa_2}{\partial \mathbf{t}_2}\right)^2 \; du\, dv, \qquad (4.9)$$

where κ_1, κ_2 again denote principal curvatures and $\mathbf{t}_1, \mathbf{t}_2$ the corresponding principal curvature directions. The discrete approximation of these so-called *minimum variation surfaces* [Moreton and Séquin 92] can be computed by the sixth-order PDE $\Delta^3 \mathbf{x} = 0$ (see Figure 4.8 (right)).

We have seen that we can compute membrane surfaces, thin-plate surfaces, and minimum variation surfaces by solving linear Laplacian systems $\mathbf{L}^k\mathbf{x} = \mathbf{0}$ of order 1, 2, and 3, respectively. Figure 4.9 shows the influence of different discretizations of the Laplace-Beltrami operator for the minimization of the thin-plate energy. The uniform Laplacian yields artifacts in regions of varying high vertex density, whereas the cotangent discretization gives the expected result.

There is an interesting connection between surface fairing and diffusion flow: for the fair surfaces discussed above, the kth-order Laplacian $\Delta^k\mathbf{x}$ vanishes on the whole surface (by construction). Since the kth-order Laplacian is also the update vector of the kth-order Laplacian flow, these surfaces are steady-states of the flow $\partial\mathbf{x}/\partial t = \Delta^k\mathbf{x}$. This confirms that fair

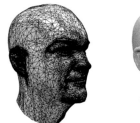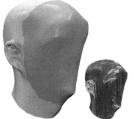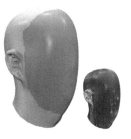

Figure 4.9. Comparison of different Laplace-Beltrami discretizations for solving $\Delta^2\mathbf{x} = \mathbf{0}$: irregular input triangle mesh (left), uniform Laplacian (center), and cotangent Laplacian (right). The small images show the respective mean curvatures. (Model courtesy of Cyberware. Image taken from [Botsch and Sorkine 08]. ©2008 IEEE.)

surfaces are indeed as smooth as possible. Furthermore, one explicit time step of the kth-order Laplacian flow is equivalent to one (damped) Jacobi iteration for solving the linear system $\Delta^k\mathbf{x} = \mathbf{0}$ (see the Appendix). Computing one implicit time step with infinite step size $h = \infty$ leads directly to $\Delta^k\mathbf{x} = \mathbf{0}$. As a consequence, Laplacian flows converge to fair surfaces.

Finally, note that the exact same framework can also be used to construct fair general functions $\mathbf{f} \colon \mathcal{S} \to \mathbb{R}^d$, which simply amounts to replacing the coordinate function $\mathbf{x}$ with $\mathbf{f}$. We will see these concepts again when computing parameterizations of minimal distortion ($\Delta\mathbf{u} = \mathbf{0}$, see Chapter 5), deformations that minimize stretching and bending ($k_s\Delta\mathbf{d} + k_b\Delta^2\mathbf{d} = \mathbf{0}$, see Chapter 9), and smooth patches for hole filling ($\Delta^2\mathbf{x} = \mathbf{0}$, see Section 8).

4.4   Summary and Further Reading

In this chapter we introduced three different but closely related approaches for smoothing 2-manifold surfaces and triangle surfaces. Manifold harmonics provide an elegant generalization of the Fourier transform to surface meshes but are computationally too expensive for most applications. Diffusion flow and higher-order Laplacian flows are easy to implement and constitute an efficient tool for removing high frequency noise. Surface fairing computes as-smooth-as-possible surfaces, which are limit surfaces of their corresponding smoothing flows.

We restricted our discussion to *isotropic* and *linear* smoothing techniques since those are easier to understand and sufficient in most situations.

For alternative techniques we refer the reader to the more sophisticated approaches mentioned below.

Anisotropic diffusion flow. Diffusion flow, as discussed so far, is an *isotropic* smoothing scheme since it diffuses high frequency noise equally in all directions. However, this process inevitably also blurs geometric features, such as sharp edges. In contrast, *anisotropic* diffusion tries to preserve features by adjusting the direction of diffusion, such that smoothing happens along, but not across features. To this end, the isotropic Laplacian $\Delta f = \text{div}\nabla f$ is extended by a data-dependent diffusion tensor $\mathbf{D}(\mathbf{x})$, yielding the anisotropic diffusion flow equation $\partial f/\partial t = \text{div}\,\mathbf{D}\,\nabla f$ [Perona and Malik 90]. Examples of anisotropic surface smoothing can be found in [Bajaj and Xu 03, Clarenz et al. 00, Desbrun et al. 00, Hildebrandt and Polthier 04].

Bilateral filtering. Bilateral filtering of images [Tomasi and Manduchi 98] preserves features by considering both the image domain (as for classic filtering) and its range (color values): each pixel becomes a weighted average of pixels with similar color values in its spatial neighborhood. Bilateral filtering was adapted to surface denoising by [Fleishman et al. 03, Jones et al. 03], who took spatial distances (image domain) as well as local variation of normal vectors (range domain) into account.

Nonlinear smoothing. For surface fairing we replaced nonlinear intrinsic properties (e.g., fundamental forms and principal curvatures) with first- and second-order partial derivatives, which eventually led to a simple linear system to be solved for the fair surface. Nonlinear smoothing approaches solve the true nonlinear minimization problem, which is numerically more difficult but provides surfaces of higher quality since they are less dependent on the initial triangulation or parameterization [Moreton and Séquin 92]. For instance, Schneider at al. [Schneider and Kobbelt 01, Schneider and Kobbelt 00] solve the nonlinear equation $\Delta H = 0$, and Bobenko and Schröder minimize the discrete Willmore flow [Bobenko and Schröder 05]. Eigensatz et al. apply a bilateral filter directly on the discrete mean curvature function and reconstruct a triangle mesh that best approximates the filtered curvature values [Eigensatz et al. 08].

PARAMETERIZATION

Different representations are used to encode the geometry of three-dimensional objects (see Chapter 1). The choice of a representation depends on the acquisition process upstream and on the application downstream. However, the representations that are the easiest to reconstruct are in most cases not optimal for the applications. The notion of parameterization attaches a "geometric coordinate system" to the object (see Chapter 3). This chapter introduces methods that compute such a parametric representation for a given polygonal mesh. This facilitates converting from one representation to another. For instance, it is possible to convert a mesh model into a piecewise bicubic spline surface, which is the type of representation used in computer-aided design (CAD) packages. In a certain sense, this retrieves an "equation" of the geometry, or constructs an *abstraction* of the geometry: once the geometry is abstracted, re-instancing it into alternative representations becomes easier.

As an initial motivation, we start by listing some important applications of mesh parameterization. We then present methods based on barycentric mapping that fix the booundary on a convex polygon. Then we study conformal mapping methods that preserve angles and that do not require fixing the bounary. We also review methods based on notions from differential geometry presented in Chapter 3, (the anisotropy ellipse and distortion analysis). Note that this chapter is limited to parameterization methods for objects with disk topology. Parameterization methods for objects with more general topology (global parameterization methods) are not covered.

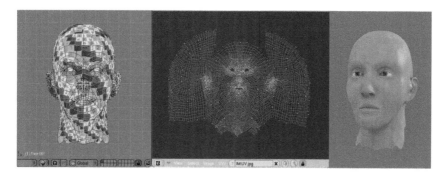

Figure 5.1. Texture mapping as one application of parameterization (least squares conformal maps as implemented in the open-source modeler Blender).

5.1 General Goals

Computing a parameterization of an object means attaching a coordinate system to it. Such a coordinate system has many possible applications. One of the main applications of mesh parameterization is *texture mapping*. Figure 5.1 shows an example of a parameterization implemented in the Blender[1] open-source modeler. The parameterization is used to put the surface into one-to-one correspondence with an image, stored in the 2D domain. It is possible to map an existing image onto the 3D model, or to define the parameter space image by directly painting the model.

With the advent of programmable graphics hardware, texture mapping can now be used to map more complex attributes onto surfaces. The example shown in Figure 5.2 illustrates a technique referred to as *normal mapping* (see, e.g., [Sander et al. 01]). The initial object is replaced with a significantly decimated version (see Chapter 7). Its visual appearance is nevertheless preserved accurately by encoding the original, high-resolution normal vectors in a texture and using a fragment shader to compute the lighting while preserving its overall visual appearance. Since details can be stored more compactly in a texture image than by using a large number of triangles, normal-mapping is an important technique for real-time rendering.

Another class of applications concerns re-meshing algorithms (see Chapter 6). Finally, the coordinate system defined by the parameterization facilitates converting from a mesh representation into an alternative one. This is of paramount importance for modeling and simulation tasks, which use representations that are completely different from the dense triangulated meshes constructed by 3D scanners and their companion reconstruction

---

[1]http://www.blender.org/

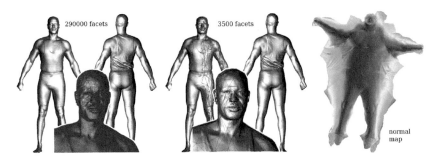

Figure 5.2. Appearance-preserving simplification as another application of parameterization: The initial object (left) is decimated to 1.5% of the original size (center). High-resolution geometric details are encoded in a normal map (right) and mapped to the simplified model, thereby preserving the original appearance. (Model courtesy of Cyberware. Image taken from [Hormann et al. 07]. ©2007 ACM, Inc. Included here by permission.)

software. More specifically, these applications require parametric representations (see Chapter 1). For instance, Figure 5.3 shows a mesh transformed into a parametric representation, using a parameterization. This fills the gap between acquisition and CAD/finite element simulations.

To summarize: formally, a parameterization of a 3D surface is a function putting this surface in one-to-one correspondence with a 2D domain. This notion plays an important role in geometry processing since it makes

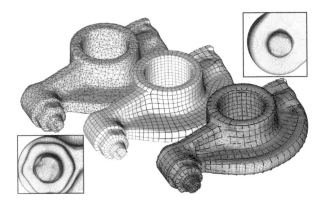

Figure 5.3. On a mesh (left), a parameterization defines a coordinate system (center) that can be used to convert the input mesh into a parametric surface (right). (Image taken from [Hormann et al. 07]. ©2007 ACM, Inc. Included here by permission.)

it possible to transform complex 3D modeling problems into a 2D space where they are simpler to solve. The next section discretizes the notion of parameterization into the context of a piecewise linear triangle mesh.

5.2   Parameterization of a Triangulated Surface

Triangulated surfaces—defined as in Chapter 2 by vertices $v_1, \ldots, v_n \in \mathcal{V}$, positions $\mathbf{p}_1, \ldots, \mathbf{p}_n$ (or $\mathbf{x}_1, \ldots, \mathbf{x}_n$), and a set $\mathcal{F}$ of triangular faces—are naturally parameterized using piecewise linear functions, whose pieces correspond to the triangles of the surface. Thus, it is possible to represent the parameterization by the set of all (u_i, v_i) coordinates associated with each vertex (x_i, y_i, z_i). Figure 5.4 shows an example of a parameterized triangulated surface in 3D space and in (u, v) parameter space.

Note that in the context of differential geometry (Chapter 3), we consider an *existing* parameterization, whereas this chapter considers the problem of constructing a parameterization for an existing surface. For this

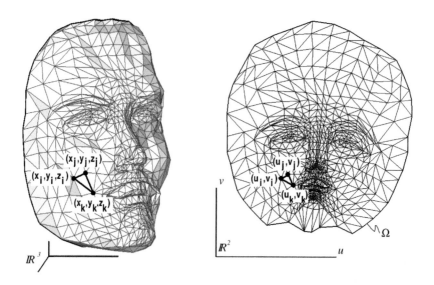

Figure 5.4. A parameterized triangulated surface in 3D space (left) and in (u, v) parameter space (right). A parameterization of a triangulated surface can be defined as a piecewise linear function, determined by the coordinates (u_i, v_i) at each vertex (x_i, y_i, z_i). (Image taken from [Hormann et al. 07]. ©2007 ACM, Inc. Included here by permission.)

reason, in contrast with the conventions of differential geometry, it is more natural to consider that we map the 3D space (known) into the 2D parameter space (unknown), shown on the left and on the right, respectively, in Figure 5.4. We will see more fundamental implications of this "swapping" when we explain the formulation and behavior of methods based on distortion analysis.

At a given point (u, v) of the parameter space Ω, the parameterization $\mathbf{x}$ is given by

$$\mathbf{x}(u, v) = \alpha\mathbf{p}_i + \beta\mathbf{p}_j + \gamma\mathbf{p}_k,$$

where (i, j, k) denotes the index triplet such that the triangle $[(u_i, v_i), (u_j, v_j), (u_k, v_k)]$ in parameter space contains the point (u, v). The triplet (α, β, γ) denotes the barycentric coordinates at point (u, v) in the triangle. See also Equations (1.3) and (1.4).

In summary, constructing a parameterization of a triangulated surface means finding a set of coordinates (u_i, v_i) associated to each vertex i. Moreover, these coordinates need to be such that the image of the surface in parameter space does not self-intersect. This means that the intersection of any two triangles in parameter space is either a common edge, a common vertex, or empty. In the following we discuss different solutions for assigning (u, v) coordinates to the vertices.

5.3   Barycentric Mapping

Barycentric map is one of the most widely used methods for constructing a parameterization of a triangulated surface. This method is based on Tutte's barycentric mapping theorem [Tutte 60], from graph theory, which states:

> Given a triangulated surface homeomorphic to a disk, if the (u, v) coordinates at the boundary vertices lie on a convex polygon, and if the coordinates of the internal vertices are a convex combination of their neighbors, then the (u, v) coordinates form a valid parameterization (without self-intersections).

Supposing that the vertices are ordered so that indices $\{1, \ldots n_{\text{int}}\}$ correspond to interior vertices and indices $\{n_{\text{int}}+1, \ldots, n\}$ correspond to boundary vertices, the second condition of the theorem can be written as

$$\forall i \in \{1, \ldots, n_{\text{int}}\} : \quad -a_{i,i} \begin{pmatrix} u_i \\ v_i \end{pmatrix} = \sum_{j \neq i} a_{i,j} \begin{pmatrix} u_j \\ v_j \end{pmatrix},$$

where the coefficients $a_{i,j}$ are such that $\forall i \in \{1, \ldots, n\}$

$$
\begin{cases}
a_{i,j} > 0 & \text{if } v_i \text{ and } v_j \text{ are connected by an edge,} \\
a_{i,i} = -\sum_{j \neq i} a_{i,j}, & \\
a_{i,j} = 0 & \text{otherwise.}
\end{cases}
\tag{5.1}
$$

The initial proof by Tutte [Tutte 60] uses sophisticated concepts from graph theory. A simpler proof was established by Colin de Verdière [de Verdierc 90]. Finally, a proof based on the notion of discrete one forms was established by [Gortler et al. 06]. Since it uses simple counting arguments, this latter proof is accessible without requiring the important graph theory background involved in the other two.

This theorem—which *characterizes* a family of valid parameterizations—can be used instead as a method to *construct* a parameterization [Floater 97]. The idea consists of first fixing the vertices of the boundary on a convex polygon. Then, the coordinates at the internal vertices are found by solving Equation (5.1). This means solving two linear systems, $\mathbf{Au} = \bar{\mathbf{u}}$ and $\mathbf{Av} = \bar{\mathbf{v}}$ of dimension n_{int}, where the vectors $\mathbf{u}$ and $\mathbf{v}$ gather all the u and v coordinates at the internal vertices, and where the righthand side $\bar{\mathbf{u}}$ (respectively $\bar{\mathbf{v}}$) contains the weighted coordinates at the vertices on the boundary:

$$
\forall i \in \{1, \ldots, n_{\text{int}}\} : \quad
\begin{cases}
\sum_{j=1}^{n_{\text{int}}} a_{i,j} u_j = \bar{u}_i = -\sum_{j=n_{\text{int}}+1}^{n} a_{i,j} u_j, \\
\sum_{j=1}^{n_{\text{int}}} a_{i,j} v_j = \bar{v}_i = -\sum_{j=n_{\text{int}}+1}^{n} a_{i,j} v_j.
\end{cases}
\tag{5.2}
$$

There are many possibilities for solving Equation (5.2). For large meshes, the most efficient ones comprise sparse iterative and sparse direct methods, discussed in the Appendix. For reasonably small meshes (up to 5K vertices), a simple Gauss-Seidel solver (see also the Appendix) can also be used. In practice, this means iteratively moving all vertices to the barycenter of their neighbors:

```
parameterize_Tutte_Floater()
    while more iterations are needed
        for i = 1 to n_int
```
$$
\begin{pmatrix} u_i \\ v_i \end{pmatrix} \leftarrow \frac{1}{a_{i,i}} \sum_{j \neq i} a_{i,j} \begin{pmatrix} u_j \\ v_j \end{pmatrix}
$$

The iterations are stopped when the (u, v) updates are smaller than a user-specified threshold or after a given maximum number of iterations.

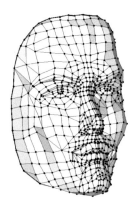 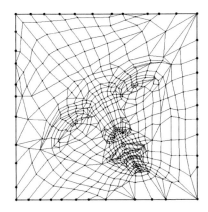

Figure 5.5. Parameterization with Floater's method. The parametric coordinates on the boundary of the surface are fixed on a convex polygon, and the interior coordinates are obtained by solving a linear system. (Image taken from [Hormann et al. 07]. ©2007 ACM, Inc. Included here by permission.)

The matrix $\mathbf{A}$ has a property that is sufficient to ensure that the Gauss-Seidel iteration converges to the solution ($\mathbf{A}$ is a M-matrix, see [Golub and Loan 89]). Figure 5.5 shows an example of a parameterization computed by this method (using weights $a_{i,j}$ detailed further).

A possible valid choice for the coefficients $a_{i,j}$ is given by $a_{i,j} = 1$ if i and j are connected by an edge, and $a_{i,i} = -|\mathcal{N}_i|$, where $|\mathcal{N}_i|$ denotes the number of one-ring neighbors of vertex i (i.e., its valence). However, these weights do not take the mesh geometry into account (such as edge lengths or triangle angles), and therefore introduce distortions that must be avoided by most applications. For this reason, the next section introduces a way of choosing these weights so as to minimize some distortions.

5.3.1 Discrete Laplacian

The Laplacian, or Laplace operator, is a generalization of the second-order derivative for multivariate functions. In flat 2D space, this operator is defined by

$$\Delta f = \frac{\partial^2 f}{\partial x^2} + \frac{\partial^2 f}{\partial y^2}.$$

The Laplacian measures the regularity (or irregularity) of a function. For instance, for a linear function the Laplacian is equal to zero. Therefore, minimizing the Laplacian of u and v results in smooth parametric coordinates; in other words, this also minimizes the distortion of the parameterization. The Laplacian can be generalized to curved surfaces, and the

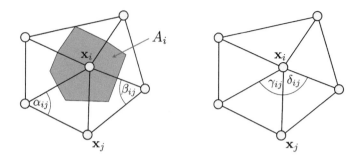

Figure 5.6. Angles and areas used by the discrete cotangent Laplacian (left) and the mean value coordinates (right).

generalized form is called the Laplace-Beltrami operator. In Chapter 3, Equation (3.11), a discrete version of this operator was derived, such that

$$a_{i,j} = \frac{1}{2A_i}\left(\cot \alpha_{i,j} + \cot \beta_{i,j}\right),$$

$$a_{i,i} = -\sum_{j \neq i} a_{i,j},$$

where the angles $\alpha_{i,j}$ and $\beta_{i,j}$ are shown in Figure 5.6 (left), and where A_i corresponds to the Voronoi area of vertex v_i. The so-defined discrete Laplacian is a matrix $(a_{i,j})$ whose nonzero pattern corresponds to the connectivity of the mesh and satisfies $a_{i,i} = -\sum_{j \neq i} a_{i,j}$. It is therefore possible to use the discrete Laplacian to define the coefficients $a_{i,j}$ used in Floater's method, as done in [Eck et al. 95]. We elaborate further on the link between the discrete Laplacian and parametric distortion in Section 5.4.3.

As already mentioned in Chapter 3, for meshes with obtuse angles, the coefficients of the discrete Laplacian may become negative. This violates the requirements of Tutte's theorem such that the validity of the mapping can no longer be guaranteed. It is possible to remove obtuse angles by subdividing the initial mesh [Rivara 84]. Another possibility is to use a different definition of weights, introduced by [Floater 03], based on the mean value theorem (instead of Stokes theorem for cotangent weights):

$$a_{i,j} = \frac{1}{\|\mathbf{x}_i - \mathbf{x}_j\|}\left(\tan\left(\frac{\delta_{i,j}}{2}\right) + \tan\left(\frac{\gamma_{i,j}}{2}\right)\right), \qquad a_{i,i} = -\sum_{j \neq i} a_{i,j},$$

where $\delta_{i,j}$ and $\gamma_{i,j}$ are the angles shown in Figure 5.6 (right). The so-defined *mean value weights* are always positive and therefore provably generate one-to-one mappings.

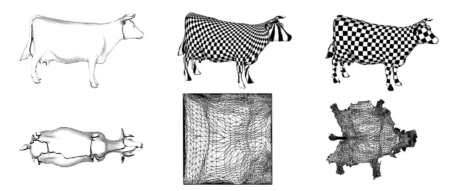

Figure 5.7. A mesh cut in a way that makes it homeomorphic to a disk, using the *seamster* algorithm [Sheffer and Hart 02] (left). Tutte-Floater parameterization obtained by fixing the boundary on a square (center). Parameterization obtained with a free-boundary parameterization [Sheffer and de Sturler 01] (right). (Image taken from [Hormann et al. 07]. ©2007 ACM, Inc. Included here by permission.)

Therefore, Tutte's theorem combined with mean value weights provides a provably correct way of constructing a valid parameterization for a disk-like surface. However, for some surfaces the necessity of fixing the boundary on a convex polygon may be problematic (see Figure 5.7), for the following reasons: (1) in general, it is difficult to find a "natural" way of fixing the boundary on a convex polygon, and (2) for some surfaces, the shape of the boundary is far from being convex. As a consequence, the obtained parameterization shows high distortions. Even if one can imagine different ways of improving the result, the so-obtained parameterization will probably not be as good as the one shown in Figure 5.7 (right), which better matches what a tanner would expect for such a mesh. The next section studies methods devised to construct parameterizations with free boundaries, based on the notion of conformal mapping.

5.4   Conformal Mapping

Conformal mapping is related to the formalism of complex analysis. Conformal mapping relies on the conformality condition, which defines a criterion with sufficient rigidity to offer good extrapolation capabilities that can compute natural boundaries. Readers interested in this formalism are referred to [Needham 94].

The anisotropy ellipse, introduced in Section 3.2.2, plays a central role in the definition of (non-distorted) parameterization methods. We now

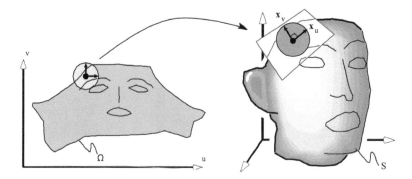

Figure 5.8. A conformal parameterization transforms a small circle into a small circle, i.e., it is locally a similarity transform. (Image taken from [Hormann et al. 07]. ©2007 ACM, Inc. Included here by permission.)

focus on a particular family of parameterization, called *conformal maps*, for which the anisotropy ellipse is a circle for all points of the surface. As shown in Figure 5.8, this also means that the two gradient vectors $\mathbf{x}_u$ and $\mathbf{x}_v$ are orthogonal and have the same norm. The condition can also be written as $\mathbf{x}_v = \mathbf{n} \times \mathbf{x}_u$, where $\mathbf{n}$ denotes the normal vector. Remarkably, if a parameterization is conformal, this is also the case for the inverse function (since the Jacobian matrix of the inverse is equal to the inverse of the Jacobian matrix). To understand that, one can also say that if the iso-u and iso-v curves are orthogonal, it is also the case for their normal vectors in the tangent plane. Finally, conformality also means that the Jacobian matrix is composed of rotation and scaling only (i.e., a *similarity transform*). Therefore, conformal mappings locally correspond to similarities. We now review various methods that compute a conformal parameterization.

5.4.1   Gradient in a Triangle

Conformality can be expressed as a relation between the gradients of parameterization. Therefore, to port the definition of conformal maps into the setting of piecewise linear triangulated surfaces, one can use the expression of the gradients as given in Section 3.3.

However, we need to stress again that our setting is slightly different from the one in Chapter 3. In our case, the 3D surface is given, and our goal is to construct the parameterization. In this setting, it seems more natural to characterize the inverse of the parameterization, i.e., the function that goes from the 3D surface $\mathcal{S}$ (known) to the parameter space Ω (unknown). This function is also piecewise linear. In this configuration, to define the gradients it is possible to provide each triangle with an

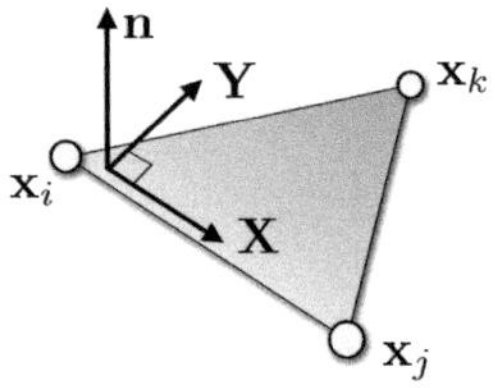

$$\mathbf{X} = \frac{\mathbf{x}_j - \mathbf{x}_i}{\|\mathbf{x}_j - \mathbf{x}_i\|}$$

$$\mathbf{n} = \frac{\mathbf{X} \times (\mathbf{x}_k - \mathbf{x}_i)}{\|\mathbf{X} \times (\mathbf{x}_k - \mathbf{x}_i)\|}$$

$$\mathbf{Y} = \mathbf{n} \times \mathbf{X}$$

Figure 5.9. Local X, Y basis in a triangle.

orthonormal basis X, Y, as shown in Figure 5.9 (we can use one of the vertices $\mathbf{x}_i$ of the triangle as the origin). In this basis, we can study the inverse of the parameterization—that is to say, the function that maps a point (X, Y) of the triangle to a point (u, v) in the parameter space. The gradients of this function are given by

$$\nabla u = \begin{bmatrix} \partial u / \partial X \\ \partial u / \partial Y \end{bmatrix} = \underbrace{\frac{1}{2 A_T} \begin{bmatrix} Y_j - Y_k & Y_k - Y_i & Y_i - Y_j \\ X_k - X_j & X_i - X_k & X_j - X_i \end{bmatrix}}_{=\mathbf{M}_T} \begin{pmatrix} u_i \\ u_j \\ u_k \end{pmatrix},$$

(5.3)

where matrix $\mathbf{M}_T$ is constant over the triangle T, and where A_T denotes the area of T. Note that these gradients are different (but strongly related to) the gradients of the $\mathcal{S} \to \Omega$ function, manipulated in Section 3.2.2: The gradient of u (respectively v) intersects the iso-u lines (respectively the iso-v lines) at a right angle (instead of being tangent to them), and its norm is the inverse of the one computed in Section 3.3. Since the inverse of a conformal map is also a conformal map, for a triangulated surface the conformality condition can be written as

$$\nabla v = \mathbf{n} \times \nabla u.$$

5.4.2 Least Squares Conformal Maps

In contrast to the exposition of the initial paper [Lévy et al. 02], we present the least squares conformal maps (LSCM) method in terms of simple geometric relations between the gradients computed in the previous subsection. We then elaborate on the complex analysis formalism and establish the relation with other methods.

The LSCM method simply expresses the conformality condition of the function that maps the surface to the parameter space. We now consider one of the triangles of the surface, provided with an orthonormal basis

(X, Y) of its supporting plane (see Section 5.4.1). In this context, conformality can be written as

$$\nabla v = (\nabla u)^{\perp} = \begin{bmatrix} 0 & -1 \\ 1 & 0 \end{bmatrix} \nabla u, \tag{5.4}$$

where $(\cdot)^{\perp}$ denotes the counterclockwise rotation of 90 degrees around $\mathbf{n}$.

Using Equation (5.3) for the gradient in a triangle, Equation (5.4), which characterizes piecewise linear conformal maps, becomes

$$\mathbf{M}_T \begin{pmatrix} v_i \\ v_j \\ v_k \end{pmatrix} - \begin{bmatrix} 0 & -1 \\ 1 & 0 \end{bmatrix} \mathbf{M}_T \begin{pmatrix} u_i \\ u_j \\ u_k \end{pmatrix} = \begin{pmatrix} 0 \\ 0 \end{pmatrix}.$$

In the continuous setting, Riemann's theorem states that any surface admits a conformal parameterization (see, e.g., [Berger 07]). However, in our specific case of piecewise linear functions, only the developable surfaces admit a conformal parameterization. For a general (non-developable) surface, LSCM minimizes an energy E_{LSCM} that corresponds to the "non-conformality" of the application and is denoted by the *conformal energy*:

$$E_{\mathrm{LSCM}} = \sum_{T=(i,j,k)} A_T \left\| \mathbf{M}_T \begin{pmatrix} v_i \\ v_j \\ v_k \end{pmatrix} - \begin{bmatrix} 0 & -1 \\ 1 & 0 \end{bmatrix} \mathbf{M}_T \begin{pmatrix} u_i \\ u_j \\ u_k \end{pmatrix} \right\|^2.$$

Note that E_{LSCM} is invariant with respect to arbitrary translations and rotations applied in parameter-space. As a consequence, E_{LSCM} does not have a unique minimizer. To have a well-defined optimization problem, it is required to reduce the degrees of freedom by fixing the (u, v) coordinates of at least two vertices.

We have considered conformal maps from the point of view of the gradients. The next section, which may be skipped in a first reading, exhibits relations between conformal maps and harmonic functions. This also shows some connections with Floater's barycentric mapping method and its generalizations.

5.4.3 Conformal Maps and Harmonic Maps

Conformal maps play a particular role in complex analysis and Riemannian geometry. The following system of equations, which is known as the *Cauchy-Riemann equations*, characterizes conformal maps:

$$\frac{\partial v}{\partial x} = -\frac{\partial u}{\partial y},$$

$$\frac{\partial v}{\partial y} = \frac{\partial u}{\partial x}.$$

They play a central role in complex analysis since they characterize differentiable complex functions (also called analytic functions).

Another interesting property of complex differentiable functions is that their first-order differentiability makes them differentiable at any order. Differentiating the Cauchy-Riemann equations once more with respect to u and v reveals interesting relations with the Laplacian (see Section 5.3.1):

$$\Delta u = \frac{\partial^2 u}{\partial x^2} + \frac{\partial^2 u}{\partial y^2} = 0,$$

$$\Delta v = \frac{\partial^2 v}{\partial x^2} + \frac{\partial^2 v}{\partial y^2} = 0.$$

In other words, the real part and the imaginary part of a conformal map are two harmonic functions (i.e., two functions with zero Laplacian). This justifies the idea of using the discrete Laplacian to define Floater's weights, mentioned in the previous section. This is the point of view adopted by Desbrun et al. to develop their conformal parameterization method [Desbrun et al. 02], equivalent to LSCM. Thus, Desbrun et al. compute two harmonic functions while letting the boundary evolve. On the boundary, a set of constraints enforce the conformality of the parameterization and introduce a coupling term between the u- and the v-coordinates.

Another way of considering both approaches, mentioned by Pinkall and Polthier [Pinkall and Polthier 93], is given by Plateau's problem [Plateau 73, Meeks 81]. Given a closed curve, this problem concerns the existence of a surface with minimum area, such that its boundary matches the closed curve. To minimize the area of a surface, Douglas [Douglas 31] and Rado [Rado 30], and later Courant [Courant 50], considered Dirichlet's energy (i.e., the integral of the squared norm of the gradients, see Equation (4.8)) easier to manipulate. A discretization of this energy was proposed by Pinkall and Polthier [Pinkall and Polthier 93], with the aim of giving a practical solution to Plateau's problem in the discrete case. Dirichlet's energy differs from the area of the surface. The difference is a term that depends on the parameterization, called the *conformal energy*, which is zero if the parameterization is conformal. The relation between these three quantities is explained below:

$$\underbrace{\int_\Omega \sqrt{\det(\mathbf{I})}\mathrm{d}A}_{\text{area of the surface}} = \underbrace{\frac{1}{2}\int_\Omega \|\mathbf{x}_u\|^2 + \|\mathbf{x}_v\|^2\,\mathrm{d}A}_{\text{Dirichlet's energy}} - \underbrace{\frac{1}{2}\int_\Omega \|\mathbf{x}_v - (\mathbf{x}_u)^\perp\|^2\,\mathrm{d}A,}_{\text{conformal energy}}$$

where $\mathbf{I}$ is the first fundamental form. This relation is easy to prove by expanding the integrated terms. Therefore, LSCM minimizes the conformal energy, and Desbrun et al.'s method minimizes Dirichlet's energy. Since the difference between these two quantities corresponds to the (constant) area of the surface, both methods are equivalent.

The conformal mapping methods mentioned above are based on relations between the gradients of the parameterization. We also refer the reader to [Zayer et al. 05c], which provides another way of "setting the boundary free" by separating computations into several steps involving simple (linear) computations. The notion of the derivative and its connection with geometry (or differential geometry) plays a central role in the conformal mapping methods mentioned above. For this reason, these methods can be referred to as *analytical* methods. In the next section, we focus on *geometric* methods, which consider the shape of the triangles.

5.4.4   Geometric Methods for Conformal Mapping

Analytical methods are reasonably easy to implement since they mean minimizing a quadratic form. For this reason they are well used in both the academic and industrial worlds. However, the necessity of pinning two vertices may generate results that are unbalanced in terms of distortions (see Figure 5.10) if the input surface has high Gaussian curvature.

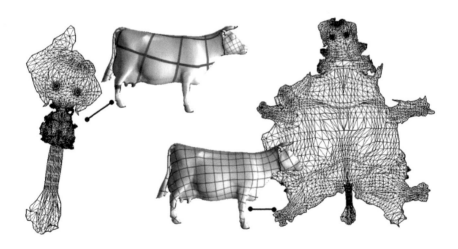

Figure 5.10. For surfaces that have a high Gaussian curvature, conformal methods may generate highly distorted results, different from what the user might expect (left). The ABF method and its variants better balance the distortions and give better results (right). (Image taken from [Hormann et al. 07]. ©2007 ACM, Inc. Included here by permission.)

We now introduce geometric methods, which do not suffer from these problems. We will review the *angle-based flattening* (ABF) method. Note that one may also classify circle packings [Bobenko and Hoffmann 01] and circle patterns [Bobenko et al. 06] in this category, but these methods are not covered here.

The ABF method, developed by Sheffer et al. [Sheffer and de Sturler 01], is based on the following observation: the parameter space is a two-dimensional triangulation, uniquely defined by all the angles at the corners of the triangles (modulo a similarity transformation in parameter space). This simple remark leads to the reformulation of the parameterization problem—finding (u_i, v_i) coordinates—in terms of angles, that is, finding the angles α_i^T, where α_i^T denotes the angle at the corner of triangle T incident to vertex i.

The energy minimized by ABF is given by

$$E_{\text{ABF}}(\boldsymbol{\alpha}) = \sum_{T \in \mathcal{F}} \sum_{k=1}^{3} \left(\frac{\alpha_k^T - \beta_k^T}{\beta_k^T} \right)^2,$$

where the sum is over all triangles T, and the energy measures the relative deviation of the unknown 2D angles α_k^T from the "optimal" angles β_k^T, measured on the 3D mesh.

To ensure that the 2D angles define a valid triangulation, a set of constraints needs to be satisfied. These can be incorporated into the energy minimization using Lagrange multipliers:

▶ The three triangle angles have to sum to π:

$$\forall T \in \mathcal{F}: \quad \alpha_1^T + \alpha_2^T + \alpha_3^T = \pi.$$

▶ For each internal vertex the incident angles have to sum to 2π (since it is a planar 2D configuration):

$$\forall v \in \mathcal{V}_{\text{int}}: \quad \sum_{(T,k) \in v^*} \alpha_k^T = 2\pi,$$

where $\mathcal{V}_{int}$ denotes the set of internal vertices, and v^* denotes the set of angles incident to vertex v.

▶ The reconstruction constraints ensure that the relations of edge lengths and angles around a vertex are consistent:

$$\forall v \in \mathcal{V}_{int}: \quad \prod_{(T,k) \in v^*} \sin \alpha_{k \oplus 1}^T = \prod_{(T,k) \in v^*} \sin \alpha_{k \ominus 1}^T.$$

The indices $k \oplus 1$ and $k \ominus 1$ denote the next and previous angle in the triangle, respectively. To understand this constraint, note that the product $\sin \alpha_{k \oplus 1}^T \cdot \sin \alpha_{k \ominus 1}^T$ corresponds to the product of the ratio between the lengths of two consecutive edges around vertex k. If they do not match, it is then possible to "turn around" vertex k without "landing" on the starting point.

Sheffer and de Sturler [Sheffer and de Sturler 01] compute a stationary point of the Lagrangian of the constrained quadratic optimization problem by using Newton's method. An improvement of the numerical solution mechanism has been proposed [Sheffer et al. 05]. To speed up computations, Zayer et al. propose a linearized approximation that solves for the approximation error [Zayer et al. 07]. The dual formulation leads to a least-norm problem, which means solving a single linear system.

5.5 Methods Based on Distortion Analysis

For texture mapping applications, it is important to minimize distortions. In particular, the distortion analysis formalism introduced in Section 3.2.2 and 5.4.1 allows us to characterize how a signal stored in a texture is distorted when mapped onto the surface. After setting up the formalism, we will start from the simpler methods and then elaborate on signal-specialized parameterizations, best suited to texture mapping.

Before going further, we need to warn the reader again about a possible source of confusion in the literature:

▶ Half of the methods study the function that goes from the surface $\mathcal{S}$ to the parameter space Ω (as in Section 5.3). This is justified by the fact that the (u, v) coordinates are unknown. Therefore, it is more natural to go from the known world (the surface) to the unknown world (the parameter space);

▶ The other half of the methods use the inverse convention and study the function that goes from parameter space Ω to the surface $\mathcal{S}$ (as in Chapter 3). This is justified by the fact that it makes the formalism compatible with classical differential geometry books [do Carmo 76] that use this convention.

Let us first reconsider the continuous distortion analysis of Section 3.2.2 and identify some common types of distortion of the $\Omega \to \mathcal{S}$ mapping:

▶ When mapping two tangent directions $\bar{\mathbf{w}}_1, \bar{\mathbf{w}}_2$ at a point $\mathbf{u} \in \Omega$ to the surface $\mathcal{S}$, the angle of their images $\mathbf{w}_1, \mathbf{w}_2$ can be computed through their (normalized) inner product

$$\frac{\mathbf{w}_1^T \mathbf{w}_2}{\sqrt{\mathbf{w}_1^T \mathbf{w}_1} \cdot \sqrt{\mathbf{w}_2^T \mathbf{w}_2}} = \frac{\bar{\mathbf{w}}_1^T \mathbf{I}(\mathbf{u}) \, \bar{\mathbf{w}}_2}{\sqrt{\bar{\mathbf{w}}_1^T \mathbf{I}(\mathbf{u}) \, \bar{\mathbf{w}}_1} \cdot \sqrt{\bar{\mathbf{w}}_2^T \mathbf{I}(\mathbf{u}) \, \bar{\mathbf{w}}_2}}.$$

Hence, the angle is preserved if the first fundamental form is a multiple of the identity, i.e., $\mathbf{I}(\mathbf{u}) = \eta(\mathbf{u})\,\mathbf{Id}$, or, equivalently, if the singular values of $\mathbf{I}$ are equal: $\sigma_1 = \sigma_2$. If this holds for all points $\mathbf{u} \in \Omega$, we get an angle-preserving or *conformal* parameterization, which was already discussed in Section 5.4. Elementary circles are mapped to elementary circles, but their radius might change.

▶ Since the area of a mapped patch $\mathbf{x}(U)$, $U \subset \Omega$, is computed as $\int_U \sqrt{\det(\mathbf{I})}\mathrm{d}A$, the parameterization is area-preserving or *equiareal* if $\det \mathbf{I} = 1$, or equivalently $\sigma_1\sigma_2 = 1$, for all points $\mathbf{u} \in \Omega$. Elementary circles are mapped to elementary ellipses of the same area.

▶ Finally, a parameterization is length-preserving or *isometric* if it is both conformal and equiareal. In this case the first fundamental form is the identity, i.e., $\sigma_1 = \sigma_2 = 1$. Elementary circles are mapped to elementary circles of the same radius.

While isometric parameterizations are ideal in the sense that they do not distort angles and areas, only surfaces of a specific class, called *developable surfaces*, admit an isometric parameterization. These surfaces have zero Gaussian curvature everywhere, which is a consequence of the first fundamental form being the identity and of the Gaussian curvature depending only on the first fundamental form (Gauss' Theorema Egregium).

In the remainder of this section, we use the $\mathcal{S} \to \Omega$ convention, and all the metric properties $\mathbf{J}_T, \mathbf{I}_T, \sigma_1, \sigma_2$ are with respect to this function (this is the inverse direction compared to Chapter 3). Note that the metric properties are constant on each triangle T. Based on these metric properties, we will review several methods and express them in a common formalism. For each method, we will take care of identifying whether the $\mathcal{S} \to \Omega$ function or the $\Omega \to \mathcal{S}$ function is used in the initial reference.

5.5.1 Metric Properties of Piecewise Linear Surfaces

We now compute the metric properties characterizing the function that maps from local triangle coordinates (X, Y) into parameter space (u, v). Using the expression of the gradient given in Equation (5.3), we compute the Jacobian

$$\mathbf{J}_T = \begin{bmatrix} \partial u/\partial X & \partial v/\partial X \\ \partial u/\partial Y & \partial v/\partial Y \end{bmatrix} = \begin{bmatrix} \mathbf{u}_X, \mathbf{u}_Y \end{bmatrix},$$

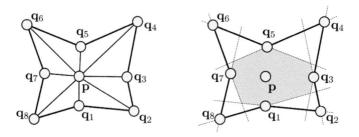

Figure 5.11. To avoid triangle flips, each vertex **p** is constrained to remain in the kernel of the polygon defined by its neighbors $\mathbf{q}_i$ (left). The kernel of a polygon—orange—is defined by the intersection of the half-planes defined by the support lines of its edges—dashed (right).

which is constant over each triangle T. From the Jacobian, we compute the fundamental form $\mathbf{I}_T$ (also constant in triangle T):

$$\mathbf{I}_T = \mathbf{J}_T^T\mathbf{J}_T = \begin{bmatrix} E & F \\ F & G \end{bmatrix} = \begin{bmatrix} \mathbf{u}_X^T\mathbf{u}_X & \mathbf{u}_X^T\mathbf{u}_Y \\ \mathbf{u}_X^T\mathbf{u}_Y & \mathbf{u}_Y^T\mathbf{u}_Y \end{bmatrix}.$$

The lengths σ_1 and σ_2 of the axes of the anisotropy ellipse (see also Section 3.2.2) are given as

$$\sigma_1 = \sqrt{1/2(E+G) + \sqrt{(E-G)^2 + 4F^2}},$$

$$\sigma_2 = \sqrt{1/2(E+G) - \sqrt{(E-G)^2 + 4F^2}}.$$

Before evoking these methods, we give two more precisions:

▶ To avoid triangle flips, some of the methods constrain each vertex **p** to remain in the kernel of the polygon defined by its neighbors $\mathbf{q}_i$. This notion is illustrated in Figure 5.11. To compute the kernel of a polygon, it is, for instance, possible to apply Sutherland and Hogdman's re-entrant polygon clipping algorithm to the polygon (clipped by itself). The algorithm is described in most general computer graphics books [Foley et al. 90].

▶ Since they are based on the eigenvalues of the first fundamental form, the objective functions involved in distortion analysis are often nonlinear and therefore difficult to minimize in an efficient way. To accelerate the computations, a commonly used technique consists of representing the surface in a multi-resolution manner, based on Hoppe's progressive mesh data structure [Hoppe 96]. The algorithm starts by optimizing a simplified version of the object, then introduces the additional vertices and optimizes them by iterative refinements.

Now that we have seen the general notions related to distortion analysis and the particular aspects that concern the optimization of objective functions involved in distortion analysis, we can review several classical methods that belong to this category.

5.5.2   Green-Lagrange Deformation Tensor

To minimize the distortions of a parameterization, one of the first methods that was developed consists of minimizing a matrix norm of the Green-Lagrange deformation tensor $\mathbf{L}$ [Maillot et al. 93]. This notion comes from mechanics, and it measures the deformation of a material. Clearly, if the metric tensor $\mathbf{I}$ is equal to the identity matrix $\mathbf{Id}$, then an elementary circle is transformed into an elementary circle of the same radius (see Section 3.2.2), and the parameterization is said to be isometric. As mentioned above, only developable surfaces admit an isometric parameterization. In the general case, for a given (possibly non-developable) surface with a parameterization, the Green-Lagrange deformation tensor is given by $\mathbf{L} = \mathbf{I} - \mathbf{Id}$ and measures the "non-isometry" of the parameterization. However, minimizing a matrix norm of $\mathbf{L}$ is extremely difficult since the function is highly nonlinear, with many local minima.

5.5.3   MIPS

The MIPS (most isometric parameterization of surfaces) method [Hormann and Greiner 00] was the first mesh parameterization method that computes a natural boundary. This method is based on the minimization of the ratio between σ_1 and σ_2, the two lengths of the axes of the anisotropy ellipse. This corresponds to the 2-norm of the Jacobian matrix:

$$E_2(\mathbf{J}_T) \;=\; \|\mathbf{J}_T\|_2 \, \left\|\mathbf{J}_T^{-1}\right\|_2 \;=\; \sigma_1/\sigma_2.$$

Since minimizing this energy is a difficult numerical problem, Hormann and Greiner have replaced the 2-norm $\|\cdot\|_2$ by the Frobenius norm $\|\cdot\|_F$, i.e., the square root of the sum of the squared singular values:

$$E_{\mathrm{MIPS}}(\mathbf{J}_T) \;=\; \|\mathbf{J}_T\|_F \, \left\|\mathbf{J}_T^{-1}\right\|_F \;=\; \frac{\mathrm{trace}(\mathbf{I}_T)}{\det(\mathbf{J}_T)}.$$

As can be seen in this equation, cancelation of terms yields a simpler expression in the end. The final expression corresponds to the ratio between the trace of the first fundamental form and the determinant of the Jacobian matrix. As indicated in the original article, this value can also be interpreted as the *Dirichlet energy per parameter-space area*: the term $\mathrm{trace}(\mathbf{I}_T)$

corresponds to the Dirichlet energy, and the Jacobian $\det(\mathbf{J}_T)$ corresponds to the ratio between a triangle's area in 3D and in parameter space (more on Dirichlet energy in Section 5.4.3 about conformal mappings). A similar approach is described in [Degener et al. 03], with a more efficient implementation of the solver for the so-defined (highly nonlinear) energy functional.

5.5.4   Signal-Specialized Parameterization

Motivated by texture mapping applications, Sander et al. studied the way a signal stored in parameter space is distorted when it is texture-mapped onto the surface (by applying the parameterization) [Sander et al. 01]. For this reason, their formalism uses the function $\Omega \to \mathcal{S}$ that maps the parameter space onto the surface (the same convention is used in Chapter 3). To relate this method with the convention adopted in this chapter, that is to say the metric properties of the $\mathcal{S} \to \Omega$ function, one can check that this simply means replacing σ_1 with $1/\sigma_2$ (and σ_2 with $1/\sigma_1$) in the computations.

A possible way of characterizing the distortions of a texture is to consider a point and a direction in parameter space and analyze how the texture is deformed along that direction. Sander et al. call this value the *stretch*. This exactly corresponds to the notion of directional derivative, introduced in Section 3.2.2. For a triangle T, they defined an energy that corresponds to the average value of the stretch for all directions:

$$E_{\text{stretch}}(T) \;=\; \sqrt{\left((1/\sigma_1)^2 + (1/\sigma_2)^2\right)/2}.$$

The local energies of each triangle T are combined into a global energy

$$E_{\text{stretch}}(\mathcal{S}) \;=\; \sqrt{\frac{\sum_T A_T E_{\text{stretch}}(T)}{\sum_T A_T}},$$

where A_T again denotes the area of the triangle T.

Figure 5.12 shows some results computed with this approach. This formalism is particularly well suited to texture mapping applications since it minimizes the distortions that are responsible for the visual artifacts that this type of application wants to avoid. Moreover, a simple modification of this method allows the contents of the texture to be taken into account, therefore defining a signal-adapted parameterization [Sander et al. 02].

5.6   Summary and Further Reading

In this chapter we gave an introduction to the notion of mesh parameterization and derived the fundamental tools of distortion analysis, based on

Figure 5.12. Some results computed by stretch L_2 minimization. (Parameterized models courtesy of Pedro Sander and Alla Sheffer. Image taken from [Hormann et al. 07]. ©2007 ACM, Inc. Included here by permission.)

the notion of metric tensor. We then built on these foundations the classical fixed boundary barycentric methods, then the free-boundary quadratic methods, and finally the nonlinear methods. These methods can be used by many applications, including texture mapping, reverse engineering, and conversion between different representations. Implementations are available in the publicly available packages CGAL,[2] OpenMesh,[3] OpenNL,[4] Graphiten,[5] and Meshlab.[6]

In this chapter we limited ourselves to methods that compute a parameterization for objects with disk topology. In particular, we did not cover global parameterization methods. The reader is referred to [Gu and Yau 03, Gu and Yau 04, Steiner and Fischer 05, Kälberer et al. 05, Ray et al. 06, Tong et al. 06] for more details.

For further reading, we mention that the fundamental aspects of mesh parameterization concern differential geometry, and more specifically Riemannian geometry. The reader is referred to the extensive survey in [Berger 07]. Riemannian geometry has strong connections with complex analysis, and these connections are very well explained in [Needham 94]. We also refer the reader to parameterization methods based on the relation between curvature and metric [Ben-Chen et al. 08, Yang et al. 08, Springborn et al. 08].

Finally, we also recommend the survey on mesh parameterization [Floater and Hormann 05] and the detailed course notes [Hormann et al. 07].

---

[2]http://www.cgal.org
[3]http://www.openmesh.org
[4]http://alice.loria.fr/index.php/software.html
[5]http://alice.loria.fr/index.php/software.html
[6]http://www.meshlab.org

REMESHING

Remeshing is a key technique for mesh quality improvement in many industrial applications such as numerical simulation and geometric modeling (e.g., shape editing, animation, morphing). As such, it has received considerable attention in recent years, and a wealth of remeshing algorithms have been developed. In this chapter we focus on surface remeshing and do not consider volumetric remeshing. The first goal of surface remeshing is to reduce the complexity of an input surface mesh, subject to certain quality criteria. This process is commonly referred to as *mesh simplification*, a topic covered in Chapter 7. The second goal of remeshing is to improve the quality of a mesh, such that it can be used as input for various downstream applications. Different applications imply different quality criteria and requirements. For more complete coverage of the topic, we refer the reader to a survey [Alliez et al. 07], which proposes this definition for remeshing: "Given a 3D mesh, compute another mesh, whose elements satisfy some quality requirements, while approximating the input acceptably." Here the term *approximation* can be understood with respect to locations as well as to normals or higher-order differential properties.

In contrast to general mesh repair (see Chapter 8), the input of remeshing algorithms is usually assumed to already be a manifold triangle mesh or part of it. The term *mesh quality* thus refers to non-topological properties, such as sampling density, regularity, size, orientation, alignment, and shape of the mesh elements. This chapter deals with these latter aspects of remeshing and presents various methods that achieve this goal. We begin our discussion by structuring the different types of remeshing algorithms and by clarifying some concepts commonly used in the remeshing literature. Beginning with Section 6.4, we discuss several remeshing methods, focusing on the key paradigms behind each of them.

6.1 Local Structure

The local structure of a mesh is described by the type, shape, orientation, and distribution of the mesh elements.

▶ Element type. The most common target element types are *triangles* and *quadrangles*. Triangle meshes are usually easier to produce, while in quadrangular remeshing one often has to content oneself with results that are only *quad-dominant*. Note that, in principle, any quadrangle mesh can be trivially converted into a triangle mesh by inserting a diagonal into each quadrangle. Converting a triangle mesh into a quadrangle mesh can be performed either by barycentric subdivision (splitting each triangle into three quadrangles by inserting its barycenter and linking it to edge midpoints) or by splitting each triangle at its barycenter into three new triangles (one-to-three split) and discarding the original mesh edges.

▶ Element shape. Elements can be classified as being either *isotropic* or *anisotropic*. The shape of isotropic elements is locally uniform in all directions. Ideally, a triangle/quadrangle is isotropic if it is close to equilateral/square (see Figure 6.1).

For triangles this roundness can be measured by the ratio of the circumcircle radius to the length of the shortest edge (see [Shewchuk 97]). Isotropic elements are favored in numerical applications (FEM or geometry processing), as the local uniform shape of their elements often leads to a better conditioning of the resulting systems (see [Shewchuk 02] for a more detailed discussion). The shape of anisotropic elements locally varies according to the orientation on the

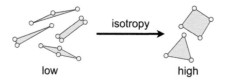

low   high

Figure 6.1. Isotropy: low (left) versus high (right). (Image taken from [Botsch et al. 06b]. ©2006 ACM, Inc. Included here by permission.)

surface. When carefully aligned and oriented (see "element alignment and orientation" below), anisotropic meshes are preferred for shape approximation because they usually need fewer elements than their isotropic pendants to achieve the same approximation quality. Anisotropic elements are commonly oriented with the principal curvature directions of the surface (see Chapter 3). Furthermore, anisotropic elements better express the structure of geometric primitives (cylinders, cones, etc.) inherent in many technical models.

▶ Element density. In a *uniform* distribution, the mesh elements are evenly spread across the entire model. In a *nonuniform* or *adaptive* distribution, the number of elements varies, e.g., smaller elements are assigned to areas with high curvature. When carefully designed, adaptive meshes need significantly fewer elements to achieve an approximation quality that is comparable to that of uniform meshes.

▶ Element alignment and orientation. Converting a mesh approximating a piecewise smooth surface into a new mesh corresponds to a resampling process. Hence, sharp features may be affected by alias artifacts. In order to prevent this, elements should align to sharp features so that they properly represent tangent discontinuities. Furthermore, the orientation of anisotropic elements plays a crucial role in faithful shape approximation [Nadler 86].

6.2   Global Structure

A vertex in a triangle mesh is called *regular* if its valence (i.e., its number of neighboring vertices) is 6 for interior vertices or 4 for boundary vertices. In quadrangle meshes, the regular valences are 4 and 3, respectively. Vertices that are not regular are called *irregular* or *extraordinary*. The global structure of a mesh can be classified as being *irregular*, *semiregular*, *highly regular*, or *regular* (see Figure 6.2):

▶ *Irregular* meshes do not exhibit any kind of regularities in their connectivity.

▶ *Semiregular* meshes are produced by regular subdivision of a coarse initial mesh. Thus, the number of extraordinary vertices in a semiregular mesh is small and constant [Eck et al. 95, Guskov et al. 00, Lee et al. 98, Kobbelt et al. 99a] under uniform refinement.

▶ In *highly regular* meshes most vertices are regular. In contrast to semiregular meshes, highly regular meshes need not be the result of a

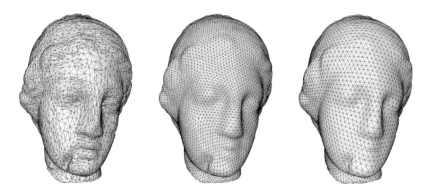

Figure 6.2. Meshes: Irregular (left), semiregular (center), and regular (right). (Model courtesy of Cyberware.)

subdivision process [Szymczak et al. 02, Surazhsky and Gotsman 03, Alliez et al. 02, Surazhsky et al. 03].

▶ In a *regular* mesh all vertices are regular. A regular mesh can compactly be represented as a 2D array that can be used for efficient rendering (a so-called *geometry image*) [Gu et al. 02, Sander et al. 03, Losasso et al. 03].

Besides this topological characterization, the suitability of a remeshing algorithm usually depends on its ability to capture the global structure of the input geometry by aligning groups of elements to the dominant geometric features. Since this corresponds to the alignment of entire submeshes, e.g., to global curvature lines of geometric primitives, it is strongly related to mesh segmentation techniques [Marinov and Kobbelt 06].

Fully regular meshes can be generated only for a very limited number of input models, namely those that topologically are (part of) a torus. All other models have to be cut into one or more topological disks before processing (and then the global regularity is broken at the seams). Furthermore, special care has to be taken to correctly identify and handle the seams that result from cutting. Semiregular meshes are, in particular, suitable for multiresolution analysis and modeling [Zorin et al. 97, Guskov et al. 00]. They define a natural parameterization of a model over a coarse base mesh. Highly regular meshes require different techniques for multiresolution analysis, and they are well suited to numerical simulations. In particular, mesh compression algorithms can take advantage of the mostly uniform valence distribution and produce a very efficient connectivity encoding [Touma and Gotsman 98, Alliez and Desbrun 01, Kälberer et al. 05].

6.3   Correspondences

All remeshing algorithms compute point locations on or near the original surface. Most algorithms furthermore iteratively relocate mesh vertices in order to improve the quality of the mesh. Thus, a key issue in all remeshing algorithms is to compute or to maintain correspondences between points $\mathbf{p}$ on the generated mesh and their counterparts $\phi(\mathbf{p})$ on the input mesh. There are a number of approaches to address this problem:

▶ Global parameterization. The input model is globally parameterized onto a 2D domain (see Chapter 5). Sample points can then be easily distributed and relocated in the 2D domain and later be lifted to three dimensions [Alliez et al. 03b, Alliez et al. 03a].

▶ Local parameterization. The algorithm maintains a parameterization of a local geodesic neighborhood around $\phi(\mathbf{p})$. When a sample leaves this neighborhood, a new neighborhood has to be computed [Surazhsky et al. 03].

▶ Projection. The sample point is projected onto the nearest element (point, edge, or triangle) of the input model [Botsch and Kobbelt 04b].

Global parameterization is, in general, expensive and may suffer from parametric distortion or discontinuities when the mesh needs to be cut into a topological disk. Naive direct projection may produce local and global fold-overs if the points are too far away from the surface. However, in practice the projection operator can be stabilized by constraining the movement of the sample points to their tangent planes. Although no theoretical guarantees can be provided, this makes sure that the samples do not move too far away from the surface, such that the projection can be safely evaluated. The local parameterization approach is stable and produces high-quality results. However, it requires expensive bookkeeping to track, cache, and re-parameterize the local neighborhoods.

6.4   Voronoi Diagrams and Delaunay Triangulations

Voronoi diagrams and Delaunay triangulations are important geometric data structures for meshing and remeshing. We now provide definitions for Voronoi diagrams and Delaunay triangulations in arbitrary dimensions, although they will later be used only in two and three dimensions.

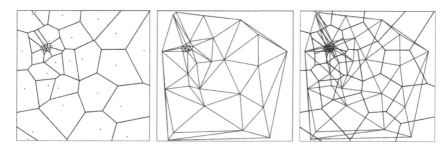

Figure 6.3. A 2D Voronoi diagram of a point set (left), 2D Delaunay triangulation of the same point set (center), and both superimposed (right).

Let $\mathcal{P} = \{\mathbf{p}_1, \ldots, \mathbf{p}_n\}$ be a set of points (so-called *sites*) in $\mathbb{R}^d$. We associate to each site $\mathbf{p}_i$ its *Voronoi region* $V(\mathbf{p}_i)$ such that

$$V(\mathbf{p}_i) = \{\mathbf{x} \in \mathbb{R}^d \colon \|\mathbf{x} - \mathbf{p}_i\| \leq \|\mathbf{x} - \mathbf{p}_j\|, \forall j \neq i\}.$$

The collection of the nonempty Voronoi regions and their faces, together with their incidence relations, constitute a cell complex called the *Voronoi diagram* of $\mathcal{P}$. See Figure 6.3 (left) for an example in two dimensions. The Voronoi diagram of $\mathcal{P}$ is a partition of $\mathbb{R}^d$ because any point of $\mathbb{R}^d$ belongs to at least one Voronoi region. The locus of points that are equidistant to two sites $\mathbf{p}_i$ and $\mathbf{p}_j$ is called a bisector, and all bisectors are affine subspaces of $\mathbb{R}^d$ (lines in two dimensions, planes in three dimensions). A Voronoi cell of a site $\mathbf{p}_i$ is also defined as the intersection of closed half-spaces bounded by bisectors. This implies that all Voronoi cells are convex since the intersection of convex sets remains convex. Note that some Voronoi cells may be unbounded with unbounded bisectors. This happens when a site $\mathbf{p}_i$ is on the boundary of the convex hull of $\mathcal{P}$. Voronoi cells have *faces* of different dimensions. In two dimensions, a face of dimension k is the intersection of $3 - k$ Voronoi cells. A Voronoi vertex is generally equidistant from three points, and a Voronoi edge is equidistant from two points. A point set $\mathcal{P} \subset \mathbb{R}^d$ is generic or non-degenerate if the affine hull of any set of k points with $1 \leq k \leq d$ is homeomorphic to $\mathbb{R}^{k-1}$ and no $d+2$ points are cospherical [Dey 06]. We refer the reader to [Okabe et al. 92, Boissonnat and Yvinec 98] for more details about Voronoi diagrams.

The dual structure to the Voronoi diagram is called the *Delaunay triangulation*; see Figure 6.3 (center). More specifically, the Delaunay triangulation of a set of sites $\mathcal{P}$ is a simplicial complex such that $k + 1$ points in $\mathcal{P}$ form a Delaunay simplex if their Voronoi cells have nonempty intersection. In two dimensions, each Delaunay triangle $(\mathbf{p}, \mathbf{q}, \mathbf{r})$ is dual to a Voronoi vertex where $V(\mathbf{p})$, $V(\mathbf{q})$, and $V(\mathbf{r})$ meet; each Delaunay edge $(\mathbf{p}, \mathbf{q})$ is dual to a Voronoi edge where $V(\mathbf{p})$ and $V(\mathbf{q})$ meet; and each Delaunay vertex $\mathbf{p}$ is dual to its Voronoi face $V(\mathbf{p})$. The Delaunay triangulation of a point set $\mathcal{P}$ covers the convex hull of $\mathcal{P}$.

The Delaunay triangulation is shown to enjoy several local and global properties due to its duality with the Voronoi diagram. One local property is the so-called *empty sphere property*. A triangulation $\mathcal{T}$ of a point set $\mathcal{P}$ such that any d-simplex of $\mathcal{T}$ has a circumsphere that does not enclose any point of $\mathcal{P}$ is a Delaunay triangulation of $\mathcal{P}$. Conversely, any k-simplex with vertices in $\mathcal{P}$ that can be circumscribed by a hypersphere that does not enclose any point of $\mathcal{P}$ is a face of the Delaunay triangulation of $\mathcal{P}$. In two dimensions, one global property is related to the smallest triangle angle: the Delaunay triangulation of a point set $\mathcal{P}$ is the triangulation of $\mathcal{P}$ that maximizes the smallest angle. Another even stronger global property is the following: the triangulation of $\mathcal{P}$ whose angular vector (the set of all triangle angles) is maximal for the lexicographic order is the Delaunay triangulation of $\mathcal{P}$. The latter two properties explain the success of the Delaunay triangulation for mesh generation, as small angles cause numerical problems in finite elements methods.

Another key notion used in Delaunay-based surface meshing algorithms is the *restricted Delaunay triangulation*. Let X denote a subset of $\mathbb{R}^d$; $\mathcal{P}$ a point set of $\mathbb{R}^d$; and $\mathrm{Del}(\mathcal{P})$ the Delaunay triangulation of $\mathcal{P}$. We call the Delaunay triangulation restricted to X the sub-complex of $\mathrm{Del}(\mathcal{P})$, denoted $\mathrm{Del}_X(\mathcal{P})$, whose dual Voronoi faces intersect X. Figure 6.4 illustrates the Delaunay triangulation of a 2D point set restricted to a planar

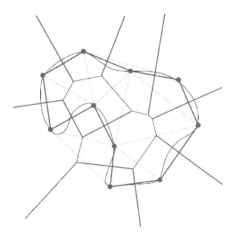

Figure 6.4. Delaunay triangulation of a point set restricted to a planar closed curve. The edges of the restricted Delaunay triangulation are depicted with solid blue lines. The Voronoi edges intersecting the curve are depicted with solid red lines.

closed curve. The 3D Delaunay triangulation restricted to a surface $\mathcal{S}$ is the set of Delaunay facets (triangles) whose dual Voronoi edges intersect $\mathcal{S}$. The notion of restricted Delaunay triangulation was introduced by Chew for meshing surfaces [Chew 93] and was later formalized [Edelsbrunner and Shah 94] and used for many reconstruction and mesh generation algorithms [Dey 06]. A key property of the Delaunay triangulation restricted to a smooth closed surface $\mathcal{S}$, denoted $\text{Del}_{\mathcal{S}}(\mathcal{P})$, is its approximation property (both in terms of geometry and topology) when $\mathcal{P}$ is sufficiently dense. More details are provided in [Boissonnat and Oudot 05].

6.5   Triangle-Based Remeshing

In an isotropic mesh all triangles are well shaped, i.e., ideally equilateral. One may further require a globally uniform vertex density or allow a smooth change in the triangle sizes, i.e., a smooth *gradation*. There are a number of algorithms for isotropic remeshing of triangle meshes (see [Alliez et al. 07]). In this section we describe three different paradigms commonly employed for isotropic surface remeshing; then we detail three representative algorithms for these paradigms.

Existing algorithms could be roughly classified as being *greedy*, *variational*, or *incremental*. Greedy algorithms commonly perform one local change at a time, such as vertex insertion, until the initially stated goal is satisfied. Variational techniques cast the initial problem as one of minimizing an energy functional such that low levels of this energy correspond to good solutions for this problem (reaching a global optimum is in general elusive). A solver for this energy commonly performs global relaxation, i.e., vertex relocations and re-triangulations until convergence. Finally, an algorithm is said to be incremental when it combines both refinement and decimation, possibly interleaved with a relaxation procedure (see [Bossen and Heckbert 96]).

6.5.1   Greedy Remeshing

The greedy surface meshing algorithm in [Boissonnat and Oudot 05] is flexible enough to be used for isotropic remeshing of smooth surfaces. The core principle behind this algorithm relies on refining and filtering a 3D Delaunay triangulation. At each refinement step one point taken on the input surface is inserted into the triangulation. The point location is chosen among the intersections of the input surface $\mathcal{S}$ with the Voronoi edges of the triangulation. In other words, the edges of the Voronoi diagram are used to probe the input surface along the refinement process. The filtering process consists of updating the Delaunay triangulation restricted to $\mathcal{S}$ (denoted

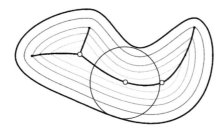

Figure 6.5. Medial axis of the complement of a planar curve. Lines parallel to the curve are depicted with thin lines. The circle bounds a medial ball.

$\mathrm{Del}_{\mathcal{S}}(\mathcal{P}))$, i.e., selecting the Delaunay facets whose dual Voronoi edges intersect $\mathcal{S}$. Before providing the pseudocode of the refinement algorithm we define several required concepts.

Surface Delaunay ball. A *surface Delaunay ball* is a ball centered at the input surface $\mathcal{S}$ that circumscribes a facet f of $\mathrm{Del}_{\mathcal{S}}(\mathcal{P})$. As there can be several surface Delaunay balls associated with a given Delaunay facet, we denote by $B_f = B(\mathbf{c}_f, r_f)$ a surface Delaunay ball circumscribing f, centered at $\mathbf{c}_f$ and of radius r_f.

Medial axis. Denote by $\mathcal{O}$ an open set of $\mathbb{R}^d$. The *medial axis* $M(\mathcal{O})$ of $\mathcal{O}$ is the closure of the set of points with at least two closest points on the boundary of $\mathcal{O}$. A ball centered on the medial axis, whose interior is contained in $\mathcal{O}$ and whose bounding sphere intersects the boundary of $\mathcal{O}$ is called a *medial ball*; see Figure 6.5 for a planar example. The *reach* (or *local feature size*) at a point $\mathbf{x} \in \mathcal{O}$, denoted $\rho(\mathbf{x})$, is the distance from $\mathbf{x}$ to the medial axis of $\mathcal{O}$. For the present application we consider the case where $\mathcal{O}$ is the complement of a surface $\mathcal{S}$ of $\mathbb{R}^3$.

   The key idea behind the refinement algorithm is to refine $\mathrm{Del}_{\mathcal{S}}(\mathcal{P})$ until all surface Delaunay balls have radius lower than a fraction of the local reach. Guaranteeing the algorithm termination requires bounding the reach away from zero, i.e., restricting ourselves to the class of $C^{1,1}$ surfaces. $C^{1,1}$ surfaces are a bit more general than C^2 (smooth) surfaces, as they admit one normal at each point and a Lipschitz normal field. Because the input surface $\mathcal{S}$ is already provided as a surface mesh in the present application, this condition is not fulfilled and hence we have to consider it as an approximation of a $C^{1,1}$ surface.

Algorithm. The algorithm maintains the set $\mathcal{P}$, the Delaunay triangulation $\mathrm{Del}(\mathcal{P})$, and its restriction $\mathrm{Del}_{\mathcal{S}}(\mathcal{P})$ to $\mathcal{S}$ as well as the list L of "bad" facets of $\mathrm{Del}_{\mathcal{S}}(\mathcal{P})$. A bad facet f herein means that its surface Delaunay ball

$B_f = B(\mathbf{c}_f, r_f)$ satisfies $r_f > \psi(\mathbf{c}_f)$, where ψ is defined over $\mathcal{S}$ and satisfies $\psi(\mathbf{x}) \geq \psi_{\text{inf}} > 0 \;\; \forall \mathbf{x} \in \mathcal{S}$. The initial point set $\mathcal{P}$ is constructed by taking at least three points sufficiently close on each connected component of $\mathcal{S}$ and runs the following refinement algorithm:

```
refine()
    while L is not empty
        pop one bad facet f from L
        c_f = dual(f) ∩ S
        insert c_f to P
        update Del(P)
        update Del_S(P)
        update L, i.e.,
            remove facets of L that are no longer facets of Del_S(P)
            add new bad facets of Del_S(P) to L
```

Under assumptions on ψ, i.e., $\psi \leq \epsilon \cdot \rho$, where $\epsilon = 0.2$ and $\rho = \text{reach}$, the algorithm summarized above is shown to terminate after a finite number of refinement steps. Upon termination, the output of the algorithm (i.e., the piecewise linear interpolation derived from the restricted Delaunay triangulation) is shown to enjoy both approximation guarantees, in terms of topology and geometry, and also quality guarantees, in terms of the shape of the mesh elements. More precisely, the restricted Delaunay triangulation is homeomorphic to the input surface $\mathcal{S}$ and approximates it in terms of its Hausdorff distance, normals, curvature, and area. All angles of the triangles are bounded, which provides us with a mesh quality amenable to reliable mesh processing operations and faithful simulations.

The elementary operation of the meshing process reduces to the insertion of a new vertex into the 3D Delaunay triangulation that interpolates the input surface. The only assumption made is that the input surface representation is amenable to simple geometric computations, namely its

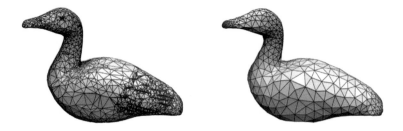

Figure 6.6. Isotropic remeshing by Delaunay refinement and filtering. The input mesh (left) is the output of an interpolatory surface reconstruction algorithm. (Model courtesy of [Dey et al. 05].)

intersection with a line. In other words, the shape to be discretized is only known through an *oracle* that provides answers to intersection predicates. The current implementations [Dey et al. 05, Boissonnat and Oudot 05] of the Delaunay-based refinement techniques commonly use octree data structures to accelerate the line-triangle queries (see Chapter 1). Figure 6.6 illustrates the remeshing of a surface triangle mesh that is the output of an interpolatory surface reconstruction algorithm.

Figure 6.7 illustrates Delaunay-based remeshing of a 2M triangle surface mesh. On this example the mesh refinement procedure is seeded by inserting into the 3D Delaunay triangulation 20 randomly chosen points from the input mesh vertices.

The main advantages of this greedy algorithm are its guaranteed properties. Moreover, the output triangle surface mesh is guaranteed not to self-intersect by construction because it is extracted from a 3D Delaunay triangulation. The latter property is often neglected by other remeshing techniques. It is also quite robust as it does not resort to any local or global parameterization technique and constructs a 3D tetrahedral mesh instead.

Figure 6.7. Remeshing by Delaunay refinement and filtering. The input (left) is an irregular surface triangle mesh obtained by surface reconstruction followed by simplification. The output (right) is an isotropic surface triangle mesh where all triangle angles are greater than 25 degrees. (Model courtesy of Pisa Visual Computing Lab.)

The following questions may arise: Can we construct a mesh of higher quality? With fewer vertices while satisfying the same set of constraints? Some of these questions are addressed by variational techniques.

6.5.2   Variational Remeshing

When high-quality meshes are sought after, it may be desirable to resort to an optimization procedure. Two questions now arise: Which criterion should we optimize? By exploiting which degrees of freedom? The optimized criterion can be directly related to the shape and size of the triangles, but we will describe next how other criteria achieve satisfactory results as well. As the number of degrees of freedom are both continuous and discrete (vertex positions and mesh connectivity), there is a need for narrowing the space of possible triangulations.

Mesh optimization, also commonly referred to as *mesh smoothing* in the meshing community, has addressed parts of these questions, although some work remains to be done in order to specialize these techniques to remeshing of surfaces. We refer the reader to a comprehensive survey of mesh optimization techniques [Eppstein 01].

Designing a variational algorithm requires defining an energy to minimize and a solver for this energy. Ideally, the solver is fast and robust and converges to a global optimum. In practice, however, the space of possible solutions is so vast that reaching a global optimum is elusive—even more so when the notion of "best possible mesh" is not well defined. The zoo of criteria used for the optimization (see, e.g., [Amenta et al. 99]) reveals the difficulty of choosing one criterion to optimize: should we optimize over the triangle angles, the edge lengths, or the compactness of the triangles? Although one optimization technique has been specifically designed for optimizing the shape of the triangles [Chen 04], a class of mesh smoothing techniques rely on the observation that isotropic 2D point samplings lead to well-shaped triangles [Eppstein 01]. Note that in three dimensions this observation does not hold anymore since sliver tetrahedra can occur. A *sliver* is an almost flat tetrahedron with its four vertices evenly distributed along the equator of its circumsphere. Isotropic remeshing can therefore be cast into the problem of isotropic point sampling, which amounts to distributing a set of points on the input mesh in as even a manner as possible.

One approach to evenly distributing a set of points in two dimensions is to construct a *centroidal Voronoi tessellation* [Du et al. 99]. Given a density function defined over a bounded domain Ω, a centroidal Voronoi tessellation (denoted CVT) of Ω is a class of Voronoi tessellations where each site coincides with the centroid (i.e., center of mass) of its Voronoi

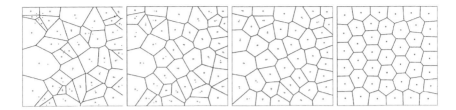

Figure 6.8. From left to right: ordinary Voronoi tessellation (sites are depicted in black; Voronoi cell centroids in red); Voronoi tessellation after one Lloyd iteration; Voronoi tessellation after three Lloyd iterations; Centroidal Voronoi tessellation obtained after convergence of the Lloyd iteration. Each site coincides with the center of mass of its Voronoi cell.

region. The centroid $\mathbf{c}_i$ of a Voronoi region V_i is calculated as

$$\mathbf{c}_i = \frac{\int_{V_i} \mathbf{x} \cdot \rho(\mathbf{x})\, d\mathbf{x}}{\int_{V_i} \rho(\mathbf{x})\, d\mathbf{x}}, \qquad (6.1)$$

where $\rho(\mathbf{x})$ is the density function, defined to control the size of the Voronoi cells. This structure turns out to have a surprisingly broad range of applications for numerical analysis, location optimization, optimal repartition of resources, cell growth, vector quantization, etc. This follows from the mathematical importance of its relationship with the energy function,

$$E(\mathbf{p}_1, \ldots, \mathbf{p}_n, V_1, \ldots, V_n) = \sum_{i=1}^{n} \int_{V_i} \rho(\mathbf{x}) \left\| \mathbf{x} - \mathbf{p}_i \right\|^2 d\mathbf{x},$$

with sites $\mathbf{p}_i$ and corresponding regions $V_i \subset \Omega$. We can show that the energy function is minimized when the $\mathbf{p}_i$ are the mass centroids $\mathbf{c}_i$ of their corresponding regions V_i. Moreover, for a fixed set of sites $\mathbf{p}_1, \ldots, \mathbf{p}_n$, the energy function is minimized if $\{V_1, \ldots, V_n\}$ is a Voronoi tessellation.

One way to build a centroidal Voronoi tessellation is to use *Lloyd's relaxation method*. The Lloyd algorithm is a deterministic, fixed-point iteration [Lloyd 82]. Given a density function and an initial set of n sites, it consists of the following three steps (see Figure 6.8):

1. Construct the Voronoi tessellation corresponding to the sites $\mathbf{p}_i$.

2. Compute the centroids $\mathbf{c}_i$ of the Voronoi regions V_i using Equation (6.1), and move the sites $\mathbf{p}_i$ to their respective centroids $\mathbf{c}_i$.

3. Repeat steps 1 and 2 until satisfactory convergence is achieved.

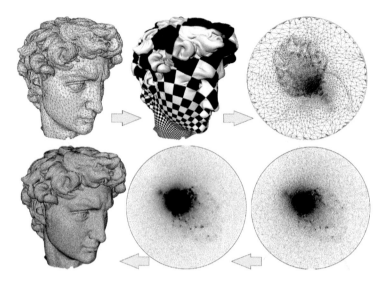

Figure 6.9. Isotropic remeshing of the head of Michelangelo's David. A planar conformal parameterization is computed (top). Isotropic sampling, then Lloyd relaxation, is applied in the parameter space in order to obtain a non-uniform centroidal Voronoi tessellation, with which the mesh is uniformly remeshed (bottom). (Image taken from [Alliez et al. 03b]. ©2003 IEEE. Model courtesy of the Stanford Computer Graphics Library.)

Alliez et al. [Alliez et al. 03b] propose a surface remeshing technique based on Lloyd relaxation. It uses a global conformal planar parameterization (see Chapter 5) and applies relaxation in the parameter space using a density function designed so as to compensate for the area distortion due to flattening (see Figure 6.9). Nonuniform isotropic meshes can also be obtained by incorporating into the density function the desired mesh sizing. Sharp features such as creases and corners are preserved by applying the Lloyd iteration over a bounded Voronoi diagram, i.e., the pseudo-dual of a constrained Delaunay triangulation (see Figure 6.10).

The remeshing algorithm is summarized by the following pseudocode:

```
isotropic_remeshing(input surface triangle mesh M)
  conformal paramerization of M
  compute density function
  perform in parameter space
    random sampling in accordance to the density function
    repeat until convergence
      Voronoi diagram
      relocate sites to Voronoi cell centroids
  lift 2D Delaunay triangulation to 3D
```

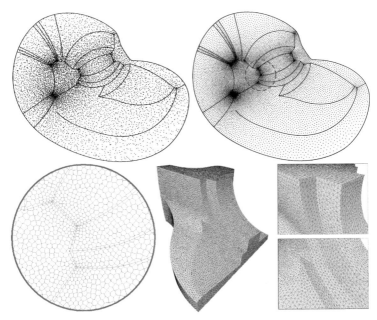

Figure 6.10. Uniform remeshing of the fandisk model with 10k vertices (the bottom of the original mesh has been removed so as to obtain a topological disk): initial sampling (top left); sampling obtained after 20 iterations of Lloyd relaxation (top right); closeup over the centroidal Voronoi tessellation after Lloyd convergence (bottom left); global view of the remeshed model (bottom center); and closeups around sharp features (bottom right). (Image taken from [Alliez et al. 03b]. ©2003 IEEE.)

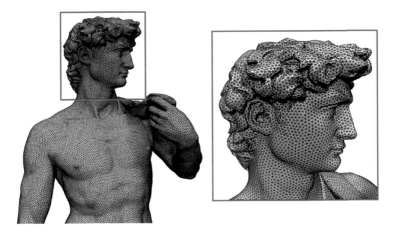

Figure 6.11. Isotropic remeshing using overlapping parameterizations. (Model courtesy of the Stanford Computer Graphics Laboratory.)

To alleviate the numerical issues for high distortion, as well as the artificial cuts required for closed or models with nontrivial topology, Surazhsky et al. [Surazhsky et al. 03] apply the Lloyd relaxation procedure on a set of local overlapping parameterizations (see Figure 6.11).

6.5.3 Incremental Remeshing

In this section we present an efficient remeshing algorithm that produces isotropic triangle meshes. The algorithm was presented in [Botsch and Kobbelt 04b] and is a simplified version of [Vorsatz et al. 03] and an extension of [Kobbelt et al. 00]. It produces results that are comparable to the ones by the original algorithm, but it has the advantage of being simpler to implement and of being robust. In particular, it does not need any parameterization nor the involved computation of (geodesic) Voronoi cells as, e.g., [Surazhsky et al. 03].

The algorithm takes as input a target edge length and repeatedly splits long edges, collapses short edges, and relocates vertices until all edges are approximately of the desired target edge length (see Figure 6.12). The algorithm runs the following loop:

```
remesh(target_edge_length)
  low = 4/5 * target_edge_length
  high = 4/3 * target_edge_length
  for i = 0 to 10 do
    split_long_edges(high)
    collapse_short_edges(low,high)
    equalize_valences()
    tangential_relaxation()
    project_to_surface()
```

Notice that the proper thresholds $\frac{4}{5}$ and $\frac{4}{3}$ are essential to converge to a uniform edge length [Botsch and Kobbelt 04b]. The values are derived from considerations to make sure that after a split or collapse function, the edge lengths are closer to the target lengths than before. A hysteresis behavior is induced by the interleaved tangential smoothing operator.

The split_long_edges(high) function visits all edges of the current mesh. If an edge is longer than the given threshold high, the edge is split at its midpoint and the two adjacent triangles are bisected (2-4 split).

```
split_long_edges(high)
  while exists edge e with length(e) > high do
    split e at midpoint(e)
```

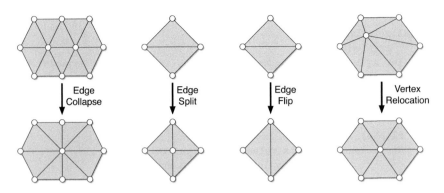

Figure 6.12. Local remeshing operators. (Image taken from [Botsch 05].)

The `collapse_short_edges(low, high)` function collapses and thus removes all edges that are shorter than a threshold `low`. Here one has to take care of a subtle problem: by collapsing along chains of short edges, the algorithm may create new edges that are arbitrarily long and thus undo the work that was done in `split_long_edges(high)`. This issue is resolved by testing before each collapse whether the collapse would produce an edge that is longer than `high`. If so, the collapse is not executed.

```
collapse_short_edges(low, high)
  while exists edge e with length(e) < low do
    let e = (a,b) and let a[1],...,a[n] be the one-ring of a
    collapse_ok = true
    for i = 1 to n do
      if length(b,a[i]) > high then
        collapse_ok = false
    if collapse_ok then
      collapse a into b along e
```

The `equalize_valences()` function equalizes the vertex valences by flipping edges. The target valence `target_val(v)` is 6 and 4 for interior and boundary vertices, respectively. The algorithm tentatively flips each edge `e` and checks whether the deviation to the target valences decreases. If not, the edge is flipped back.

```
equalize_valences()
  for each edge e do
    let a, b, c, d be the vertices of the two triangles adjacent to e
    deviation_pre = abs(valence(a)-target_val(a))
                  + abs(valence(b)-target_val(b))
                  + abs(valence(c)-target_val(c))
                  + abs(valence(d)-target_val(d))
    flip(e)
    deviation_post = abs(valence(a)-target_val(a))
                   + abs(valence(b)-target_val(b))
                   + abs(valence(c)-target_val(c))
                   + abs(valence(d)-target_val(d))
    if deviation_pre ≤ deviation_post do
      flip(e)
```

The `tangential_relaxation()` function applies an iterative smoothing filter to the mesh. Here, the vertex movement has to be constrained to the vertex tangent plane in order to stabilize the following projection operator. Let $\mathbf{p}$ be an arbitrary vertex in the current mesh, let $\mathbf{n}$ be its normal, and let $\mathbf{q}$ be the position of the vertex as calculated by a smoothing algorithm with uniform Laplacian weights (see Chapter 4):

$$\mathbf{q} = \frac{1}{|\mathcal{N}_1(\mathbf{p})|} \sum_{\mathbf{p}_j \in \mathcal{N}_1(\mathbf{p})} \mathbf{p}_j .$$

The new position $\mathbf{p}'$ of $\mathbf{p}$ is then computed by projecting $\mathbf{q}$ onto $\mathbf{p}$'s tangent plane:

$$\mathbf{p}' = \mathbf{q} + \mathbf{n}\mathbf{n}^T(\mathbf{p} - \mathbf{q}).$$

Again, this can be implemented as follows:

```
tangential_relaxation()
  for each vertex v do
    q[v] = the barycenter of v's neighbor vertices
  for each vertex v do
    let p[v] and n[v] be the position and normal of v, respectively
    p[v] = q[v] + dot(n[v],(p[v] - q[v])) * n[v]
```

Finally, the `project_to_surface()` function maps the vertices back to the surface.

Feature preservation. A few rules are added to make sure that the remeshing algorithm preserves the features of the input model (see Figure 6.13). We assume that the feature edges and vertices have already been marked in the input model, e.g., by automatic feature detection algorithms or by manual specification [Vorsatz et al. 03, Botsch 05].

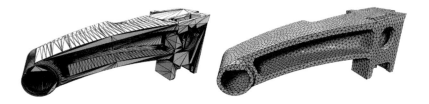

Figure 6.13. Isotropic, feature-sensitive remeshing (right) of a CAD model (left).

▶ Corner vertices with more than two or exactly one incident feature edge have to be preserved and are excluded from all topological and geometric operations.

▶ Feature vertices may only be collapsed along their incident feature edges.

▶ Splitting a feature edge creates two new feature edges and a feature vertex.

▶ Feature edges are never flipped.

▶ Tangential smoothing of feature vertices is restricted to univariate smoothing along the corresponding feature lines.

As shown by Figures 6.13 and 6.14, the algorithm above produces quite good results. It is also possible to incorporate additional regularization

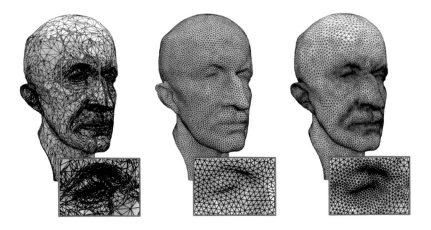

Figure 6.14. Isotropic remeshing: Max Planck model at full resolution (two leftmost images), uniform mesh (center), and adaptive mesh (right).

terms by adjusting the weights that are used in the smoothing phase. This
allows one to achieve a uniform triangle area distribution or to implement
an adaptive remeshing algorithm that produces finer elements in regions of
high curvature.

6.6 Quad-dominant Remeshing

Partitioning a surface into quadrangle tiles is a common requirement in
computer graphics, computer-aided geometric design, and reverse engineering. Such quad tilings are amenable to a variety of subsequent applications
due to their tensor-product nature, such as B-spline fitting, simulation, texture atlasing, and rendering with highly detailed modulation maps. Quad
meshes are also useful in modeling as they aptly capture the symmetries of
natural or man-made geometry.

In an anisotropic mesh the elements should orient to the principal
curvature directions, i.e., they are elongated along the minimum curvature direction and shortened along the maximum curvature direction (see
Chapter 3). Anisotropic triangle meshes of a given target complexity can
easily be produced by incrementally decimating the input model down to
a desired target complexity (see also Chapter 7). No matter whether one
uses quadric error metrics, (one-sided) Hausdorff distance, or the normal
deviation to rank the priorities of removal operations, the result will always
be an anisotropic triangle mesh that naturally orients to the principal curvature directions. The meshes that are produced by this method satisfy the
definition of being anisotropic, but unfortunately they do not convey the
orthogonal structure of the curvature lines. To produce such a structure,
it is usually better to first compute a quadrangle mesh.

Automatically converting a triangulated surface (issued, e.g., from a
3D scanner) into a quad mesh is a notoriously difficult task. Stringent
topological conditions make quadrangulating a surface a rather constrained
and global problem compared to triangulating it. Further hurdles are added
by application-dependent meshing requirements such as edge orthogonality,
sizing, mesh regularity, and orientation and alignment of the elements with
the geometry.

Several paradigms have been proposed for generating quadrangle
meshes:

▶ Quadrangulation. A number of techniques have been proposed to quad-
rangulate point sets. A subset of these techniques allows generating
all-convex quadrangles by adding Steiner points [Bremner et al. 01]
and well-shaped quadrangles using circle packing [Bern and Eppstein 00]. Quadrangle meshing thus amounts to carefully placing
a set of points, which are then automatically quadrangulated. In the

context of surface remeshing, the main issue with this paradigm is the lack of control over the orientation and alignment of the edges as well as over the mesh regularity.

▶ Conversion. One way to generate quadrangle meshes is to first generate a triangle or polygon mesh, then convert it to a quadrangle mesh. Examples of such approaches commonly proceed by pairwise triangle merging and 4-8 subdivision, or by bisection of hex-dominant meshes followed by barycentric subdivision [Boier-Martin et al. 04]. As for quadrangulation of point sets, this approach provides the user with little control over the orientation and alignment of the mesh edges.

▶ Curve-based sampling. One way to control the edge alignment and orientation of the mesh edges is to place a set of curves that are everywhere tangent to direction fields. The vertices of the final mesh are obtained by intersecting the networks of curves. When using lines of curvatures, the output meshes are quad-dominant, although not pure quadrangle meshes as T-junctions can appear due to the greedy process used for tracing the lines of curvatures. Another curve-based approach consists of placing a set of minimum-bending curves [Marinov and Kobbelt 06].

▶ Contouring. When pure quadrangle meshes are sought after (without T-junctions), a robust approach consists of computing two scalar functions and extracting a quadrangle surface tiling by contouring these functions along well-chosen isovalues.

We restrict ourselves to the approaches based on curve-based sampling and refer to Chapter 5 for methods based on contouring, as they are very close to parameterization techniques.

6.6.1 Lines of Curvatures

The remeshing technique introduced by Alliez et al. generates a quad-dominant mesh that reflects the symmetries of the input shape by sampling the input shape with curves instead of the usual points [Alliez et al. 03a] (see overview in Figure 6.15).

The algorithm comprises three main stages. The first stage recovers a continuous model from the input triangle mesh by estimating one 3D curvature tensor per vertex (see Chapter 3). The normal component of each tensor is then discarded, and a 2D piecewise linear curvature tensor field is built after computing a discrete conformal parameterization. This tensor field is then altered by linear convolution with a Gaussian kernel to obtain smoother principal curvature directions. The singularities of the tensor field (the umbilics) are also extracted. (See Figure 6.16.)

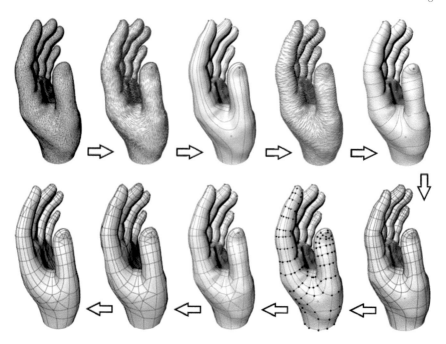

Figure 6.15. Anisotropic remeshing: From an input-triangulated geometry, the curvature tensor field is estimated, then smoothed, and its umbilics are deduced (colored dots). Lines of curvatures (following the principal directions) are then traced on the surface, with local density guided by the principal curvatures, while usual point-sampling is used near umbilic points (spherical regions). The final mesh is extracted by subsampling and conforming-edge insertion. The result is an anisotropic mesh, with elongated quads oriented to the original principal directions and triangles in isotropic regions. (Image taken from [Alliez et al. 03a]. ©2003 ACM, Inc. Included here by permission.)

The second stage consists of resampling the original mesh in parameter space by building a network of lines of curvatures (a set of "streamlines" approximated by polylines) following the principal curvature directions on anisotropic areas. On isotropic areas the algorithm resorts to common point sampling (see Figure 6.17). A user-prescribed approximation precision in conjunction with the estimated curvatures is used to define the local density of lines of curvatures at each point in parameter space during the integration of streamlines.

The third stage deduces the vertices of the new mesh by intersecting the lines of curvatures in anisotropic areas and by selecting a subset of the umbilics in isotropic areas (estimated to be spherical). The edges are obtained

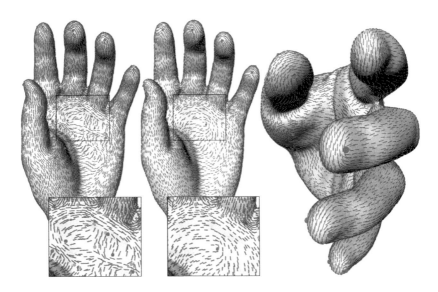

Figure 6.16. Estimating and smoothing the principal direction fields: Initial minimal curvature direction field (left); the color dots indicate umbilics. Minimal curvature directions after smoothing (center). Another view of the smoothed direction field (right). (Image taken from [Alliez et al. 03a]. ©2003 ACM, Inc. Included here by permission.)

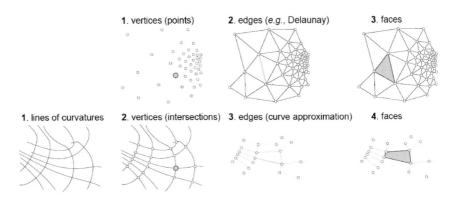

Figure 6.17. Point-based sampling versus curve-based sampling. Point-sampling and Delaunay triangulation are used on near-isotropic areas where principal directions are meaningless (top). Lines of curvatures are sampled on anisotropic areas to find vertex positions by intersection. These lines are then simplified by straightening edges, and the faces are deduced (bottom). (Image taken from [Alliez et al. 03a]. ©2003 ACM, Inc. Included here by permission.)

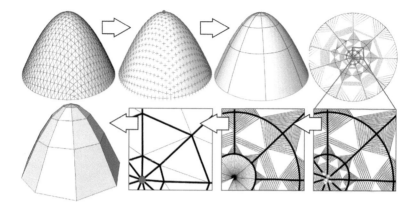

Figure 6.18. Remeshing a dome-like shape. All curvature line segments (red/blue) and boundary edges (green) are added as constraints to a dense 2D constrained Delaunay triangulation in parameter space (top). A decimation process trims all dangling constrained edges, simplifies the chains of constrained edges between the intersection points, and inserts umbilics into the constrained Delaunay triangulation. What remains is a coarser quad-dominant mesh (bottom). (Image taken from [Alliez et al. 03a]. ©2003 ACM, Inc. Included here by permission.)

by straightening the lines of curvatures in between the newly extracted vertices in anisotropic areas and are deduced from the Delaunay triangulation in isotropic areas (see Figure 6.18). The final output is a polygon mesh with mostly elongated quadrangle elements in anisotropic areas and triangles on isotropic areas. Quads are placed mostly in regions with two estimated axes of symmetry, while triangles are used to either tile isotropic areas or to generate conforming convex polygonal elements. On flat areas the infinite spacing of streamlines will not produce any polygons, except for the sake of convex decomposition.

Marinov and Kobbelt [Marinov and Kobbelt 04] propose a variant of Alliez et al.'s algorithm, which differs from the original work in two aspects (see Figure 6.19):

▶ Curvature line tracking and meshing are all done in 3D space. There is no need to compute a global parameterization such that objects of arbitrary genus can be processed.

▶ The algorithm is able to compute a quad-dominant, anisotropic mesh even in flat regions of the model, where there are no reliable curvature estimates, by extrapolating directional information from neighboring anisotropic regions.

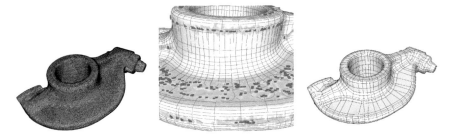

Figure 6.19. Quad-dominant remeshing: The input is a manifold triangle mesh (left). In regions of low confidence, the curvature lines are not well defined (center). The algorithm bridges these regions by extrapolation and produces the result shown (right). (Image taken from [Marinov and Kobbelt 04]. ©2008 IEEE.)

In addition to mere curvature directions, a confidence value for each face and vertex of the input mesh is estimated as well. The estimate is based on the coherence of the principal directions at the face's vertices. This confidence estimate is then used to propagate the curvature tensors from regions of high confidence (highly curved regions) into regions of low confidence (flat regions and noisy regions). Curvature lines are traced directly on the 3D mesh, i.e., at any time a line sample position is identified by a tuple $(f, (u, v, w))$, where f is the index of a triangle and u, v, and w are the barycentric coordinates of the sample within that triangle. To advance the current sample point, the face f and its neighborhood are locally flattened, either by a *hinge map* (if the curvature line crosses an edge of f) or by a *polar map* (if the curvature line crosses one of f's vertices); see Figure 6.20.

When a streamline enters a region of low confidence, the algorithm switches the tracing mode: instead of integrating along the principal curvatures, the line is simply extrapolated from its last sample points along a geodesic curve until it enters a region of high confidence again. At this point the line is then "snapped" to the most similar principal curvature direction.

Due to the strong visual and structural importance of curvatures, remeshing algorithms that track these lines produce results that are similar to those that would have been created by a human designer. However, reliably estimating and tracking the principal curvatures on a discrete triangle mesh is not that easy, in particular for coarse or noisy meshes. Alliez et al.'s algorithm outsources most of the computationally hard work to a constrained Delaunay triangulation [CGAL 09] by globally parameterizing the whole input model. Apart from being hard to compute for large models,

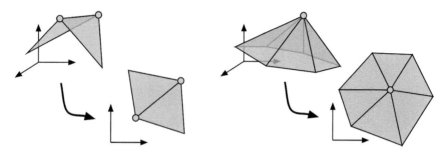

Figure 6.20. Examples of a hinge map (left) and a polar map (right). (Image taken from [Botsch et al. 06b]. ©2006 ACM, Inc. Included here by permission.)

a global parameterization restricts the inputs to genus-0 manifolds with a single boundary loop. Higher-genus objects have to be cut open along each handle. The approach of Marinov et al. is parameterization-free and hence has no restrictions on the topology of the input model. However, the extraction of the final mesh might lead to non-manifold configurations that have to be fixed in a post-processing step.

6.7   Summary and Further Reading

We have provided a brief overview of surface remeshing techniques with a focus on isotropic triangle meshes and quad-dominant meshes. Isotropic remeshing is now a well-studied problem, and robust software components are available for large meshes. Although the variational or incremental approaches generate the best results, the greedy technique based on Delaunay refinement and filtering provides guarantees over the shape of the elements as well as over other useful properties, such as the absence of self-intersection. The latter property is of crucial importance for generating volumetric meshes for simulation.

Regarding isotropic triangle-based remeshing, the Lloyd-based isotropic remeshing approach has been extended in several directions: one uses the geodesic distance on triangle meshes to generate a centroidal geodesic-based Voronoi diagram [Peyré and Cohen 04]; one is a discrete analog of the Lloyd relaxation applied onto the input mesh triangles [Valette and Chassery 04]; and another applies a quasi-Newton version of the Lloyd relaxation over a Voronoi diagram restricted to the input surface mesh [Yan et al. 09]. Regarding quad-dominant remeshing, a recent work [Bommes et al. 09] uses a mixed-integer solver in order to compute a set of parameterizations that tile the input surface mesh without any T-junctions.

SIMPLIFICATION & APPROXIMATION

Mesh simplification and approximation describes a class of algorithms that transform a given polygonal mesh into another mesh with fewer faces, edges, and vertices [Gotsman et al. 02, Luebke et al. 03]. The simplification or approximation procedure is usually controlled by user-defined quality criteria, which favor meshes that preserve specific properties of the original data as much as possible. Typical criteria include geometric distortion (e.g., Hausdorff distance, normals) or visual appearance (e.g., colors, features, etc.) [Cignoni et al. 98a].

There are many applications for simplification and approximation algorithms. First, they obviously can be used to *adjust the complexity* of a geometric data set. This makes geometry processing a scalable task where differently complex models can be used on computers with varying computing performance. Second, since many decimation schemes work iteratively, i.e., they decimate a mesh by removing one vertex at a time, they usually can be inverted. Running a decimation scheme backwards means reconstructing the original data from a decimated version by inserting more and more detail information. This inverse decimation can be used for adaptive refinement and *progressive transmission* of geometry data [Hoppe 96]. Obviously, in order to make progressive transmission effective, we have to use decimation operators whose inverses can be encoded compactly (see Figure 7.3).

There are several conceptual approaches to mesh simplification. In principle we can think of the complexity reduction as a one-step operation or as an iterative procedure. The vertex positions of the decimated mesh can be obtained as a subset of the original set of vertex positions, as a set of weighted averages of original vertex positions, or by resampling the original piecewise linear surface. In the literature the different approaches are classified into

- ▶ vertex clustering algorithms;

- ▶ incremental decimation algorithms;

- ▶ resampling algorithms;

- ▶ mesh approximation algorithms.

Vertex clustering algorithms are usually very efficient and robust. The computational complexity is typically linear in the number of vertices. However, the quality of the resulting meshes is not always satisfactory.

Incremental algorithms in most cases lead to higher-quality meshes. The iterative decimation procedure can take arbitrary user-defined criteria into account, according to which the next removal operation is chosen. However, its total computational complexity in the average case is $O(n \log n)$ and can go up to $O(n^2)$ in the worst case, especially when a global error threshold is to be respected.

Resampling algorithms are the most general approach to mesh decimation. Here, new sample points are more or less freely distributed over the original surface mesh. By connecting these samples, a completely new mesh is constructed. One major motivation for resampling techniques is that they can force the resulting mesh to have a special connectivity structure, i.e., subdivision connectivity (or semi-regular connectivity). By this they can be used to build multiresolution representations based on subdivision basis functions [Eck et al. 95]. The most serious disadvantage of resampling, however, is that aliasing errors can occur if the sampling pattern is not perfectly aligned to features in the original geometry. To avoid aliasing effects, many resampling schemes to some degree require manual pre-segmentation of the data for reliable feature detection. Resampling techniques are discussed in detail in Chapter 6.

Mesh approximation algorithms are devised to minimize well-defined error metrics through various mesh optimization strategies [Hoppe et al. 93, Alliez et al. 99, Cohen-Steiner et al. 04].

In the following sections we explain in more detail the various approaches to mesh simplification and approximation. Usually there are many choices for the different ingredients and sub-procedures in each algorithm, and we will point out the advantages and disadvantages for each class.

7.1 Vertex Clustering

The basic idea of vertex clustering is as follows: For a given approximation tolerance ε we partition the bounding space around the given object into cells with diameter smaller than the tolerance. For each cell we compute a representative vertex position, which we assign to all vertices that fall into this cell. By this clustering step, original faces degenerate if two or three of their corners lie in the same cell and consequently are mapped to the same position. The decimated mesh is eventually obtained by removing all degenerate faces [Rossignac and Borrel 93].

The remaining faces correspond to those original triangles whose corners all lie in different cells. Stated otherwise, if $\mathbf{p}$ is the representative vertex for the vertices $\mathbf{p}_0, \ldots, \mathbf{p}_n$ in the cluster P, and $\mathbf{q}$ is the representative for the vertices $\mathbf{q}_0, \ldots, \mathbf{q}_m$ in the cluster Q, then $\mathbf{p}$ and $\mathbf{q}$ are connected in the decimated mesh if and only if at least one pair of vertices $(\mathbf{p}_i, \mathbf{q}_j)$ was connected in the original mesh.

One drawback of vertex clustering is that the resulting mesh might no longer be 2-manifold, even if the original mesh was. Topological changes occur when a part of a surface that collapses into a single point is not homeomorphic to a disk, i.e., when two different sheets of the surface pass through a single ε-cell. However, this disadvantage can also be considered as an advantage. Since the scheme is able to change the topology of the given model, we can very effectively reduce the object complexity. Consider, e.g., applying mesh decimation to a 3D model of a sponge. Here, any decimation scheme that preserves the surface topology cannot reduce the mesh complexity significantly since all the small holes have to be preserved.

The computational efficiency of vertex clustering is determined by the effort it takes to map the mesh vertices to clusters. For simple uniform spatial grids this can be achieved in linear time with small constants. Then, for each cell, a representative has to be found that might require involved computations. But the number of clusters is usually much smaller than the number of vertices.

Another apparently nice aspect of vertex clustering is that it automatically guarantees a global approximation tolerance by defining the clusters accordingly. However, in practice it turns out that the actual approximation error of the decimated mesh is usually much smaller than the radius of the clusters. This indicates that, for a given error threshold, vertex clustering algorithms do not achieve optimal complexity reduction. Consider, as an extreme example, a very fine planar mesh. Here, decimation down to a single triangle without any approximation error would be possible. The result of vertex clustering instead will always keep one vertex for every ε-cell.

7.1.1   Computing Cluster Representatives

Different vertex clustering algorithms vary mainly in how they compute the representative. Simply taking the center of each cell or the straight average of its associated vertices are obvious choices, but these methods rarely lead to satisfying results (see Figure 7.1).

A more reasonable choice is based on finding the optimal vertex position as a least-squares approximation. For this we exploit the fact that for sufficiently small ε the polygonal surface patch that lies within one ε-cell is expected to be piecewise flat, i.e., either the associated normal cone has a small opening angle (totally flat) or the patch can be split into a small number of sectors for which the normal cone has a small opening angle. The optimal representative vertex position should have a minimum deviation from all the (regression) tangent planes that correspond to these sectors. If these approximate tangent planes do not intersect in a single point, we need to compute a solution in the least-squares sense.

Consider one triangle t_i within the current cell of interest. Let us denote by $P_i = (\mathbf{x}_i, \mathbf{n}_i)$ the supporting plane of this triangle, with $\mathbf{x}_i$ an arbitrary vertex on the plane and $\mathbf{n}_i$ the unit normal vector of t_i. With $d_i = \mathbf{n}_i^T \mathbf{x}_i$ the squared distance of a point $\mathbf{x}$ from the plane P_i can be computed as

$$\mathrm{dist}^2(\mathbf{x}, P_i) \;=\; \left(\mathbf{n}_i^T \mathbf{x} - d_i\right)^2.$$

Using homogeneous coordinates $\bar{\mathbf{x}} = (\mathbf{x}, 1)$ and $\bar{\mathbf{n}}_i = (\mathbf{n}_i, -d_i)$ the above equation simplifies to

$$\mathrm{dist}^2(\mathbf{x}, P_i) \;=\; \left(\bar{\mathbf{n}}_i^T \bar{\mathbf{x}}\right)^2 \;=\; \bar{\mathbf{x}}^T \bar{\mathbf{n}}_i \bar{\mathbf{n}}_i^T \bar{\mathbf{x}} \;=:\; \bar{\mathbf{x}}^T \mathbf{Q}_i \bar{\mathbf{x}},$$

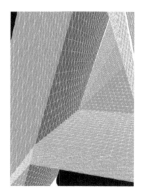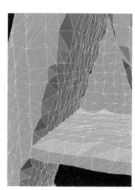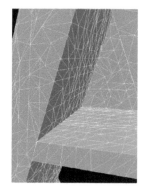

Figure 7.1.   Different choices for the representative vertex when decimating a mesh using clustering: original (left), average (center), and quadric-based (right). (Image taken from [Botsch et al. 06b]. ©2006 ACM, Inc. Included here by permission.)

with a symmetric 4×4 matrix $\mathbf{Q}_i = \bar{\mathbf{n}}_i \bar{\mathbf{n}}_i^T$. The sum of the quadratic distances to the supporting planes P_i of all triangles t_i within a cell C is given by

$$E(\mathbf{x}) \;=\; \sum_{t_i \in C} \bar{\mathbf{x}}^T \mathbf{Q}_i \bar{\mathbf{x}} \;=\; \bar{\mathbf{x}}^T \left(\sum_{t_i \in C} \mathbf{Q}_i \right) \bar{\mathbf{x}} \;=:\; \bar{\mathbf{x}}^T \mathbf{Q}\, \bar{\mathbf{x}}. \qquad (7.1)$$

The error function is a quadratic form, the isocontours of which are ellipsoids, and consequently the resulting error measure is called the *quadric error metric* (QEM). The coefficients of the quadric are stored in the symmetric 4×4 matrix $\mathbf{Q}$, no matter how many triangle planes P_i contribute to the error [Garland and Heckbert 97, Lindstrom 00].

The optimal position $\mathbf{x}$ minimizing the quadric error can be computed as the solution of the least squares system

$$\underbrace{\left(\sum_i \mathbf{n}_i\, \mathbf{n}_i^T \right)}_{\mathbf{A}} \mathbf{x} \;=\; \underbrace{\left(\sum_i \mathbf{n}_i\, d_i \right)}_{\mathbf{b}}, \qquad (7.2)$$

which can be obtained from the matrix $\mathbf{Q}$ as

$$\mathbf{Q} \;=\; \begin{bmatrix} \mathbf{A} & -\mathbf{b} \\ -\mathbf{b}^T & c \end{bmatrix}.$$

If the matrix $\mathbf{A}$ has full rank, i.e., if the normal vectors of the patch do not lie in a plane, then Equation (7.2) could be solved directly. However, to avoid special case handling and to make the solution more robust, a pseudo-inverse based on singular value decomposition is preferred [Lindstrom 00].

Note that for irregular triangulations, a weighted sum of squared distances can improve the result, where typically triangle areas $|t_i|$ are used as weights w_i. This leads to an error function $E(\mathbf{x}) = \sum_i w_i \operatorname{dist}^2(\mathbf{x}, P_i)$, which simply corresponds to a quadric matrix $\mathbf{Q} = \sum_i w_i \mathbf{Q}_i$. Based on the blocks of this matrix as defined above, the optimal point is again computed as the solution of $\mathbf{A}\mathbf{x} = \mathbf{b}$.

7.2   Incremental Decimation

Incremental algorithms remove one mesh vertex at a time (see Figure 7.2). In each step, the best candidate for removal is determined based on user-specified criteria. Those criteria can be either *binary* (removal is or is not allowed) or *continuous* (rate the quality of the mesh after the removal). Binary criteria usually refer to the global approximation tolerance or to other

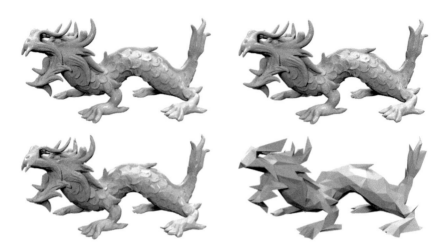

Figure 7.2. Decimation of the dragon mesh consisting of 577,512 triangles (top left) to a simplified version with 10% (top right), 1% (bottom left), and 0.1% (bottom right) of the original triangle count. (Model courtesy of the Stanford Computer Graphics Laboratory.)

minimum requirements, e.g., minimum aspect ratio of triangles. Continuous criteria measure the *fairness* of the mesh with respect to the approximation error or in some other sense such as, e.g., isotropic triangles are better than anisotropic ones, and small normal jumps between neighboring triangles are better than large normal jumps.

Every time a removal is executed, the surface geometry in the vicinity changes. Therefore, the quality criteria must be re-evaluated. During the iterative procedure, this re-evaluation is computationally the most expensive part. To preserve the order of the candidates, they are usually kept in a modifiable *heap data structure* with the best removal operation on top. Whenever removal candidates have to be re-evaluated, they are deleted from the heap and re-inserted with their new value. By this procedure, the complexity of the update step increases only about $O(\log n)$ for large meshes if the criteria evaluation itself has constant complexity.

7.2.1 Topological Operations

There are several different choices for the basic removal operation. The major design goal is to keep the operation as simple as possible. In particular, this means that we do not want to remove large parts of the original mesh at once but rather want to remove a single vertex at a time. Strong decimation is then achieved by applying many simple decimation steps instead of a few complicated ones. If mesh consistency, i.e., topological correctness,

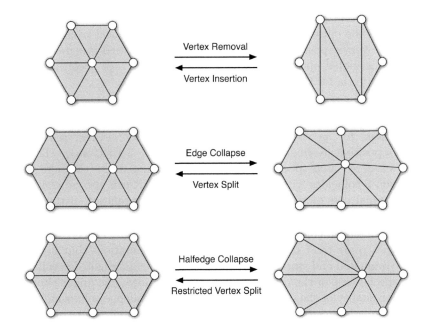

Figure 7.3. Euler operations and inverses for incremental mesh decimation: vertex removal (top), general edge collapse (middle), and halfedge collapse (bottom).

matters, then the decimation operator must be an *Euler operator* so as to preserve the Euler characteristic (see Equation (1.5), [Hoppe et al. 93]).

Vertex removal. The first operator one might think of *deletes one vertex* plus its adjacent triangles. For a vertex with valence k, this leaves a k-sided hole. This hole can be fixed by any polygon triangulation algorithm [Schroeder et al. 92]. Although there are several combinatorial degrees of freedom, the number of triangles will always be $k - 2$. Hence, the removal operation decreases the number of vertices by one, the number of edges by three, and the number of triangles by two (see Figure 7.3 (top)).

Edge collapse. Another decimation operator takes two adjacent vertices, $\mathbf{p}$ and $\mathbf{q}$, and collapses the edge between them, i.e., both vertices are moved to the same new point location $\mathbf{r}$ [Hoppe 96] (see Figure 7.3 (middle)). By this operation, two adjacent triangles degenerate and can be removed from the mesh. In total this operator also removes one vertex, three edges, and two triangles. The degrees of freedom in this *edge collapse* operator emerge from the freedom to choose the new point location $\mathbf{r}$.

Both operators that we discussed so far are not unique. In either case there is some optimization involved to find the best local triangulation or the best vertex position. Conceptually this is not well designed since it mixes the global optimization (which candidate is best according to the sorting criteria for the heap) with local optimization.

Halfedge collapse. A possible way out is the so-called *halfedge collapse* operation: for an ordered pair (**p**, **q**) of adjacent vertices, **p** is moved to **q**'s position [Kobbelt et al. 98a] (see Figure 7.3 (bottom)). This can be considered as a special case of edge collapsing where the new vertex position **r** coincides with **q**. On the other hand, it can also be considered as a special case of vertex deletion where the triangulation of the k-sided hole is generated by connecting all neighboring vertices with vertex **q**.

The halfedge collapse has no degrees of freedom. Notice that **p** → **q** and **q** → **p** are treated as independent removal operations that both have to be evaluated and stored in the candidate heap. Since halfedge collapsing is a special case of the other two removal operations, one might expect an inferior quality of the decimated mesh. In fact, halfedge collapsing merely sub-samples the set of original vertices while the full edge collapse can act as a low-pass filter where new vertex positions are computed, e.g., by averaging original vertex positions. However, in practice this effect becomes noticeable only for extremely strong decimation where the exact location of individual vertices really matters.

The big advantage of halfedge collapsing is that for moderate decimation, the global optimization (i.e., candidate selection based on user-specified criteria) is completely separated from the decimation operator that makes the design of mesh decimation schemes more modular.

Note that an edge collapse or halfedge collapse can lead to a topologically invalid configuration. Collapsing an edge (**p**, **q**) is a valid operation if and only if the following two criteria hold [Hoppe et al. 93]:

▶ If both **p** and **q** are boundary vertices, then the edge (**p**, **q**) has to be a boundary edge.

▶ For all vertices **r** incident to both **p** and **q** there has to be a triangle (**p**, **q**, **r**). In other words, the intersection of the one-rings of **p** and **q** consists of vertices opposite the edge (**p**, **q**) only.

Another formulation of these criteria is the so-called *link condition* [Dey et al. 99, Edelsbrunner 06], which states under which conditions an edge collapse preserves the mesh topology. Examples of illegal edge collapses are shown in Figure 7.4.

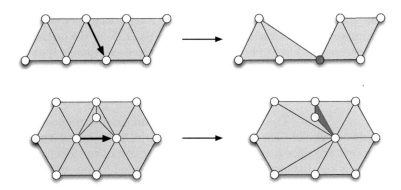

Figure 7.4. Two examples for topologically illegal (half-)edge collapses **p** → **q**. Collapsing two boundary vertices through the interior leads to a non-manifold pinched vertex (top). The one-rings of **p** and **q** intersect in more than two vertices, which after collapsing results in a duplicate fold-over triangle and a non-manifold edge (bottom).

Vertex contraction. If the above criteria are satisfied, all of the above removal operations preserve the mesh consistency and consequently the topology of the underlying surface. No holes in the original mesh will be closed, no handles will be removed, and no connected component will be eliminated. If a decimation scheme should be able to also simplify the topology of the input model, we have to use non-Euler removal operators. The most common operator in this class is *vertex contraction*, where two vertices **p** and **q** can be contracted into one new vertex **r** even if they are not connected by an edge [Garland and Heckbert 97, Schroeder 97]. This operation reduces the number of vertices by one but keeps the number of triangles constant. The implementation of mesh decimation based on vertex contraction requires flexible data structures that are able to represent non-manifold meshes, since the surface patch around vertex **r** after the contraction might no longer be homeomorphic to a (half-)disk.

7.2.2   Distance Measures

Guaranteeing an approximation tolerance during decimation is the most important requirement for most applications. Usually an upper bound ε is prescribed, and the decimation scheme looks for the mesh with the least number of triangles that stays within ε to the original mesh. However, exactly computing the geometric distance between two polygonal mesh models is computationally expensive [Klein et al. 96, Cignoni et al. 98b], and hence conservative approximations are used that can be evaluated quickly.

The generic situation during mesh decimation is that each triangle t_i in the decimated mesh is associated with a sub-patch $\mathcal{S}_i$ of the original mesh. Distance measures have to be computed between each triangle t_i and either the vertices or faces of $\mathcal{S}_i$. Depending on the application, we have to take the maximum distance or we can average the distance over the patch.

Error accumulation. The simplest of these techniques is error accumulation [Schroeder et al. 92]. For example, each edge collapse operation modifies the adjacent triangles t_i by shifting one of their corner vertices from $\mathbf{p}$ or $\mathbf{q}$ to $\mathbf{r}$. Hence, the distance of $\mathbf{r}$ to t_i is an upper bound for the approximation error introduced in this step. Error accumulation means that we store an error value for each triangle and simply add the new error contribution for every decimation step. The error accumulation can be done based either on scalar distance values or on distance vectors. Vector addition takes into account the effect that approximation error estimates in opposite directions can cancel each other.

Error quadrics. Another distance measure assigns distance values to the vertices $\mathbf{p}_j$ of the decimated mesh. It is based on estimating the sum of squared distances of $\mathbf{p}_j$ from all the supporting planes of triangles in the patches $\mathcal{S}_i$ that are associated with the triangles t_i surrounding $\mathbf{p}_j$. This is, in fact, what the quadric error metric does [Garland and Heckbert 97].

Initially we compute the error quadric $\mathbf{Q_p}$ for each original vertex $\mathbf{p}$ according to Equation (7.1) by summing over all triangles that are directly adjacent to $\mathbf{p}$. Then, whenever the edge between two vertices $\mathbf{p}$ and $\mathbf{q}$ is collapsed, the error quadric for the new vertex $\mathbf{r}$ is accumulated as $\mathbf{Q_r} = \mathbf{Q_p} + \mathbf{Q_q}$. The error of collapsing $\mathbf{p}$ and $\mathbf{q}$ into $\mathbf{r}$ is computed according to Equation (7.1) as $E_{\mathbf{r}}(\mathbf{r}) = \bar{\mathbf{r}}^T \mathbf{Q_r} \bar{\mathbf{r}}$. The optimal position for $\mathbf{r}$ is given by the solution of Equation (7.2).

By summing up the quadrics of the edge's endpoints, the new quadric $\mathbf{Q_r}$ represents the sum of squared distances to all planes stored in either $\mathbf{Q_p}$ or $\mathbf{Q_q}$. Consequently, triangle planes can occur multiple (at most three) times, which can overestimate the error. Approximating the distance from a triangle by the distance to a plane can underestimate the true error. Hence, the quadric error metric gives neither a strict upper nor a strict lower bound on the true geometric error.

On the other hand, error quadrics have major advantages regarding memory consumption and computational efficiency: each vertex $\mathbf{x}$ stores a symmetric 4×4 matrix $\mathbf{Q}$ only, and the error can efficiently be computed in constant time as $\bar{\mathbf{x}}^T \mathbf{Q} \bar{\mathbf{x}}$—no matter how many planes are associated to vertex $\mathbf{x}$ during decimation. Because of this, error quadrics are one of the most frequently employed techniques in mesh decimation.

Hausdorff distance. Finally, the most expensive but also the sharpest distance error estimate is the *Hausdorff distance* [Klein et al. 96]. This distance measure is defined to be the maximum minimum distance, i.e., if we have two sets $\mathcal{A}$ and $\mathcal{B}$ then $H(\mathcal{A},\mathcal{B})$ is found by computing the minimum distance $d(\mathbf{a},\mathcal{B})$ for each point $\mathbf{a} \in \mathcal{A}$ and then taking the maximum of those values:

$$H(\mathcal{A},\mathcal{B}) \;=\; \max_{\mathbf{a}\in\mathcal{A}} \min_{\mathbf{b}\in\mathcal{B}} \|\mathbf{a}-\mathbf{b}\|\,.$$

Notice that, in general, $H(\mathcal{A},\mathcal{B}) \neq H(\mathcal{B},\mathcal{A})$ and hence the *symmetric Hausdorff distance* is the maximum of both values.

If we assume that the vertices of the original mesh represent sample points measured on some original geometry, then the faces have been generated by some triangulation preprocess and should be considered as piecewise linear approximations to the original shape. From this point of view, the correct error estimate for the decimated mesh would be the *one-sided* Hausdorff distance $H(\mathcal{A},\mathcal{B})$ from the original sample points $\mathcal{A}$ to the decimated mesh $\mathcal{B}$.

To efficiently compute the Hausdorff distance, we have to keep track of the assignment of original vertices to the triangles of the decimated mesh. Whenever an edge collapse operation is performed, the removed vertices $\mathbf{p}$ and $\mathbf{q}$ (or $\mathbf{p}$ alone in the case of a halfedge collapse) are assigned to the nearest triangle in a local vicinity. In addition, since the edge collapse changes the shape of the adjacent triangles, the data points that previously have been assigned to these triangles must be re-distributed. By this, every triangle t_i of the decimated mesh at any time maintains a list of original vertices belonging to the currently associated patch $\mathcal{S}_i$. The Hausdorff distance is then evaluated by finding the most distant point in this list.

A special technique for exact distance computation is suggested in [Cohen et al. 96], where two offset surfaces to the original mesh are computed to bound the space in which the decimated mesh has to stay. The method of Borouchaki and Frey performs an approximate computation of the Hausdorff distance [Borouchaki and Frey 05].

7.2.3   Fairness Criteria

The distance measures can be used to decide which removal operations among the candidates are legal and which are not (because they violate the global error threshold ε). In an incremental mesh decimation scheme we have to provide an additional criterion that ranks all the legal removal operations. This criterion determines the ordering of candidates in the heap.

One straightforward solution is to use the distance measure for the ordering as well. This implies that the decimation algorithm will always remove that vertex in the next step that increases the approximation error least. While this is a reasonable heuristic in general, we can use other criteria to optimize the resulting mesh for special application-dependent requirements.

For example, we might prefer triangle meshes with faces that are as close as possible to equilateral. In this case we can measure the quality of a vertex removal operation, e.g., by the ratio of the circumcircle radius to the length of the shortest edge [Shewchuk 97] of all incident triangles after the removal.

If we prefer visually smooth meshes, we can use the maximum or average normal jump between adjacent triangles after the removal as a sorting criterion. In order to prevent triangles from flipping over due to a collapse operation, the angle between the normals of each incident triangle before and after the collapse should be computed. If this angle is close to 180 degrees, then the collapse should not be performed, e.g., by assigning it a very high cost in the priority queue.

Other criteria might include color deviation or texture distortion if the input data does not consist of pure geometry but also has color and texture attributes attached [Cignoni et al. 99, Cohen et al. 98, Garland and Heckbert 98].

All these different criteria for sorting vertex removal operations are called *fairness criteria* since they rate the quality of the mesh beyond the mere approximation tolerance. If we keep the fairness criterion separate from the other modules in an implementation of incremental mesh decimation, we can adapt the algorithm to arbitrary user-defined requirements by simply exchanging that one procedure. This gives rise to a flexible toolbox for building custom-tailored mesh decimation schemes [Kobbelt et al. 98a].

7.3   Shape Approximation

Cohen-Steiner et al. [Cohen-Steiner et al. 04] have introduced a *variational shape approximation* (VSA) algorithm. VSA is highly sensitive to features and symmetries and produces anisotropic meshes of high approximation quality. In VSA the input shape is approximated by a set of proxies. The approximation error is iteratively decreased by clustering faces into best-fitting regions. In contrast to some remeshing methods, VSA does not require a parameterization of the input or local estimates of differential quantities. VSA techniques can also be used in mesh segmentation.

Let $\mathcal{M}$ be a triangle mesh and let $\mathcal{R} = \{\mathcal{R}_1, \ldots, \mathcal{R}_k\}$ be a partition of $\mathcal{M}$ into k regions, i.e., $\mathcal{R}_i \subset \mathcal{M}$ and

$$\mathcal{R}_1 \cup \cdots \cup \mathcal{R}_k = \mathcal{M}.$$

Furthermore, let $\mathcal{P} = \{P_1, \ldots, P_k\}$ be a set of *proxies*. A proxy $P_i = (\mathbf{x}_i, \mathbf{n}_i)$ is simply a plane in space through the point $\mathbf{x}_i$ with normal direction $\mathbf{n}_i$. Cohen-Steiner et al. consider two metrics that measure a generalized distance of a region $\mathcal{R}_i$ to its proxy P_i. The standard $\mathcal{L}^2$ metric is defined as

$$\mathcal{L}^2(\mathcal{R}_i, P_i) = \int_{\mathbf{x} \in \mathcal{R}_i} \left(\mathbf{n}_i^T \mathbf{x} - \mathbf{n}_i^T \mathbf{x}_i\right)^2 \mathrm{d}A,$$

where the integrand is just the squared orthogonal distance of $\mathbf{x}$ from the plane P_i. They also introduce a new shape metric $\mathcal{L}^{2,1}$ that is based on a measure of the normal field:

$$\mathcal{L}^{2,1}(\mathcal{R}_i, P_i) = \int_{\mathbf{x} \in \mathcal{R}_i} \|\mathbf{n}(\mathbf{x}) - \mathbf{n}_i\|^2 \mathrm{d}A.$$

The goal of variational shape approximation is then the following: given a number k and an error metric E (i.e., either $E = \mathcal{L}^2$ or $E = \mathcal{L}^{2,1}$), find a set $\mathcal{R} = \{\mathcal{R}_1, \ldots, \mathcal{R}_k\}$ of regions and a set $\mathcal{P} = \{P_1, \ldots, P_k\}$ of proxies such that the global distortion

$$E(\mathcal{R}, \mathcal{P}) = \sum_{i=1}^{k} E(\mathcal{R}_i, P_i) \qquad (7.3)$$

is minimized. We can then extract a mesh of the original input from the proxies.

In the following sections we describe and compare two algorithms for computing an (approximate) minimum of Equation (7.3). The first algorithm is due to Cohen-Steiner et al. and uses Lloyd clustering to produce the regions $\mathcal{R}_i$. The second method is a greedy approximation to VSA with additional injectivity guarantees.

7.3.1 Variational Shape Approximation

Cohen-Steiner et al. [Cohen-Steiner et al. 04] use a method to minimize Equation (7.3) that is inspired by Lloyd's clustering algorithm, which has been used for mesh segmentation in [Sander et al. 03]. The algorithm iteratively alternates between a *geometry partitioning* phase and a *proxy fitting* phase. In the geometry partitioning phase, the algorithm computes a set of regions that best fit a given set of proxies. In the proxy fitting phase, the partitioning is kept fixed and the proxies are adjusted.

Geometry partitioning. In the geometry partitioning phase, the algorithm modifies the set $\mathcal{R}$ of regions to achieve a lower approximation error (Equation (7.3)) while keeping the proxies $\mathcal{P}$ fixed. It does so by selecting a number of seed triangles and greedily growing new regions $\mathcal{R}_i$ around them.

First, the algorithm picks the triangle t_i from each region $\mathcal{R}_i$ that is most similar to its associated proxy P_i. This is done through iterating once over all triangles t in $\mathcal{R}_i$ and finding the one that minimizes $E(t, P_i)$.

After initializing $\mathcal{R}_i = \{t_i\}$, the algorithm simultaneously grows the sets $\mathcal{R}_i$. A priority queue contains candidate pairs (t, P_i) of triangles and proxies. The priority of a triangle-proxy pair (t, P_i) is naturally given as $E(t, P_i)$. For each seed triangle t_i, its neighboring triangles r are found and the pairs (r, P_i) are inserted into the queue. The algorithm then iteratively pops pairs (t, P_i) from the queue, checks whether t has already been conquered by the region growing process, and if not assigns t to $\mathcal{R}_i$. Again, the unconquered neighbor triangles r of t are selected, and the pairs (r, P_i) are inserted to the queue. This process is iterated until the queue is empty and all triangles are assigned to a region. Note that a given triangle can appear up to three times simultaneously in the queue. Instead of checking whether a triangle is already in the queue, the algorithm keeps a status bit *conquered* for each triangle and checks this bit before assigning a triangle to a region. The following pseudocode summarizes the geometry partitioning procedure:

```
partition(R = {R₁,...,Rₖ}, P = {P₁,...,Pₖ})

    // find the seed triangles and initialize the priority queue
    queue = ∅
    for i = 1 to k do
        select the triangle t ∈ Rᵢ that minimizes E(t, Pᵢ)
        Rᵢ = {t}
        set t to conquered
        for all neighbors r of t do
            insert (r, Pᵢ) into queue

    // grow the regions
    while the queue is not empty do
        get (t, Pᵢ) from the queue that minimizes E(t, Pᵢ)
        if t is not conquered then
            set t to conquered
            Rᵢ = Rᵢ ∪ {t}
            for all neighbors r of t do
                if r is not conquered then
                    insert (r, Pᵢ) into queue
```

The algorithm is initialized by randomly picking k triangles $t_1, \ldots, t_k$ on the input model, setting $\mathcal{R}_i = \{t_i\}$, and initializing $P_i = (\mathbf{x}_i, \mathbf{n}_i)$, where $\mathbf{x}_i$ is an arbitrary point on t_i and $\mathbf{n}_i$ is t_i's normal. Then, regions are grown as in the geometry partitioning phase.

Proxy fitting. In the proxy fitting phase, the partition $\mathcal{R}$ is kept fixed while the proxies $P_i = (\mathbf{x}_i, \mathbf{n}_i)$ are adjusted in order to minimize Equation (7.3).

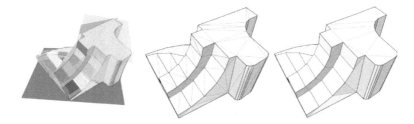

Figure 7.5. Variational shape approximation applied to the fandisk model.

For the $\mathcal{L}^2$ metric, the best proxy is the least-squares fitting plane. It can be found using integral principal component analysis [Cohen-Steiner et al. 04]. When using the $\mathcal{L}^{2,1}$ metric, the proxy normal $\mathbf{n}_i$ is just the area-weighted average of the triangle normals. The base point $\mathbf{x}_i$ is irrelevant for $\mathcal{L}^{2,1}$, but it is set to the barycenter of $\mathcal{R}_i$ for remeshing purposes.

Mesh extraction. From an optimal partitioning $\mathcal{R} = \{\mathcal{R}_1, \ldots, \mathcal{R}_k\}$ and corresponding proxies $\mathcal{P} = \{P_1, \ldots, P_k\}$, one can now extract an anisotropic remesh as follows: First, all vertices in the original mesh that are adjacent to three or more different regions are identified. These vertices are projected onto each proxy, and their average position is computed. These so-called anchor vertices are then connected by tracing the boundaries of the regions $\mathcal{R}$. The resulting faces are triangulated by performing a "discrete" analog of the Delaunay triangulation over the input triangle mesh (see the example in Figure 7.5).

7.3.2 Greedy Shape Approximation

In [Marinov and Kobbelt 05], a greedy algorithm to compute an approximate minimum of Equation (7.3) is proposed (see Figure 7.6). Its main advantages are that

▶ the algorithm naturally generates a multiresolution hierarchy of shape approximations (Figure 7.6),

▶ the output is guaranteed to be free of fold-overs and degenerate faces.

On the downside, due to its greedy approach, it is more likely that the algorithm will get stuck in a local minimum (although this is rarely observed in practice). Furthermore, its implementation is involved and requires the robust computation of Delaunay triangulations.

Setup. In addition to the partition $\mathcal{R} = \{\mathcal{R}_1, \ldots, \mathcal{R}_k\}$ and the proxies $\mathcal{P} = \{P_1, \ldots, P_k\}$, the algorithm maintains a set of polygonal faces $\mathcal{F} =$

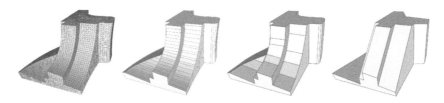

Figure 7.6. A multiresolution hierarchy of differently detailed meshes that was created by greedy shape approximation. (Image taken from [Marinov and Kobbelt 05].)

$\{f_1, \ldots, f_k\}$. Each face f_i can be an arbitrary connected polygon, i.e., it has an outer boundary and possibly a number of inner boundaries around interior holes. At the beginning of the algorithm, we initialize the sets $\mathcal{R}$, $\mathcal{P}$, and $\mathcal{F}$ as follows:

▶ $\mathcal{R}_i = \{t_i\}$, i.e., each triangle makes up a region on its own.

▶ The proxy of $\mathcal{R}_i$ is set to $P_i = (\mathbf{x}_i, \mathbf{n}_i)$, where $\mathbf{x}_i$ is an arbitrary point on t_i and $\mathbf{n}_i$ is t_i's normal.

▶ $f_i = t_i$, in particular the projection of f_i onto P_i is injective.

Algorithm invariant. The goal of the algorithm is to guarantee a valid shape approximation that is free of fold-overs and degenerate faces. This is achieved by maintaining the following invariant at all times during the run of the algorithm:

Injectivity constraint: The projection of f_i onto P_i is injective.

Note that the initial settings for the sets $\mathcal{R}$, $\mathcal{P}$, and $\mathcal{F}$ satisfy this constraint.

Due to the injectivity constraint, one is able to extract a valid triangle mesh at all times during the run of the algorithm. To produce a triangulation $\mathcal{D}_i$ of a face f_i, one simply projects f_i onto P_i (which is a plane), performs a (planar) constrained Delaunay triangulation there, and lifts the triangles of the Delaunay triangulation back to f_i.

Greedy optimization. The partitioning is now greedily optimized in a loop that stops when a predefined maximum error or a predefined number of regions is reached. In each iteration one selects (subject to the injectivity constraint) two regions $\mathcal{R}_i$ and $\mathcal{R}_j$ and merges them into a new region $\mathcal{R}' = \mathcal{R}_i \cup \mathcal{R}_j$. (The order in which the merging is performed is described in the next paragraph.) Then, a new proxy $P' = (\mathbf{x}', \mathbf{n}')$ is computed as an area-weighted average of P_i and P_j for

$$\mathbf{n}' = \frac{a_i \mathbf{n}_i + a_j \mathbf{n}_j}{\|a_i \mathbf{n}_i + a_j \mathbf{n}_j\|} \quad \text{and} \quad \mathbf{x}' = \frac{a_i \mathbf{x}_i + a_j \mathbf{x}_j}{a_i + a_j},$$

where $a_i = \text{area}(\mathcal{R}_i)$. Finally, a new face f' is computed by identifying and removing the common boundary edges of f_i and f_j. The algorithm then checks for valence-2 vertices: If it finds an interior valence-2 vertex, it is immediately removed. Boundary valence-2 vertices are only removed if their distance from the proxy is smaller than a user-defined threshold.

Note again that all the operations described above (merging of faces, removal of valence-2 vertices) are performed only if the injectivity constraint is not violated by the operation.

Merge priorities. For each adjacent pair $\mathcal{R}_i$ and $\mathcal{R}_j$ of regions, we could compute the shape measure $E(\mathcal{R}', P')$ as described in Equation (7.3) and order the region pairs by increasing shape error. In order to speed up the algorithm, the exact $\mathcal{L}^2$ measure is approximated by

$$L^2(f') = \mathcal{L}^2(\mathcal{D}_i, P') + \mathcal{L}^2(\mathcal{D}_j, P').$$

Since $\mathcal{D}_i$ usually contains much fewer triangles than $\mathcal{R}_i$, this will significantly speed up the algorithm. The $\mathcal{L}^{2,1}$ error is replaced by

$$L^{2,1}(f') = a_i \left\| \mathbf{n}_i - \mathbf{n}' \right\|^2 + a_j \left\| \mathbf{n}_j - \mathbf{n}' \right\|^2,$$

where $a_i = \text{area}(\mathcal{R}_i)$ as before. The two error measures are combined into a single, scale-independent measure,

$$E(f') = \left(1 + L^2(f')\right) \cdot \left(1 + L^{2,1}(f')\right),$$

which does not require any user-defined weight parameters.

Cohen-Steiner's algorithm generally produces high-quality results with low approximation error. However, the mesh extraction step might produce degenerate triangles and fold-overs. The extensions presented by Marinov produce a hierarchy of reconstructions that are guaranteed to be free of fold-overs. However, due to the greedy approach, Marinov's algorithm is more likely to get stuck in a local optimum. To achieve acceptable running times, they furthermore have to resort to an approximation of the true $\mathcal{L}^2$ or $\mathcal{L}^{2,1}$ errors.

7.4   Out-of-Core Methods

Mesh simplification is frequently applied to very large data sets that are too complex to fit into main memory. To avoid severe performance degradation due to virtual memory swapping, *out-of-core* algorithms have been proposed that allow an efficient decimation of polygonal meshes without requiring the entire data set to be present in main memory. The challenge here is to design suitable data structures that avoid random access to parts of the mesh during the simplification.

Lindstrom presented an approach based on vertex clustering combined with quadric error metrics for computing the cluster representatives [Lindstrom 00] (see Section 7.1). This algorithm requires only limited connectivity information and processes meshes stored as a triangle soup, where each triangle is represented as a triplet of vertex coordinates. Using a single pass over the mesh data, an in-core representation of the simplified mesh is build incrementally. A dynamic hash table is used for fast localization, and quadrics associated with a cluster are aggregated until all triangles have been processed. The final simplified mesh is then produced by computing a representative from the per-cluster quadrics and the corresponding connectivity information as described above.

Lindstrom and Silva improved on this approach by removing the requirement for the output model to fit into main memory using a multi-pass approach [Lindstrom and Silva 01]. Their method requires only a constant amount of memory that is independent of the size of the input and output data. This improvement is achieved by a careful (slower, but cheaper) use of disk space, which typically leads to performance overheads between a factor of two and five, as compared to [Lindstrom 00]. To avoid storing the list of occupied clusters and associated quadrics in main memory, the required information from each triangle to compute the quadrics is stored to disk. This file is then sorted according to the grid locations using an external sort algorithm. Finally, quadrics and final vertex positions are computed in a single linear sweep over the sorted file. The authors also apply a scheme similar to the one proposed in [Garland and Heckbert 97] to better preserve boundary edges.

Wu and Kobbelt proposed a streaming approach to out-of-core mesh decimation based on edge collapse operations in connection with a quadric error metric [Wu and Kobbelt 04]. Their method uses a fixed-size active working set and is independent of the input and output model complexity. In contrast to the previous two approaches for out-of-core decimation, their method allows prescribing the size of the output mesh exactly and supports explicit control over the topology during the simplification. The basic idea is to sequentially stream the mesh data and incrementally apply decimation operations on an active working set that is kept in main memory. Assuming that the geometry stream is approximately pre-sorted, e.g., by one coordinate, the spatial coherency then guarantees that the working set can be small as compared to the total model size (see Figure 7.7). For decimation they apply randomized multiple-choice optimization, which has been shown to produce results of similar quality as those produced by the common greedy optimization. The idea is to select a small random set of candidate edges for contraction and only collapse the edge with smallest

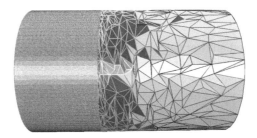

Figure 7.7. This snapshot of a stream decimation shows the as-yet-unprocessed part of the input data (left), the current in-core portion (middle), and the already decimated output (right). The data in the original file happened to be pre-sorted from right to left. (Image taken from [Wu and Kobbelt 04].)

quadric error. This significantly reduces computation costs, since no global heap data structure has to be maintained during the simplification process. In order to avoid inconsistencies during the simplification, edges can only be collapsed if they are not part of the boundary between the active working set and the parts of the mesh that are held out-of-core. Since no global connectivity information is available, this boundary cannot be distinguished from the actual mesh boundary of the input model. Thus, the latter can only be simplified after the entire mesh has been processed, which can be problematic for meshes with large boundaries.

Isenburg et al. introduced *mesh processing sequences*, which represent a mesh as a fixed interleaved sequence of indexed vertices and triangles [Isenburg et al. 03]. Processing sequences can be used to improve the out-of-core decimation algorithms described above. Both memory efficiency and mesh quality are improved for the vertex clustering method of [Lindstrom 00], while increased coherency and explicit boundary information help to reduce the size of the active working set in [Wu and Kobbelt 04].

Shaffer and Garland propose a scheme that combines an out-of-core vertex clustering step with an in-core iterative decimation step [Shaffer and Garland 01]. The central observation, which is also the rationale behind the randomized multiple choice optimization, is that the exact ordering of edge collapses is only relevant for very coarse approximations. Thus, the decimation process can be simplified by combining many edge collapse operations into single vertex clustering operations to obtain an intermediate mesh, which then serves as input for the standard greedy decimation (Section 7.2). Shaffer and Garland use quadric error metrics for both types of decimation and couple the two simplification steps by passing the quadrics computed during clustering to the subsequent iterative edge collapse pass. This coupling achieves significant improvements when compared to simply applying the two operations in succession.

7.5   Summary and Further Reading

We have presented an overview of the main paradigms used for the simplification and approximation of surface meshes. Incremental mesh decimation using repeated edge collapses is the most popular algorithm and is widely used in applications. This approach has been extended in many variants, such as efficient view-dependent simplification [Hu et al.], maximum error tolerances (Hausdorff distance) [Botsch et al. 04, Borouchaki and Frey 05], and intersection-free simplification [Gumhold et al. 03].

In [Wu and Kobbelt 05] the variational shape approximation approach is taken a step further by allowing for proxies other than simple planes, e.g., spheres, cylinders, and rolling-ball blends. Apart from requiring fewer primitives to achieve a certain fitting approximation, this method can also recover to some extent the semantic structure of the input model. In [Julius et al. 05] a similar idea is used to decompose the input mesh into nearly developable segments. Another extension of this algorithm to handling general quadric proxies has been elaborated in [Yan et al. 06].

MODEL REPAIR

Model repair is the process of removing artifacts from a geometric model in order to generate an output model suitable for further processing by downstream applications that require certain quality guarantees for their input. The specification of what kind of "models" are considered, what exactly constitutes an "artifact," and what is meant by "suitable for further processing" depends on the particular application scenario: generally, there is not one single algorithm that is applicable in all situations.

Model repair is necessary in a wide range of geometry processing applications. For example, consider the design cycle encountered in automotive CAD/CAM. Car models are typically manually designed in CAD systems that use trimmed NURBS surfaces as the underlying data structure for representing freeform surface geometry. However, numerical fluid simulations for shape analysis and optimization cannot handle such NURBS patches directly but rather need a watertight, manifold triangle mesh as input. Thus, there is a need for an intermediate stage that converts the NURBS model into a triangle mesh. Unfortunately, this conversion process is prone to producing meshing artifacts that cannot be handled by simulation packages. Thus, the converted model has to be repaired—usually in a tedious manual post-process, which often takes longer than the simulation itself.

This chapter has two purposes: to give a practical overview of the kinds of artifacts that typically occur in geometric models (Section 8.1) and to introduce the most common algorithmic approaches to removing these artifacts (Section 8.2). From a top-level view we distinguish model repair schemes that explicitly identify and resolve artifacts from those that rely on an intermediate volumetric representation, which automatically enforces topological consistency. In Section 8.3 we review the various characteristics of input models that emerge from different data sources in practical applications. We describe the specific artifacts and problems of each type and explain their origins. We also reference algorithms that are designed to process such meshes.

Finally, in Sections 8.4 and 8.5, we present in more detail some of the standard model repair algorithms. Some of these algorithms are relatively straightforward while others are more involved such that we can only discuss their basic mechanisms. We give a short description of how each algorithm works and to which types of model it is applicable. This provides a deeper understanding of the often subtle problems that occur in model repair and offers ways to address these problems.

8.1   Types of Artifacts: The "Freak Show"

The chart in Figure 8.1 shows the most common types of artifacts that occur in typical input models. Note that this collection is by no means complete and, in particular, in CAD models one often encounters further artifacts like self-intersecting (trimming) curves, feature points that do not lie on their defining geometric primitive, and so on. While some of these artifacts (e.g., complex edges) have a precise definition, others, like the distinction between small-scale and large-scale overlaps, are described intuitively rather than by strict definitions. Particularly tricky are (self-) intersections since they do not affect the proper mesh connectivity and are sometimes hard to detect. Non-topological artifacts such as badly shaped triangles are usually removed by remeshing techniques (see Chapter 6).

8.2   Types of Repair Algorithms

Most model repair algorithms can roughly be classified as being either *surface-oriented* or *volumetric*. Understanding these concepts already helps one to evaluate the strengths and weaknesses of a given algorithm and the quality that can be expected of its output.

Surface-oriented algorithms operate directly on the input data and try to explicitly identify and resolve artifacts on the surface. For example, gaps could be removed by snapping boundary elements (vertices and edges) onto each other or by stitching triangle strips in between the gap. Holes can be

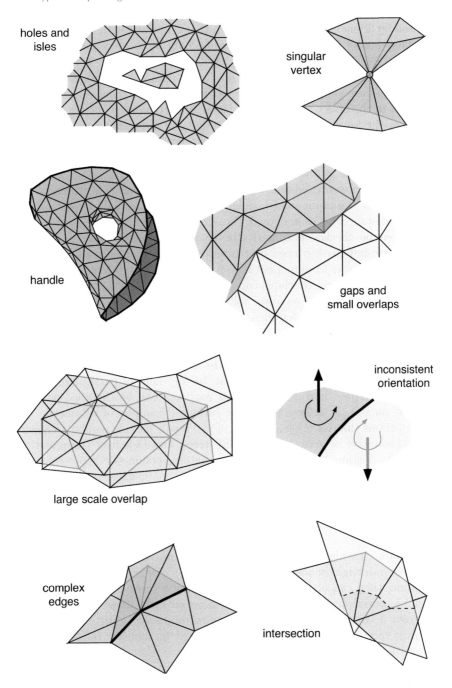

Figure 8.1. The freak show. (Image taken from [Botsch et al. 06b]. ©2006 ACM, Inc. Included here by permission.)

closed by filling in a triangulated patch that is optimal with respect to some surface quality functional. Intersections could be located and resolved by explicitly splitting edges and triangles.

Surface-oriented repair algorithms only minimally perturb the input model and are able to preserve the polygonal mesh structure in areas that are not in the direct vicinity of artifacts. In particular, geometric structure that might be encoded in the connectivity of the input (e.g., curvature lines) or material properties that are associated with triangles or vertices are usually well preserved. Furthermore, these algorithms introduce only a small number of additional triangles.

To guarantee a valid output, surface-oriented repair algorithms usually require that the input model already satisfy certain quality requirements (error tolerances). Often enough these requirements cannot be guaranteed nor even be checked automatically, so these algorithms are rarely fully automatic but instead need user interaction and manual post-processing. Furthermore, due to numerical inaccuracies, certain types of artifacts (like intersections or large overlaps) cannot be resolved robustly. Other artifacts, like gaps between two separate solids that are geometrically close to each other, cannot even be identified.

Volumetric algorithms convert the input model into an intermediate volumetric representation from which the output model is then extracted. Here, a volumetric representation can be any kind of partitioning of the embedding space into cells such that each cell can be classified as being *inside*, *outside*, or *intersected* by the surface. Examples of volumetric representations that have been used in model repair include regular Cartesian grids, adaptive octrees, kd-trees, BSP-trees, and Delaunay triangulations (see also Section 1.4). By their very nature, volumetric representations do not allow for artifacts like intersections, holes, gaps, overlaps, or inconsistent normal orientations. Depending on the type of extraction algorithm, one can often also guarantee the absence of complex edges and singular vertices. Spurious handles, however, might still be present in the reconstruction.

Volumetric algorithms are typically fully automatic and produce guaranteed watertight models (see Section 1.5.2). Depending on the type of volume, they can often be implemented very robustly. In particular, the combinatorial neighborhood relation between cells allows one to reliably extract a consistent topology of the repaired model. Furthermore, well-known morphological operators can be used to robustly remove handles from the volume.

On the downside, the conversion to and from a volume leads to a resampling of the model. It often introduces aliasing artifacts and loss of model features, and it destroys any structure that might have been present in the connectivity of the input model. The number of triangles in the output of a volumetric algorithm is usually much higher than that of the input model and thus has to be decimated in a post-processing step. Also, the quality of the output triangles often degrades and has to be improved afterwards. Finally, volumetric representations are quite memory-intensive so it is hard to run them at very high resolutions.

8.3   Types of Input

In this section we list the most common types of input models that occur in practice. For each type we describe its typical artifacts (see also Section 8.1) and give references to algorithms that can be used to remove them.

Registered range scans are a set of patches (usually triangle meshes)

that represent overlapping parts of the surface S of a scanned object. While large overlaps are a distinct advantage in registering the scans, they pose severe problems when these patches are to be fused into a single consistent triangle mesh. The main geometric problem in this setup is the potentially very large overlap of the scans such that a point x on S is often described by multiple patches that, due to measurement inaccuracies, do not necessarily agree on x's position. Furthermore, each patch has its own connectivity that is usually not compatible to the connectivity of the other patches. This is in particular a problem for surface-oriented repair algorithms. (Image taken from [Botsch et al. 06b]. ©2006 ACM, Inc. Included here by permission.)

There are only a few surface-oriented algorithms for fusing range images (e.g., Turk et al.'s mesh zippering algorithm [Turk and Levoy 94]). The most well-known volumetric method is that of Curless and Levoy [Curless and Levoy 96].

Fused range scans are manifold meshes with boundaries (i.e., gaps, holes and islands). Either these artifacts are due to obstructions in the line of sight of the scanner or they result from bad surface properties of the scanned model, such as transparency or glossiness. The goal is to identify and fill these holes (see Section 8.4.2). In the simplest case, the filling is a patch that minimizes some bending energy and connects smoothly to the boundary of the hole. Advanced algorithms either synthesize new geometric detail that resembles the detail present in a local neighborhood of the hole or they transplant geometry from other parts of the model in order to increase the realism of the reconstruction [Sharf et al. 04]. The main obstacles in hole filling are the incorporation of islands into the

reconstruction and the avoidance of geometric self-intersections. (Image taken from [Botsch et al. 06b]. ©2006 ACM, Inc. Included here by permission.)

Kliencsek proposes an algorithm based on dynamic programming for finding minimum-weight triangulations of planar polygons [Klincsek 80]. This algorithm is a key ingredient in a number of other model repair algorithms. Liepa proposes a surface-oriented method to smoothly fill holes such that the vertex densities around the hole are interpolated [Liepa 03]. Podolak et al. cast hole filling as a graph-cut problem and present an algorithm that is guaranteed to produce non-intersecting patches [Podolak and Rusinkiewicz 05]. Davis et al. propose a volumetric method that diffuses a signed distance function into empty regions of the volume [Davis et al. 02]. Pauly et al. use a database of geometric priors from which they select shapes to fill in regions of missing data [Pauly et al. 05].

Triangle soups are mere sets of triangles with little or no connectivity information. They most often arise in CAD models that are manually created

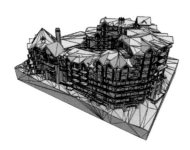

in a boundary representation where users typically assemble predefined elements (taken from a library) without bothering about consistency constraints. Due to the manual layout, these models typically are made of only a few thousands triangles, but they may contain all kinds of artifacts. Thus, triangle soups are well suited for visualization but cannot be used in most geometry-processing applications. (Image taken from [Botsch et al. 06b]. ©2006 ACM, Inc. Included here by permission.)

Intersecting triangles are one of the most common types of artifacts in triangle soups because the detection and in particular the resolution of intersecting geometry during interactive modeling would be much too time-consuming and numerically unstable. Complex edges and singular vertices are often intentionally created to avoid the duplication of vertices and the subsequent need to keep these duplicate vertices consistent. Other artifacts include inconsistent normal orientations, small gaps, and excess interior geometry.

Surface-oriented methods can efficiently remove some of these artifacts in simple cases [Guéziec et al. 01] (see Section 8.4.3) but methods that are able to automatically and robustly repair general triangle soups are not known. However, there are a number of volumetric methods that can be applied to triangle soups: Murali et al. produce a BSP tree from the triangle soup and automatically compute for each leaf a solidity [Murali and Funkhouser 97] (see Section 8.5.3). Nooruddin et al. use ray-casting and filtering to convert the triangle soup into a volumetric representation from which they then extract a consistent, watertight model [Nooruddin and Turk 03] (see Section 8.5.1). Shen et al. create an implicit representation by generalizing the moving least-squares approach from point sets to triangle soups [Shen et al. 04]. Bischoff et al. convert the soup into a binary grid, use morphological operators to determine inside/outside information, and then invoke a feature-sensitive extraction algorithm [Bischoff et al. 05] (see Section 8.5.2). Greß and Klein use a kd-tree to improve the geometric fidelity of the volumetric reconstruction [Greß and Klein 03].

Triangulated NURBS patches typically are a set of connected triangle mesh

patches that contain gaps and small overlaps along the boundaries of the patches. These artifacts arise when triangulating two or more trimmed NURBS patches that join at a common boundary curve. Usually, each patch is triangulated separately; thus the common boundary is sampled differently from each side. Other artifacts present in such models include intersecting patches and inconsistent normal orientations. Triangulated NURBS patches are usually repaired using surface-oriented methods. These methods first try to establish a consistent orientation of the input patches. Then they identify corresponding parts of the boundary and snap these parts onto each other. Thus, any structure that might be present in the triangulation (isolines, curvature lines, etc.) is preserved. (Image taken from [Botsch et al. 06b]. ©2006 ACM, Inc. Included here by permission.)

Barequet and Sharir use a geometric hashing technique to identify and bridge boundary parts that have a similar shape [Barequet and Sharir 95]. Barequet and Kumar describe an algorithm that identifies geometrically close edges and snaps them onto each other [Barequet and Kumar 97]. Borodin et al. generalize the vertex-contraction operator to a vertex-edge contraction operator and thus are able to progressively close gaps [Borodin et al. 02] (see Section 8.4.4). Bischoff and Kobbelt use a volumetric repair method locally around the artifacts and stitch the resulting patches into the remaining mesh [Bischoff and Kobbelt 05]. Borodin et al. propose an algorithm to consistently orient the normals that takes visibility information into account [Borodin et al. 04].

Contoured meshes are meshes that have been extracted from a volumetric dataset by Marching Cubes [Lorensen and Cline 87], Dual Contouring [Ju et al. 02], or other polygon mesh extraction algorithms. Provided that the correct triangulation look-up tables are used, contoured meshes are always guaranteed to be watertight and manifold (Section 1.5.2). However, these meshes often contain other topological artifacts, such as small spurious handles. (Image taken from [Botsch et al. 06b]. ©2006 ACM, Inc. Included here by permission.)

Volumetric data arises most often in medical imaging (CT, MRI, etc.), as an intermediate representation when fusing registered range scans, or in constructive solid geometry (CSG). In a volumetric dataset, each point in space is usually assigned a scalar value with negative values indicating points that lie inside of the object and positive values indicating points that lie outside of the object. Hence the surface itself corresponds to the zero-contour of the scalar field. In a discrete voxel representation, each voxel can be classified as being either *inside*, *outside*, or *on* the surface depending on the sign of the scalar field.

Unfortunately, due to the finite resolution of the underlying grid, voxels are often classified incorrectly, leading to the so-called *partial volume effect*. The term refers to topological artifacts in the reconstruction, such as small handles or disconnected components, that are not consistent with the model that should be represented by the volume. A well-known failure case is MRI datasets of the human brain. From anatomy it is well known that the cortex of the brain is homeomorphic to a sphere, but all too often a model of higher genus is extracted because anatomically separate features lie closer together than the size of a voxel. Hence sub-voxel precision is required to identify separate features [Bischoff and Kobbelt 03].

While disconnected components and small holes can easily be detected and removed from the main part of the model, handles are more problematic. Due to the simple connectivity of the underlying Cartesian grid, it is usually easier to remove them from the volume dataset before applying the contouring algorithm or to identify and resolve them during reconstruction [Wood et al. 04]. Guskov and Wood present one of the few surface-oriented algorithms to remove handles from an input mesh [Guskov and Wood 01] (see Section 8.4.5).

Badly meshed manifolds contain degenerate elements such as triangles with

zero area, *caps* (one inner angle close to π), *needles* (one edge length close to zero), and triangle flips (normal jump between adjacent faces close to π). These meshes sometimes result from the tessellation of CAD models or are the output of Marching Cubes–like algorithms—in particular if they are enhanced by feature-preserving techniques. Although badly meshed manifolds are in principle manifold and even

often watertight, the degenerate shapes of the elements prevent further processing (e.g., in finite element mesh generators), and lead to instabilities in numerical simulations. The improvement of such meshes is called *remeshing*, and we discuss this issue in depth in Chapter 6. (Image taken from [Botsch et al. 06b]. ©2006 ACM, Inc. Included here by permission.)

8.4   Surface-Oriented Algorithms

In this section we describe some of the most common surface-oriented repair algorithms. These algorithms work directly on the input mesh and try to remove artifacts by explicitly modifying the geometry and the connectivity of the input.

8.4.1   Consistent Normal Orientation

Consistently orienting the normals of an input model is part of most surface-oriented repair algorithms and can even improve the performance of volumetric algorithms. Usually the orientation of the normals is propagated along a minimum spanning tree between neighboring patches either in a preprocessing step or implicitly during traversal of the input [Hoppe et al. 92].

Borodin et al. describe a more sophisticated algorithm that additionally takes visibility information into account [Borodin et al. 04]. The input is a set of arbitrarily oriented polygons. In a preprocessing phase the polygons are assembled into larger, manifold patches (possibly with boundaries) as described in Section 8.4.3. The algorithm then builds up a connectivity graph of neighboring patches where the label of each edge encodes the *normal coherence* of the two patches. Furthermore, for each side of every patch, a *visibility coefficient* is computed that describes how much of the patch is visible when viewed from the outside. Finally, a globally consistent orientation is computed by a greedy optimization algorithm: if the coherence of two patches is high, normal consistency is favored over front-face visibility and vice versa for low coherence.

8.4.2   Surface-Based Hole Filling

In this section we describe an algorithm for computing a smooth triangulation of a hole. The algorithm was proposed by Liepa [Liepa 03] and builds on work of Klincsek [Klincsek 80] and of Barequet and Sharir [Barequet and Sharir 95]. It is a basic building block of many other repair algorithms.

The goal is to produce a triangle mesh with a prescribed boundary polygon $\mathbf{p}_0, \ldots, \mathbf{p}_{n-1}$ that fits into a hole of the mesh to be repaired. The new patch should be optimized with respect to some surface quality functional. In the context of mesh repair, this quality functional typically measures the fairness of the triangulation (e.g., its area, the variation of the triangle normals, or the curvature distribution; see also Section 4.3).

Let $\phi(i, j, k)$ be a quality function that is defined on the set of all triangles $(\mathbf{p}_i, \mathbf{p}_j, \mathbf{p}_k)$ that could possibly be generated during construction of the triangulation, and let $w_{i,j}$ be the optimal total quality score that can be achieved in triangulating the subpolygon $\mathbf{p}_i, \ldots, \mathbf{p}_j$, $0 \le i < j < n$. Then, $w_{i,j}$ can be computed recursively as

$$w_{i,j} = \min_{i < m < j} w_{i,m} + w_{m,j} + \phi(i, m, j).$$

In this formulation, the triangulation that minimizes the overall quality score $w_{0,n-1}$ can be computed by a dynamic programming algorithm that caches the intermediate values $w_{i,j}$ (see Figure 8.2).

Liepa suggests a quality functional ϕ that is designed to take into account the dihedral angles between neighboring triangles as well as the triangle's area. It produces tuples

$$\phi(i, j, k) = (\alpha, A),$$

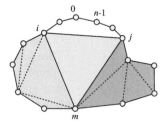

Figure 8.2.   Example of producing a triangulation of a polygonal hole. (Image taken from [Botsch et al. 06b]. ©2006 ACM, Inc. Included here by permission.)

where α is the maximum of the dihedral angles to the neighbors of $(\mathbf{p}_i, \mathbf{p}_j, \mathbf{p}_k)$ and A is its area. Note that this quality functional in particular penalizes foldovers. When comparing different values of ϕ, a low normal variation is favored over a low area:

$$(\alpha_1, A_1) < (\alpha_2, A_2) \quad : \Leftrightarrow \quad (\alpha_1 < \alpha_2) \vee (\alpha_1 = \alpha_2 \wedge A_1 < A_2).$$

Note that when evaluating ϕ one has to take into account that the neighboring triangles can either belong to the mesh that surrounds the hole or to the patch that is currently being created. A triangulation of a hole that is produced using this weight function is shown in Figure 8.3.

To produce a smooth hole filling, Liepa suggests producing a tangent-continuous fill-in of minimal thin plate energy: First, the holes are identified and filled by a coarse triangulation as described above. These patches are then refined such that their vertex densities and average edge lengths match those of the mesh surrounding the holes (see Chapter 6). Finally, the patch is smoothed so as to blend with the geometry of the surrounding mesh (see Chapter 4).

This algorithm reliably fills holes in models with smooth patches. The density of the vertices matches that of the surrounding surface (see Figure 8.4). The complexity of building the initial triangulation is $O(n^3)$, which is acceptable for most holes that occur in practice. However, the algorithm does not check or avoid geometric self-intersections and does not detect or incorporate islands into the filling patch.

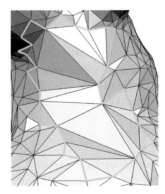

Figure 8.3. A hole triangulation that minimizes normal variation and total area. (Image taken from [Botsch et al. 06b]. ©2006 ACM, Inc. Included here by permission.)

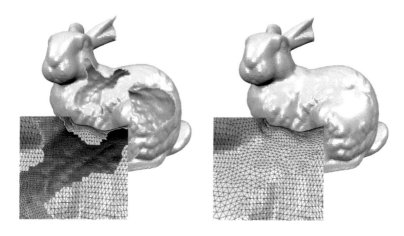

Figure 8.4. Liepa's hole-filling algorithm. Note that the vertex density of the fill-in matches that of the surrounding mesh. (Image taken from [Botsch et al. 06b]. ©2006 ACM, Inc. Included here by permission.)

8.4.3 Conversion to Manifolds

Guéziec et al. propose a method to remove complex edges and singular vertices from non-manifold input models [Guéziec et al. 01]. The output is guaranteed to be a clean manifold triangle mesh, possibly with boundaries. As the algorithm operates solely on the connectivity of the input model, it does not suffer from numerical robustness issues. In a preprocessing phase all complex edges and singular vertices are identified by counting the number of adjacent faces. The input is then cut along these complex edges into separate manifold patches. Finally, pairs of matching edges (i.e., edges that have geometrically the same endpoints) are identified and merged, if possible, in a topologically consistent manner.

The scope of this algorithm is limited to the removal of complex edges and singular vertices. This, however, is done efficiently and robustly.

8.4.4 Gap Closing

A number of surface-oriented algorithms have been proposed to close the gaps and small overlaps that are typical for triangulated NURBS models.

Barequet and Sharir proposed one of the first algorithms to fill gaps and remove small overlaps [Barequet and Sharir 95]. The algorithm identifies matching parts of the boundaries by a geometric hashing technique and fills the gaps by patching them with triangle strips or by the technique presented in Section 8.4.2.

Barequet and Kumar propose an algorithm to repair CAD models that identifies and merges pairs of boundary edges [Barequet and Kumar 97]. For each pair of boundary edges, the area between the two edges normalized by the edge lengths is computed. This score measures the geometric error that would be introduced by merging the two edges. Pairs of boundary edges are then iteratively merged in order of increasing score.

Borodin et al. propose an algorithm that snaps boundary vertices to nearby boundary edges [Borodin et al. 02]. The algorithm is based on a standard mesh-decimation technique, but it generalizes the vertex-vertex contraction operator into a vertex-edge contraction operator that merges boundary vertices v and boundary edges e. Let c be the closest point to v on e. If c is an interior point of e, c is inserted into e by splitting the adjacent triangle in two. Finally, v and c are merged. The cost of a vertex-edge collapse is defined as the distance of v to c. The algorithm maintains a priority queue of vertex/edge pairs and snaps them in order of increasing distance.

The semantics of these surface-oriented algorithms are well defined, and they are usually easy to implement. If the input data is well behaved and the user parameters are chosen in accordance with the error that was accepted during triangulation, they manage to produce satisfying results. However, there are no guarantees on the quality of the output. Due to the simple heuristics, many artifacts remain unresolved. Therefore, these algorithms are usually run in an interactive loop that allows the user to override the decisions made by the algorithms or to interactively steer the algorithms towards the expected result.

8.4.5 Topology Simplification

Guskov and Wood proposed an algorithm that detects and resolves all handles up to a given size ε in a manifold triangle mesh [Guskov and Wood 01]. Handles are removed by cutting the input along a non-separating closed path and sealing the two resulting holes by triangle patches (see Figure 8.5).

Given a seed triangle s, the algorithm conquers a geodesic region $\mathcal{R}_\varepsilon(s)$ around s in the order that is given by Dijkstra's algorithm on the dual graph of the input mesh $\mathcal{M}$. Note that Dijkstra's algorithm not only computes the length of a shortest path from each triangle t to the seed s but also produces a parent relation $p(t)$ such that the sequence $t, p(t), p^2(t), \ldots, s$ traces a shortest path from t back to the seed s.

The boundary of $\mathcal{R}_\varepsilon(s)$ consists of one or more boundary loops. Whenever a boundary loop touches itself along an edge, it is split into two new loops and the algorithm proceeds. However, when two different loops touch along a common edge $e_{1,2}$, a handle is detected. Let t_1 and t_2 be the two

   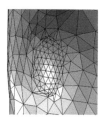

Figure 8.5. The Happy Buddha model (far left) contains more than 100 spurious handles. From left to right: a close-up of a handle; a non-separating closed cycle along a handle; the handle was removed by cutting along the non-separating cycle and filling the two resulting holes with triangle patches. (Model courtesy of the Stanford Computer Graphics Laboratory. Image taken from [Botsch et al. 06b]. ©2006 ACM, Inc. Included here by permission.)

triangles that are adjacent to the common edge $e_{1,2}$ and let $p^{n_1}(t_1) = p^{n_2}(t_2)$ be a common ancestor of t_1 and t_2. Then the closed path

$$p^{n_1}(t_1), \ldots, p(t_1), t_1, t_2, p(t_2), \ldots, p^{n_2}(t_2)$$

is a cycle of adjacent triangles that traces around the handle. The input model is cut along this triangle strip and the two boundary loops that are created by this cut are sealed (e.g., by the method presented in Section 8.4.2).

To detect all handles of the input mesh $\mathcal{M}$, one has to perform the region growing for every triangle $s \in \mathcal{M}$. Guskov and Wood describe a method to considerably reduce the necessary number of seed triangles and thus are able to significantly speed up the algorithm [Guskov and Wood 01].

The proposed method reliably detects small handles up to a user-prescribed size and removes them effectively. However, the algorithm is slow, does not detect long, thin handles, and cannot guarantee that no geometric self-intersections are created after a handle is removed.

8.5   Volumetric Repair Algorithms

This section presents more recent repair algorithms that use an intermediate volumetric representation to implicitly remove the artifacts of a model. This volumetric representation might be as simple as a regular Cartesian voxel grid or as complex as a hierarchical binary space partition.

8.5.1   Volumetric Repair on Regular Grids

Nooruddin and Turk proposed one of the first volumetric techniques to repair arbitrary models that contain gaps, overlaps, and intersections [Nooruddin and Turk 03]. Additionally, they employed morphological operators to resolve topological artifacts like holes and handles.

First, the model is converted into a Cartesian voxel grid: a set of projection directions $\{\mathbf{d}_i\}$ is produced (e.g., by subdividing an octahedron or icosahedron). Then the model is projected along these directions onto an orthogonal planar grid. For each grid point $\mathbf{x}$, the algorithm records the first and last intersection points of the ray $\mathbf{x} + \lambda\mathbf{d}_i$ with the input model. A voxel is classified by such a ray as *inside* if it lies between these two extremal depth samples; otherwise, it is classified as *outside*. The final classification of each voxel is derived from the majority vote of all the rays passing through that voxel. The Marching Cubes algorithm is then applied to extract the surface between inside and outside voxels.

In an optional second step, thin handles and holes are removed from the volume by applying *morphological operators* that are also known from image processing [Haralick et al. 87]. The *dilation* operator D_ε computes the distance from each outside voxel to the inside component. All voxels that are within a distance of ε to the inside are also set to be *inside*. Thus, the dilation operator closes small handles and bridges small gaps. The *erosion* operator E_ε works exactly the other way around and removes thin bridges and handles. Usually, dilation and erosion are used in conjunction, $E_\varepsilon \circ D_\varepsilon$, to avoid expansion or shrinkage of the model.

The classification of inside and outside voxels in this algorithm is rather heuristic and often not reliable. Furthermore, the algorithm is not feature-sensitive.

8.5.2   Volumetric Repair on Adaptive Grids

Bischoff et al. propose an improved volumetric technique to repair arbitrary triangle soups [Bischoff et al. 05] (see Figure 8.6). The user provides an error tolerance ε and a maximum diameter ρ up to which gaps should be closed. The algorithm first creates an adaptive octree representation of the input model where each cell stores the triangles intersecting with it. From these triangles a feature-sensitive sample point can be computed for each cell. Then, a sequence of morphological operations is applied to the octree to determine the topology of the model. Finally, the connectivity and geometry of the reconstruction are derived from the octree structure and samples, respectively.

Let us assume that the triangle soup is scaled to fit into the root cell of the octree. We set the maximum depth of the octree cells such that the diameter of the finest-level cells is smaller than ε. Each cell stores

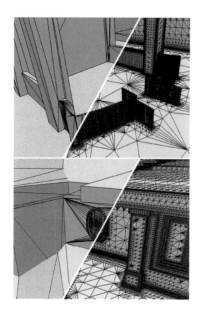
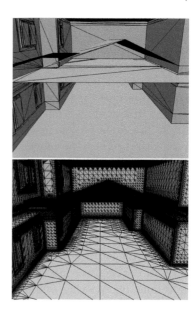

Figure 8.6. Repaired version (green) of a triangle soup model (blue). The reconstruction is a watertight mesh that is refined near the model features (left). The volumetric approach reliably detects and removes excess interior geometry from the input (right). (Image taken from [Bischoff et al. 05]. ©2005 ACM, Inc. Included here by permission.)

references to the triangles that intersect with it, and initially all triangles are associated with the root cell. Then, cells that are not yet on maximum depth are recursively split if they either contain a boundary edge or if the triangles within the cell deviate too much from a common regression plane. Whenever a cell is split, its triangles are distributed to its children. The result is a memory-efficient octree with large cells in planar or empty regions and fine cells along the features and boundaries of the input model (see Figure 8.7).

In the second phase, each leaf cell of the octree is classified as being either *inside* or *outside*. First, all cells that contain a boundary of the model are dilated by $n := \rho/\varepsilon$ layers of voxels such that all gaps of diameter $\leq \rho$ are closed. A flood fill algorithm then propagates the outside label from the boundary of the octree into its interior. Finally, the outside component is dilated again by n layers to avoid an expansion of the model.

A Dual Contouring algorithm then reconstructs the interface between the outside and the inside cells by connecting sample points. These sample points are the minimizers of the squared distances to their supporting tri-

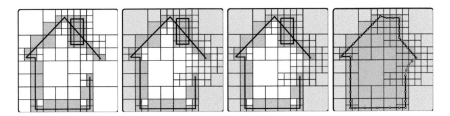

Figure 8.7. From left to right: Adaptive octree (boundary cells are marked red). Dilated boundary (green) and outside component (orange). Outside component dilated back into the boundary cells. Final reconstruction. (Image taken from [Botsch et al. 06b]. ©2006 ACM, Inc. Included here by permission.)

angle planes; thus, features like edges and corners are well preserved (see also Chapter 7 on quadric error metrics). If no such planes are available (e.g., because the cell was one of the dilated boundary cells), the corresponding sample point position is determined by a smoothing operator in a post-processing step (Chapter 4).

As this algorithm is based on a volumetric representation, it produces guaranteed manifold output (see Figure 8.6). Features are also well preserved. However, despite the adaptive octree, the resolution of the reconstruction is limited.

8.5.3 Volumetric Repair with BSP Trees

A unique method for converting triangle soups to manifold surfaces is presented by Murali and Funkhouser [Murali and Funkhouser 97]. The polygon soup is first converted into a BSP tree, where the supporting planes of the input polygons serve as splitting planes for the space partition (Figure 8.8 (left)). The leaves of the tree thus correspond to closed convex spatial regions C_i. For each C_i a *solidity coefficient* $s_i \in [-1, 1]$ is computed (Figure 8.8 (center)). Negative solidity coefficients designate empty regions while positive coefficients designate solid regions.

All unbounded cells naturally lie outside the object and thus are assigned a solidity value of -1. Let C_i be a bounded cell, and let $\mathcal{N}(i)$ be the indices of all its face neighbors. Thus, for each $j \in \mathcal{N}(i)$, the intersection $P_{ij} = C_i \cap C_j$ is a planar polygon that might be partially covered by the input geometry. For each $j \in \mathcal{N}(i)$, let t_{ij} be the transparent area, o_{ij} the opaque area, and $a_{i,j}$ the total area of P_{ij}. The solidity s_i is then related to the solidities s_j of its face neighbors by

$$s_i = \frac{1}{A_i} \sum_{j \in \mathcal{N}(i)} (t_{ij} - o_{ij}) s_j, \tag{8.1}$$

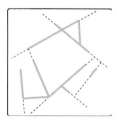 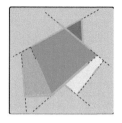 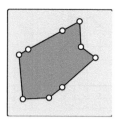

Figure 8.8. A BSP tree (left), its solidity coefficients (center), and reconstruction (right). (Image taken from [Botsch et al. 06b]. ©2006 ACM, Inc. Included here by permission.)

where $A_i = \sum_j a_{i,j}$ is the total area of the boundary of C_i. Note the two extreme cases: If P_{ij} is fully transparent, $t_{ij} - o_{ij} = a_{i,j} > 0$ (i.e., the correlation of s_i and s_j is positive), indicating that both cells should be solid or both cells should be empty. If, on the other hand, P_{ij} is fully opaque, $t_{ij} - o_{ij} = -a_{i,j} < 0$, and the negative correlation indicates that one cell should be solid and the other empty. Collecting all Equations (8.1) leads to a sparse linear system

$$\mathbf{M}\,(s_1,\ldots,s_n)^T = \mathbf{b},$$

which can be solved efficiently using a sparse solver (see the appendix). It can be shown that $\mathbf{M}$ is always invertible and that the solidity coefficients of the solution in fact lie in the range $[-1, 1]$.

Finally, the surface of the solid cells is extracted by enumerating all neighboring pairs of leaf cells (C_i, C_j). If one of them is empty and the other is solid, the corresponding (triangulated) boundary polygon P_{ij} is added to the reconstruction (see Figure 8.8 (right)).

This method does not need (but also cannot incorporate) any user parameters to automatically produce watertight models. The output might contain complex edges and singular vertices, but these can be removed using the algorithm presented in Section 8.4.3. Unfortunately, a robust and efficient computation of the combinatorial structure of the BSP is hard to accomplish.

8.5.4   Volumetric Repair on the Dual Grid

Ju proposes a volumetric algorithm to repair arbitrary triangle soups [Ju 04]. While the boundary loops are explicitly traced and filled, the overall scheme is volumetric.

The algorithm first approximates the input model (Figure 8.9 (far left)) by a subset $\mathcal{F}$ of the faces of a Cartesian grid (Figure 8.9 (second from left)). For memory efficiency, these faces are stored in an adaptive octree. Additionally, a sample point (and possibly a normal) from the input model are associated with each face to allow for a more accurate reconstruction. The boundary $\partial \mathcal{F}$ of $\mathcal{F}$ is defined as the subset of the grid edges that are incident to an odd number of faces in $\mathcal{F}$. A simple counting argument reveals that if $\mathcal{G}$ is another face set, such that $\partial \mathcal{G} = \partial \mathcal{F}$, then $\partial(\mathcal{F} \ominus \mathcal{G}) = \emptyset$. Here, the *symmetric difference* (xor) of two sets $\mathcal{A}$ and $\mathcal{B}$ is defined as $\mathcal{A} \ominus \mathcal{B} = (\mathcal{A} \cup \mathcal{B}) \setminus (\mathcal{A} \cap \mathcal{B})$. Another observation is that if $\partial \mathcal{F} = \emptyset$, then the grid voxels can be two-colored by *inside* and *outside* labels such that two adjacent voxels have the same label, while two voxels that are separated by a face of $\mathcal{F}$ have different labels.

For each boundary loop B_i of $\mathcal{F}$, the algorithm now constructs a minimal face set $\mathcal{G}_i$ such that $\partial \mathcal{G}_i = B_i$. Then, $\mathcal{F}$ is replaced by

$$\mathcal{F}' = \mathcal{F} \ominus \mathcal{G}_1 \ominus \cdots \ominus \mathcal{G}_n;$$

thus $\partial \mathcal{F}' = \emptyset$ (Figure 8.9 (second from right)). As voxels at the corners of the bounding box are known to be *outside*, they are used as seeds for propagating the *inside/outside* information across the grid. The interface between inside and outside voxels is then extracted using either the Marching Cubes [Lorensen and Cline 87] or the Dual Contouring algorithm [Ju et al. 02] to produce the final reconstruction (Figure 8.9 (far right)).

Ju's algorithm uses a volumetric representation and thus can be tuned to produce guaranteed manifold output. The algorithm is quite memory efficient, i.e., it is insensitive to the size of the input and thus can process arbitrarily large input meshes in an out-of-core fashion. On the other hand, the algorithm has problems in handling thin structures. In particular, if the discrete approximation that is used in the hole-filling step overlaps with the input geometry, this part of the mesh may disappear or be shattered into many unconnected pieces. Due to the volumetric representation, the whole input model is resampled and the output might become extremely large for fine voxel resolutions.

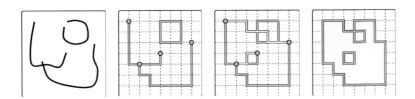

Figure 8.9. From left to right: input, face set, patches, and reconstruction. (Image taken from [Botsch et al. 06b]. ©2006 ACM, Inc. Included here by permission.)

8.6   Summary and Further Reading

In this chapter we have presented several methods for repairing surface meshes, primarily distinguishing between surface-oriented and volumetric algorithms. Over the years we have observed an increasing trend towards volumetric algorithms, which by construction provide a number of guaranteed properties in the output—even if they require local resampling of the input geometry. This is why *hybrid methods* are receiving more and more attention. They combine volumetric and surface-oriented approaches in order to exploit the superior precision that is achieved from processing polygons directly but at the same time taking advantage of the robustness of volumetric voxel operations and the efficiency of hierarchical space partitions.

An important special case of the mesh repair problem that we did not address in this chapter is the removal of geometric self-intersections in 3D models that are not necessarily reflected by inconsistencies in the topological connectivity structure of the mesh. Recently, there have been some powerful algorithms proposed in response to this special case (e.g., [Campen and Kobbelt 10, Attene 10]).

As knowledge advances in the field, it is tempting to think that model repair is a necessity that will disappear if and when all other algorithms along the geometry processing pipeline would be able generate artifact-free outputs (note that ironically, some algorithms in the literature do not guarantee for their output the very properties they require of their input). However, with more and more data emerging from physical measurements and coming from heterogeneous sources, the processing of geometric data will continue to require frequent data format conversions and this will increase the probability of inconsistencies and flaws due to numerical inaccuracies. For these reasons, model repair will remain one of the most enduring problems and it will be critical for further streamlining the geometry processing pipeline.

In today's industrial design and development processes compute-intensive steps like simulation and shape analysis become faster and faster due to improved (parallel) algorithms and more powerful hardware. However, conversion and repair steps cannot be accelerated as long as the user has to control this process manually. Hence, providing automatic conversion and repair techniques will have maximum impact on the overall process optimization measured in wall clock time, which is what actually matters in industrial practice. Nonetheless, the inherent ill-posed nature of the model repair problem explains the parallel development of semiautomatic methods that provide topology control [Hétroy et al. 08] to the user.

Finally, we recommend for further reading a recent comprehensive survey by Tao Ju [Ju 09].

DEFORMATION

In this chapter we introduce techniques for interactively deforming a given triangle mesh. This topic is challenging, since complex mathematical formulations (1) have to be hidden behind an intuitive user interface and (2) have to be implemented in a sufficiently efficient and robust manner to allow for interactive applications. This chapter gives an overview of different shape deformation techniques, classifies them into different categories, and shows their interrelations.

The deformation of a given surface $\mathcal{S}$ into the desired surface $\mathcal{S}'$ is mathematically described by a displacement function $\mathbf{d}$ that associates to each point $\mathbf{p} \in \mathcal{S}$ a displacement vector $\mathbf{d}(\mathbf{p})$. By this it maps the given surface $\mathcal{S}$ to its deformed version $\mathcal{S}'$:

$$\mathcal{S}' := \{\mathbf{p} + \mathbf{d}(\mathbf{p}) \mid \mathbf{p} \in \mathcal{S}\}.$$

For a discrete triangle mesh the displacement function $\mathbf{d}$ is piecewise linear, such that it is fully defined by the displacement vectors $\mathbf{d}_i = \mathbf{d}(\mathbf{p}_i)$ of the original mesh vertices $\mathbf{p}_i \in \mathcal{S}$.

The user controls the deformation by prescribing displacements $\bar{\mathbf{d}}_i$ for a set of so-called *handle* points $\mathbf{p}_i \in \mathcal{H} \subset \mathcal{S}$, and by constraining certain parts $\mathcal{F} \subset \mathcal{S}$ to stay *fixed* during the deformation (see Figure 9.1):

$$\begin{aligned}
\mathbf{d}(\mathbf{p}_i) &= \bar{\mathbf{d}}_i, \quad \forall\, \mathbf{p}_i \in \mathcal{H}, \\
\mathbf{d}(\mathbf{p}_i) &= \mathbf{0}, \quad \forall\, \mathbf{p}_i \in \mathcal{F}.
\end{aligned}$$

Figure 9.1. A given surface $\mathcal{S}$ is deformed into $\mathcal{S}'$ by a displacement function $\mathbf{d}(\mathbf{p})$. The user controls the deformation by moving a handle region $\mathcal{H}$ (yellow) and keeping the region $\mathcal{F}$ (gray) fixed. The unconstrained deformation region $\mathcal{R}$ (blue) should deform in an intuitive, physically-plausible manner.

The main question is how to determine the displacement vectors $\mathbf{d}_i$ for all the remaining unconstrained vertices $\mathbf{p}_i \in \mathcal{R} = \mathcal{S} \setminus (\mathcal{H} \cup \mathcal{F})$, such that the resulting shape deformation meets the user's expectations.

We discuss two classes of shape deformations in this chapter:

▶ We start with *surface-based deformations* in Sections 9.1–9.4. Here, the displacement function $\mathbf{d} \colon \mathcal{S} \to \mathbb{R}^3$ lives *on* the original surface $\mathcal{S}$ and is found by computations *on* the triangle mesh. These methods offer a high degree of control, since each vertex can be constrained individually. On the downside, the robustness and efficiency of the involved computations are strongly affected by the mesh complexity and the triangle quality of the original surface $\mathcal{S}$.

▶ *Space deformations* employ a displacement function $\mathbf{d} \colon \mathbb{R}^3 \to \mathbb{R}^3$ that warps the whole embedding space $\mathbb{R}^3$ and by this implicitly also deforms the surface $\mathcal{S}$. The deformation does not require computations on the triangle mesh $\mathcal{S}$, and therefore such methods are less affected by the complexity or triangle quality of $\mathcal{S}$. Space deformations are discussed in Sections 9.5 and 9.6.

All methods that we will describe are *linear* deformation techniques, i.e., they require the solution of a system of *linear* equations only, typically in order to minimize some quadratic deformation energy. These methods have the advantage that linear systems can be solved very efficiently (as described in the appendix). However, these methods can lead to counterintuitive results for large-scale deformations, as demonstrated in Section 9.7. Nonlinear deformation techniques overcome these limitations by minimizing more accurate nonlinear energies, which, however, requires more involved numerical schemes. We will only mention some nonlinear methods in Section 9.8.

9.1 Transformation Propagation

A simple and popular approach for shape deformation works by propagating the user-defined handle transformation within the deformation region (see Figure 9.2). After specifying the support region $\mathcal{R}$ of the deformation and a handle region $\mathcal{H}$ within it, the handle is transformed using some modeling interface. Its transformation $\mathbf{T}(\mathbf{x})$ is propagated and damped within the support region, leading to a smooth blending between the transformed handle $\mathcal{H}' = \mathbf{T}(\mathcal{H})$ and the fixed region $\mathcal{F}$.

This smooth blend is controlled by a scalar field $s \colon \mathcal{S} \to [0, 1]$, which is 1 at the handle $\mathcal{H}$ (full deformation), 0 in the fixed region $\mathcal{F}$ (no deformation), and smoothly blends between 1 and 0 within the support region. One way to construct this scalar field is to compute the distances $\mathrm{dist}_{\mathcal{F}}(\mathbf{p})$ and $\mathrm{dist}_{\mathcal{H}}(\mathbf{p})$ from $\mathbf{p}$ to the fixed part $\mathcal{F}$ and the handle region $\mathcal{H}$, respectively, and to define

$$s(\mathbf{p}) \;=\; \frac{\mathrm{dist}_{\mathcal{F}}(\mathbf{p})}{\mathrm{dist}_{\mathcal{F}}(\mathbf{p}) + \mathrm{dist}_{\mathcal{H}}(\mathbf{p})}. \tag{9.1}$$

The distances can be either geodesic distances on the surface [Bendels and Klein 03] or Euclidean distances in space [Pauly et al. 03], where the first typically gives better results but is more complex to compute [Kimmel and Sethian 98, Surazhsky et al. 05, Bommes and Kobbelt 07].

As an alternative, the scalar field can also be computed as a harmonic field on the surface, i.e., $\Delta s = 0$, with Dirichlet constraints 1 and 0 for the

Figure 9.2. After specifying the blue support region and the green handle region (left), a smooth scalar field is constructed that is 1 at the handle and 0 outside the support (center). Its isolines are visualized in black and red, where red is the $\frac{1}{2}$-isoline. This scalar field is used to propagate and damp the handle's transformation within the support region (right). (Image taken from [Botsch et al. 06b]. ©2006 ACM, Inc. Included here by permission.)

regions $\mathcal{H}$ and $\mathcal{F}$, respectively:

$$\Delta s(\mathbf{p}_i) = 0, \quad \mathbf{p}_i \in \mathcal{R},$$
$$s(\mathbf{p}_i) = 1, \quad \mathbf{p}_i \in \mathcal{H}, \qquad\qquad (9.2)$$
$$s(\mathbf{p}_i) = 0, \quad \mathbf{p}_i \in \mathcal{F}.$$

Computing $s(\mathbf{p}_i)$ from the constraints in Equation (9.2) amounts to solving a linear Laplacian system (see the appendix).

While this is computationally more expensive than the distance-based scalar field of Equation (9.1), it is guaranteed to be smooth, whereas the distance-based fields can have C^1-discontinuities. The scalar field $s(\mathbf{p})$ of either (9.1) or (9.2) can be adjusted further through a transfer function $t \colon [0,1] \to [0,1]$, which provides more control and flexibility for the blending process [Pauly et al. 03].

The resulting scalar field is then used to damp the handle transformation $\mathbf{T}$ for each vertex $\mathbf{p}_i \in \mathcal{R}$ as

$$\mathbf{p}'_i = s(\mathbf{p}_i)\, \mathbf{T}(\mathbf{p}_i) + (1 - s(\mathbf{p}_i))\, \mathbf{p}_i.$$

Alternatively, the damping can be performed separately on the rotation, scale/shear, and translation components (see, e.g., [Pauly et al. 03]).

This shape deformation approach is simple and efficient to compute and yields a smooth blending of the transformed handle $\mathcal{H}$ and the fixed region $\mathcal{F}$. However, as shown in Figure 9.3, a problem of this method is that the distance-based propagation of transformations will typically not result in the geometrically most intuitive solution. This would require the smooth interpolation of the handle transformation by the displacement function $\mathbf{d}$, while otherwise minimizing some physically-motivated deformation energies, as shown in the next section.

Figure 9.3.   A sphere is deformed by lifting a closed handle polygon (left). Propagating this translation based on geodesic distance causes a dent in the interior of the handle polygon (center). A more intuitive solution can be achieved by minimizing physically-motivated deformation energies (right). (Image taken from [Botsch 05].)

9.2   Shell-Based Deformation

More intuitive surface deformations $\mathbf{d}$ with prescribed geometric constraints $\mathbf{d}(\mathbf{p}_i) = \bar{\mathbf{d}}_i$ can be modeled by minimizing physically-inspired deformation energies. The surface is assumed to behave like a physical skin or sheet that stretches and bends as forces are acting on it. Mathematically, this behavior can be captured by an energy functional that penalizes both stretching and bending.

Let us for the following derivations assume $\mathcal{S}$ and $\mathcal{S}'$ to be given as smooth parametric surfaces, i.e., by functions $\mathbf{p}\colon \Omega \to \mathbb{R}^3$ and $\mathbf{p}'\colon \Omega \to \mathbb{R}^3$. Similarly, the displacement function is defined as $\mathbf{d}\colon \Omega \to \mathbb{R}^3$.

As introduced in Chapter 3, the first and second fundamental forms, $\mathbf{I}(u, v)$ and $\mathbf{I\!I}(u, v)$, can be used to measure geometrically intrinsic (i.e., parameterization independent) properties of $\mathcal{S}$, such as lengths, areas, and curvatures. When the surface $\mathcal{S}$ is deformed to $\mathcal{S}'$, such that its fundamental forms change to $\mathbf{I}'$ and $\mathbf{I\!I}'$, the difference of the fundamental forms can be used as an elastic thin shell energy that measures stretching and bending [Terzopoulos et al. 87]:

$$
\begin{aligned}
E(\mathcal{S}') = \iint_\Omega &\, k_s \left\| \mathbf{I}'(u, v) - \mathbf{I}(u, v) \right\|_F^2 \\
+ &\, k_b \left\| \mathbf{I\!I}'(u, v) - \mathbf{I\!I}(u, v) \right\|_F^2 \, \mathrm{d}u\,\mathrm{d}v.
\end{aligned}
\tag{9.3}
$$

The stiffness parameters k_s and k_b are used to control the resistance to stretching and bending, respectively, and $\|\cdot\|_F$ is a (weighted) Frobenius norm. In a modeling scenario one has to minimize the elastic energy (9.3) subject to user-defined deformation constraints. As shown in Figure 9.1, this typically means fixing certain surface parts $\mathcal{F}$ and prescribing displacements for the handle region(s) $\mathcal{H}$.

However, minimizing the nonlinear energy (9.3) is computationally too expensive for interactive applications. It is therefore simplified by replacing the difference of fundamental forms by partial derivatives of the displacement function $\mathbf{d}$ (difference of positions) [Celniker and Gossard 91, Welch and Witkin 92]. This leads to the following *thin-shell energy*:

$$
\begin{aligned}
E(\mathbf{d}) = \iint_\Omega &\, k_s \left(\|\mathbf{d}_u(u, v)\|^2 + \|\mathbf{d}_v(u, v)\|^2 \right) \\
+ &\, k_b \left(\|\mathbf{d}_{uu}(u, v)\|^2 + 2\|\mathbf{d}_{uv}(u, v)\|^2 + \|\mathbf{d}_{vv}(u, v)\|^2 \right) \, \mathrm{d}u\,\mathrm{d}v,
\end{aligned}
\tag{9.4}
$$

where we use the notation $\mathbf{d}_u = \frac{\partial}{\partial u}\mathbf{d}$ and $\mathbf{d}_{uv} = \frac{\partial^2}{\partial u \partial v}\mathbf{d}$ to denote partial derivatives. Note that the stretching and bending terms of this energy are almost the same as the membrane and thin plate energies employed in

Figure 9.4. A planar surface is deformed by fixing the gray part $\mathcal{F}$, lifting the yellow handle region $\mathcal{H}$, and minimizing the shell-energy of Equation (9.4) in the blue region $\mathcal{R}$. The energy consists of stretching and bending terms, and the examples show the following: pure stretching with $k_s = 1$, $k_b = 0$, (left); pure bending with $k_s = 0$, $k_b = 1$, (center); and a weighted combination with $k_s = 1$, $k_b = 10$ (right). (Image taken from [Botsch and Sorkine 08]. ©2008 IEEE.)

Section 4.3 to measure/minimize surface area and surface curvature. The only difference is that we now use displacements $\mathbf{d}$ instead of positions $\mathbf{p}$ and by this minimize the *change of* area and *change of* curvature, i.e., we minimize stretching and bending of the surface (see Figure 9.4).

For the efficient minimization of (9.4), we apply variational calculus analogously to Section 4.3. This yields the corresponding *Euler-Lagrange* equation that characterizes the minimizer of (9.4), again subject to user constraints:

$$-k_s\Delta\mathbf{d} + k_b\Delta^2\mathbf{d} \; = \; \mathbf{0}. \tag{9.5}$$

Hence, in order to minimize the energy (9.4), we simply have to solve the PDE (9.5). At this point we can switch back from continuous parametric surfaces to discrete triangle meshes and simply replace the continuous Laplacian in Equation (9.5) by the discrete cotangent Laplacian (3.11) introduced in Chapter 3. The bi-Laplacian can be defined recursively as the Laplacian of Laplacians:

$$\Delta^2\mathbf{d}_i \; := \; \frac{1}{2A_i} \sum_{v_j \in \mathcal{N}_1(v_i)} (\cot\alpha_{i,j} + \cot\beta_{i,j})\,(\Delta\mathbf{d}_j - \Delta\mathbf{d}_i),$$

where $\mathbf{d}_i = \mathbf{d}(\mathbf{p}_i) = \mathbf{d}(v_i)$ denotes the per-vertex displacements. Equation (9.5) can now be discretized to one condition per vertex:

$$\begin{aligned}
-k_s\Delta\mathbf{d}_i + k_b\Delta^2\mathbf{d}_i &= \mathbf{0}, & \mathbf{p}_i &\in \mathcal{R}, \\
\mathbf{d}_i &= \bar{\mathbf{d}}_i, & \mathbf{p}_i &\in \mathcal{H}, \\
\mathbf{d}_i &= \mathbf{0}, & \mathbf{p}_i &\in \mathcal{F}.
\end{aligned} \tag{9.6}$$

These conditions can be formulated as a linear system of equations, whose unknowns are the displacements $\mathbf{d}_1, \dots, \mathbf{d}_n$ of the free vertices $\mathcal{R}$. The known displacements for $\mathcal{H}$ and $\mathcal{F}$ are moved to the right-hand side $\mathbf{b}$:

$$
\left[-k_s \mathbf{L} + k_b \mathbf{L}^2\right] \underbrace{\begin{pmatrix} \mathbf{d}_1^T \\ \vdots \\ \mathbf{d}_n^T \end{pmatrix}}_{\mathbf{x}} = \underbrace{\begin{pmatrix} \mathbf{b}_1^T \\ \vdots \\ \mathbf{b}_n^T \end{pmatrix}}_{\mathbf{b}}, \tag{9.7}
$$

with $\mathbf{L}$ being the Laplace matrix described in the appendix. Note that $\mathbf{x}$ and $\mathbf{b}$ are $(n \times 3)$ matrices and that the linear system therefore must be solved three times—once for each column of $\mathbf{x}$ and $\mathbf{b}$, i.e., for the x, y, and z-coordinates of the unknown displacements $\mathbf{d}_1, \ldots, \mathbf{d}_n$.

Minimizing (9.4) by solving (9.7) allows for C^1 continuous surface deformations, as can also be observed in Figure 9.4. On a discrete triangle mesh, the C^1 constraints are defined solely by the position/displacements of the first two rings of fixed vertices $\mathcal{F}$ and handle vertices $\mathcal{H}$ [Kobbelt et al. 98b]. The other vertices of $\mathcal{F} \cup \mathcal{H}$ have no influence on the solution and hence do not have to be taken into account in (9.6) and (9.7).

Interactively manipulating the handle region $\mathcal{H}$ changes the boundary constraints $\bar{\mathbf{d}}_i$ of the optimization, i.e., the right-hand side $\mathbf{B}$ of the linear system (9.7). As a consequence, this system has to be solved each time the user manipulates the handle region. In the appendix we discuss efficient linear system solvers that are particularly suited for this so-called *multiple-right-hand-side problem*. Also notice that restricting to *affine* transformation of the handle region $\mathcal{H}$ (which is usually sufficient) allows one to pre-compute basis functions of the deformation, such that instead of solving (9.7) in each frame, only the basis functions have to be evaluated [Botsch and Kobbelt 04a].

Compared to the transformation propagation of Section 9.1, the shell-based approach is computationally more expensive since a linear system must be solved for each frame. This, however, can still be performed at interactive rates using suitable linear solvers. The main advantage of the shell-based approach is that the resulting deformations are usually much more intuitive since they are derived from physical principles.

9.3 Multi-Scale Deformation

The shell-based deformation of the previous section yields physically-based, smooth and fair surface deformations. Interactive performance is achieved by simplifying the nonlinear shell energy (9.3) such that only a linear system has to be solved for the deformed surface $\mathcal{S}'$. However, as a consequence of this linearization, the method does not correctly handle fine-scale surface details, as depicted in Figure 9.5. The local rotation of geometric details

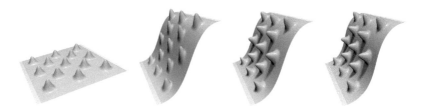

Figure 9.5. From left to right: The right strip $\mathcal{H}$ of the bumpy plane is lifted. The intuitive local rotations of geometric details cannot be achieved by a linearized deformation alone. A multi-scale approach based on normal displacements correctly rotates local details, but also distorts them, which can be seen in the leftmost row of bumps. The more accurate result of a nonlinear technique is shown. (Image taken from [Botsch and Sorkine 08]. ©2008 IEEE.)

is an inherently nonlinear behavior and therefore cannot be modeled by a purely linear technique. One way to better preserve geometric details, while still using a linear deformation approach, is to use *multi-scale* techniques, as described in this section.

The main idea of multi-scale deformations is to decompose the object into two frequency bands using the smoothing and fairing techniques introduced in Chapter 4; the low frequencies correspond to the smooth global shape, while the high frequencies correspond to the fine-scale details. Our goal is to deform the low frequencies (global shape) while preserving the high-frequency details, resulting in the desired multi-scale deformation. Figure 9.6 shows a simple 2D example of this concept.

The multi-scale deformation process is depicted in Figure 9.7. First a low-frequency representation of the given surface $\mathcal{S}$ is computed by removing the high frequencies, yielding a smooth base surface $\mathcal{B}$. The geometric details $\mathcal{D} = \mathcal{S} \ominus \mathcal{B}$, i.e., the fine surface features that have been removed, represent the high frequencies of $\mathcal{S}$ and are stored as detail information.

Figure 9.6. A multi-scale deformation of a sine wave. A frequency decomposition yields the dashed line as its low frequency component (left). Bending this line and adding the higher frequencies back onto it results in the desired global shape deformation (right). (Image taken from [Botsch 05].)

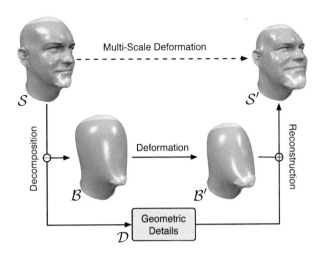

Figure 9.7. A general multi-scale editing framework consists of three main operators: the decomposition operator, which separates the low and high frequencies; the editing operator, which deforms the low frequency components; and the reconstruction operator, which adds the details back onto the modified base surface. Since the lower part of this scheme is hidden in the multi-scale kernel, only the multi-scale edit in the top row is visible to the designer. (Image taken from [Botsch and Sorkine 08]. ©2008 IEEE. Model courtesy of Cyberware.)

This allows reconstructing the original surface $\mathcal{S}$ by adding the geometric details back onto the base surface: $\mathcal{S} = \mathcal{B} \oplus \mathcal{D}$. The special operators $\ominus$ and $\oplus$ are called the *decomposition* and the *reconstruction* operator of the multi-scale framework, respectively.

This multi-scale surface representation is now enhanced by a *deformation* operator that is used to deform the smooth base surface $\mathcal{B}$ into a modified version $\mathcal{B}'$. Adding the geometric details onto the deformed base surface then results in a multi-scale deformation $\mathcal{S}' = \mathcal{B}' \oplus \mathcal{D}$.

Notice that, in general, more than one decomposition step can be used to generate a hierarchy of meshes $\mathcal{S} = \mathcal{S}_0, \mathcal{S}_1, \ldots, \mathcal{S}_k = \mathcal{B}$ with decreasing geometric complexity. In this case the frequencies that are lost from one level $\mathcal{S}_i$ to the next smoother level $\mathcal{S}_{i+1}$ are stored as geometric details $\mathcal{D}_{i+1} = \mathcal{S}_i \ominus \mathcal{S}_{i+1}$, such that after deforming the base surface to $\mathcal{B}'$, the modified original surface can be reconstructed by $\mathcal{S}' = \mathcal{B}' \oplus_{i=0}^{k-1} D_{k-i}$. Since the generalization to several hierarchy levels is straightforward, we restrict our explanations to the simpler case of a two-level decomposition, as shown in Figure 9.7.

A complete multi-scale deformation framework has to provide the three basic operators shown in Figure 9.7: the decomposition operator, the deformation operator, and the reconstruction operator. The decomposition is typically performed by mesh smoothing or fairing (Chapter 4), and for surface deformation we can employ the techniques discussed in the previous sections. The missing component is a suitable representation for the geometric detail $\mathcal{D} = \mathcal{S} \ominus \mathcal{B}$, which we describe next.

9.3.1 Displacement Vectors

The straightforward representation for multi-scale details is a displacement of the base surface $\mathcal{B}$. The detail information is a vector-valued displacement function $\mathbf{h} \colon \mathcal{B} \to \mathbb{R}^3$ that associates a displacement vector $\mathbf{h}(\mathbf{b})$ to each point $\mathbf{b}$ on the base surface. In most cases $\mathcal{S}$ and $\mathcal{B}$ have the same connectivity, leading to per-vertex *displacement vectors* $\mathbf{h}_i = (\mathbf{p}_i - \mathbf{b}_i)$ [Zorin et al. 97, Kobbelt et al. 98b, Guskov et al. 99] such that

$$\mathbf{p}_i = \mathbf{b}_i + \mathbf{h}_i, \quad \mathbf{h}_i \in \mathbb{R}^3,$$

where $\mathbf{b}_i \in \mathcal{B}$ is the vertex corresponding to $\mathbf{p}_i \in \mathcal{S}$. The vectors $\mathbf{h}_i$ have to be encoded in *local frames* with regard to $\mathcal{B}$ [Forsey and Bartels 88, Forsey and Bartels 95], determined by the normal vector $\mathbf{n}_i$ and two tangent vectors $\mathbf{t}_{i,1}$ and $\mathbf{t}_{i,2}$ of the base surface $\mathcal{B}$ at point $\mathbf{b}_i$:

$$\mathbf{h}_i = \alpha_i \, \mathbf{n}_i + \beta_i \, \mathbf{t}_{i,1} + \gamma_i \, \mathbf{t}_{i,2}. \tag{9.8}$$

When the base surface $\mathcal{B}$ is deformed to $\mathcal{B}'$, the displacement vectors rotate according to the rotations of the base surface's local frames, which then leads to a plausible detail reconstruction for $\mathcal{S}'$ (see Figure 9.8):

$$\mathbf{p}_i' = \mathbf{b}_i' + \alpha_i \, \mathbf{n}_i' + \beta_i \, \mathbf{t}_{i,1}' + \gamma_i \, \mathbf{t}_{i,2}'.$$

Figure 9.8. Representing the displacements with regard to the global coordinate system does not lead to the desired result (left). The geometrically intuitive solution is achieved by storing the details with regard to local frames that rotate according to the local tangent plane's rotation of $\mathcal{B}$ (right). (Image taken from [Botsch 05].)

While the normal vector $\mathbf{n}_i$ is well defined, it is not obvious how to compute the tangent axes $\mathbf{t}_{i,1}$ and $\mathbf{t}_{i,2}$. One heuristic is to choose $\mathbf{t}_{i,1}$ as the projection of the first edge incident to $\mathbf{p}_i$ into the tangent plane and to pick $\mathbf{t}_{i,2}$ to be orthogonal to $\mathbf{n}_i$ and $\mathbf{t}_{i,1}$.

9.3.2   Normal Displacements

As we will see next, long displacement vectors might lead to instabilities, in particular for bending deformations. As a consequence, the displacement vectors should be as short as possible, which is the case if they connect vertices $\mathbf{p}_i \in \mathcal{S}$ to their *closest* surface points on $\mathcal{B}$ instead of to their corresponding vertices $\mathbf{b}_i \in \mathcal{B}$.

This idea leads to *normal displacements* that are perpendicular to $\mathcal{B}$, i.e., parallel to its normal field $\mathbf{n}(\mathbf{b})$:

$$\mathbf{p}_i = \mathbf{b}_i + h_i \cdot \mathbf{n}_i, \quad h_i \in \mathbb{R}.$$

Since the per-vertex displacements $\mathbf{h}_i$ of (9.8) are in general not parallel to the surface normal $\mathbf{n}_i$, normal displacements require a re-sampling of either $\mathcal{S}$ or $\mathcal{B}$. Shooting rays in normal direction from each base vertex $\mathbf{b}_i \in \mathcal{B}$ and deriving new vertex positions $\mathbf{p}_i$ as their intersections with the detailed surface $\mathcal{S}$ leads to a resampling of the latter [Guskov et al. 00, Lee et al. 00]. Because $\mathcal{S}$ might be a detailed surface with high-frequency features, such a resampling is likely to introduce alias artifacts.

Hence we go the other direction, following [Kobbelt et al. 99b]. For each point $\mathbf{p}_i \in \mathcal{S}$, a local Newton iteration finds a base point $\mathbf{b}_i \in \mathcal{B}$ such that $(\mathbf{p}_i - \mathbf{b}_i)$ is parallel to the surface normal $\mathbf{n}_i = \mathbf{n}(\mathbf{b}_i)$. Note that $\mathbf{b}_i$ is now an arbitrary surface point on $\mathcal{B}$ (not necessarily a vertex). This point is contained in a triangle $(\mathbf{a}, \mathbf{b}, \mathbf{c}) \subset \mathcal{B}$ and therefore can be represented by barycentric interpolation (see Equation (1.3)):

$$\mathbf{b}_i = \alpha \, \mathbf{a} + \beta \, \mathbf{b} + \gamma \, \mathbf{c}.$$

Its normal vector $\mathbf{n}_i$ is computed by barycentric interpolation of the vertex normals, similar in concept to Phong shading :

$$\mathbf{n}_i = \frac{\alpha \, \mathbf{n_a} + \beta \, \mathbf{n_b} + \gamma \, \mathbf{n_c}}{\|\alpha \, \mathbf{n_a} + \beta \, \mathbf{n_b} + \gamma \, \mathbf{n_c}\|}.$$

Using this continuous normal field $\mathbf{n}(\mathbf{b})$ on the base surface $\mathcal{B}$, a local Newton iteration can find the barycentric coordinates (α, β, γ) of the base point $\mathbf{b}_i$ as the root of the function

$$f(\alpha, \beta, \gamma) = (\mathbf{p}_i - \mathbf{b}_i) \times \mathbf{n}_i.$$

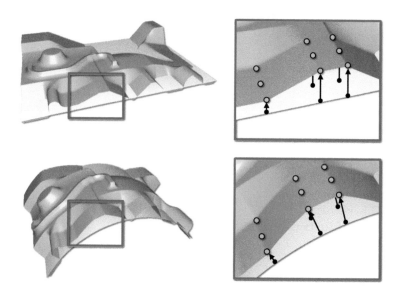

Figure 9.9. Top: The original surface $\mathcal{S}$ (orange) is decomposed into a low-frequency base surface $\mathcal{B}$ (yellow) and high-frequency normal displacements $\mathcal{D}$ (top right). Bottom: When the base surface is deformed to $\mathcal{B}'$, the normal vectors rotate accordingly and the displaced surface $\mathcal{S}' = \mathcal{B}' \oplus \mathcal{D}$ gives the desired result.

The process is initialized with the triangle closest to $\mathbf{p}_i$. If a barycentric coordinate becomes negative during the Newton iteration, one proceeds to the respective neighboring triangle.

Once the triangle $(\mathbf{a}, \mathbf{b}, \mathbf{c})$ and the barycentric coordinates (α, β, γ) have been found, the deformed point $\mathbf{p}'_i$ can be efficiently computed as a normal displacement of the deformed base surface $\mathcal{B}'$ (see Figure 9.9):

$$\mathbf{p}'_i = \left(\alpha\, \mathbf{a}' + \beta\, \mathbf{b}' + \gamma\, \mathbf{c}' \right) + h_i \cdot \frac{\alpha\, \mathbf{n}'_\mathbf{a} + \beta\, \mathbf{n}'_\mathbf{b} + \gamma\, \mathbf{n}'_\mathbf{c}}{\| \alpha\, \mathbf{n}'_\mathbf{a} + \beta\, \mathbf{n}'_\mathbf{b} + \gamma\, \mathbf{n}'_\mathbf{c} \|}.$$

This process avoids a resampling of $\mathcal{S}$ and therefore allows for the preservation of all of its sharp features (see also [Pauly et al. 06] for a comparison and discussion). Since the base points $\mathbf{b}_i$ are arbitrary surface points of $\mathcal{B}$, the connectivity of $\mathcal{S}$ and $\mathcal{B}$ is no longer restricted to be identical. This can be exploited in order to remesh the base surface $\mathcal{B}$ for the sake of higher numerical robustness [Botsch and Kobbelt 04b].

The difference in length of general displacement vectors and normal displacements typically depends on how much $\mathcal{B}$ differs from $\mathcal{S}$. For instance, in Figure 9.7 the general displacements are in average about 9 times longer than normal displacements. Besides being shorter, normal displacements

Figure 9.10. For the bending of the bumpy plane, normal displacements distort geometric details and almost lead to self-intersections (left), whereas displacement volumes (center) and deformation transfer (right) achieve more natural results. (Image taken from [Botsch et al. 06c].)

have the additional advantage that they do not require the heuristic computation of the tangent directions $\mathbf{t}_{i,1}$ and $\mathbf{t}_{i,2}$.

9.3.3   Advanced Techniques

While normal displacements are extremely efficient, their main problem is that neighboring displacement vectors are not coupled in any way. When strongly bending the surface in a convex or concave manner, the angle between neighboring displacement vectors increases or decreases, leading to an undesired distortion of geometric details (see Figures 9.5 and 9.10). In the extreme case of neighboring displacement vectors crossing each other (which happens if the curvature of $\mathcal{B}'$ becomes larger than the displacement length h_i), the surface even self-intersects locally. These problems are addressed by the advanced detail encoding techniques sketched in this section.

Displacement volumes. Both problems—the unnatural change of the volume and the local self-intersections—are addressed by displacement *volumes* instead of displacement *vectors* [Botsch and Kobbelt 03]. Each triangle $(\mathbf{p}_i, \mathbf{p}_j, \mathbf{p}_k)$ of $\mathcal{S}$, together with the corresponding points $(\mathbf{b}_i, \mathbf{b}_j, \mathbf{b}_k)$ on $\mathcal{B}$, defines a triangular prism. The volumes of those prisms are used as detail coefficients $\mathcal{D}$ and are kept constant during deformations. For a modified base surface $\mathcal{B}'$, the reconstruction operator therefore has to find $\mathcal{S}'$ such that the enclosed prisms have the same volumes as the original shape. The local volume preservation leads to more intuitive results and avoids local self-intersections (see Figures 9.5 and 9.10). However, the improved detail preservation comes at the price of higher computational cost compared to a linear detail reconstruction process.

Deformation transfer. [Botsch et al. 06c] use the deformation transfer approach of [Sumner and Popović 04] to transfer the base surface deformation $\mathcal{B} \mapsto \mathcal{B}'$ onto the detailed surface $\mathcal{S}$, resulting in a multi-scale deformation $\mathcal{S}'$. This method yields results similar in quality to displacement volumes (see Figures 9.5 and 9.10), but it only requires solving a sparse linear Poisson system. Both in terms of results and of computational efficiency, this method can be considered as lying in between displacement vectors and displacement volumes.

9.4 Differential Coordinates

While multi-scale deformation is an effective tool for enhancing shape deformations by fine-scale detail preservation, the generation of such a hierarchy can become quite involved for geometrically or topologically complex models. To avoid the explicit multi-scale decomposition, another class of methods modifies differential surface properties instead of spatial coordinates and then reconstructs a deformed surface having the desired differential coordinates. We first describe two typical differential representations—gradients and Laplacians—and how to derive the deformed surface from the manipulated differential coordinates. We then explain how to compute the local transformations of differential coordinates based on the user's deformation constraints.

9.4.1 Gradient-Based Deformation

Gradient-based methods [Yu et al. 04, Zayer et al. 05a] deform the surface by manipulating the original surface gradients and then finding the deformed surface that matches the target gradient field in the least-squares sense. This two-step deformation process is depicted by Figure 9.11.

For the manipulation of gradients, let us first consider a piecewise linear function $f: \mathcal{S} \to \mathbb{R}$ that lives on the original mesh and is defined by its values f_i at the mesh vertices. Its gradient $\nabla f: \mathcal{S} \to \mathbb{R}^3$ is a piecewise constant vector field, i.e., a constant vector $\mathbf{g}_T \in \mathbb{R}^3$ for each triangle T.

If instead of a scalar function f the piecewise linear coordinate function $\mathbf{p}: \mathcal{S} \to \mathbb{R}^3$, $v_i \mapsto \mathbf{p}_i$, is considered, then the gradient within a face T is a constant 3×3 Jacobian matrix:

$$\nabla \mathbf{p}|_T = \begin{bmatrix} \nabla \mathbf{p}_x|_T \\ \nabla \mathbf{p}_y|_T \\ \nabla \mathbf{p}_z|_T \end{bmatrix} =: \mathbf{J}_T \in \mathbb{R}^{3 \times 3}.$$

The rows of $\mathbf{J}_T$ are just the gradients of the x-, y-, and z-coordinates of

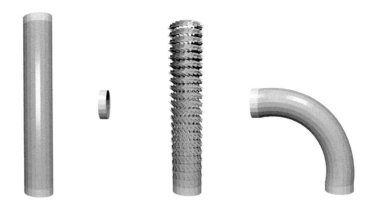

Figure 9.11. Using gradient-based editing to bend the cylinder by $90°$ (left). Rotating the handle and propagating its damped local rotation to the individual triangles (resp. their gradients $\mathbf{J}_T$) breaks up the mesh (center), but solving the Poisson system (9.10) reconnects it and yields the desired result (right). (Image taken from [Botsch and Sorkine 08]. ©2008 IEEE.)

the function $\mathbf{p}$ within triangle T, respectively, which can be computed by Equation (3.9).

The face gradients $\mathbf{J}_T$ are then modified by multiplying them by a 3×3 matrix $\mathbf{M}_T$ that represents the desired local rotation/scale/shear for the triangle T, yielding the new, desired gradients $\mathbf{J}'_T$:

$$\mathbf{J}'_T = \mathbf{M}_T \mathbf{J}_T.$$

How to actually determine the local transformation $\mathbf{M}_T$ from the user-defined handle transformation is discussed in Section 9.4.3. For a better understanding, Figure 9.11 (center) shows the transformations $\mathbf{M}_T$ applied to the individual triangles T, thereby breaking up the mesh.

The remaining step is to find new vertex positions $\mathbf{p}'_i$, such that the gradients $\nabla \mathbf{p}'|_T$ of the deformed mesh are as close as possible to the target gradients $\mathbf{J}'_T$. Intuitively this means reconnecting the triangles of Figure 9.11 (center) while changing their orientations as little as possible.

In the continuous setting, the analogous problem would be to find a function $f \colon \Omega \to \mathbb{R}$ that best matches a given gradient field $\mathbf{g}$. This amounts to minimizing the following energy functional:

$$E(f) = \iint_\Omega \|\nabla f(u, v) - \mathbf{g}(u, v)\|^2 \, du\, dv.$$

Applying variational calculus yields the Euler-Lagrange equation

$$\Delta f = \operatorname{div} \mathbf{g}, \tag{9.9}$$

which has to be solved for the optimal function f. Replacing f by the x-, y-, and z-coordinates of the deformed vertices $\mathbf{p}'_i$ and discretizing (9.9) by the discrete Laplace (3.11) and divergence (3.12) yields the linear system

$$
\mathbf{L} \cdot \begin{pmatrix} \mathbf{p}'_1{}^T \\ \vdots \\ \mathbf{p}'_n{}^T \end{pmatrix} = \begin{pmatrix} \operatorname{div} \mathbf{J}'(v_1) \\ \vdots \\ \operatorname{div} \mathbf{J}'(v_n) \end{pmatrix}.
\tag{9.10}
$$

This linear system is solved three times for the x-, y-, and z-coordinates of the deformed vertices, with the right hand side being the divergence of the modified x-, y-, and z-gradients (the rows of the modified Jacobians $\mathbf{J}'$). Note that, analogously to Equation (9.7), proper constraints have to be employed to make the system non-singular, e.g., by prescribing positions $\mathbf{p}'_i$ for handle and fixed vertices in $\mathcal{H}$ or $\mathcal{F}$.

Comparing Equation (9.10) to Equation (9.7), gradient-based editing must solve a Poisson system only, which is sparser and hence slightly more efficient than solving the bi-Laplacian system of the shell-based approach. On the other hand, the Poisson system allows for C^0 continuity at the boundary of the deformed region $\mathcal{R}$ only, whereas the shell-based approach yields C^1 continuous deformations.

9.4.2   Laplacian-Based Deformation

The second class of deformation methods based on differential coordinates is *Laplacian editing* [Lipman et al. 04, Sorkine et al. 04, Zhou et al. 05, Nealen et al. 05]. The setting is very similar to the gradient-based editing of the previous section, but now we manipulate per-vertex Laplacians instead of per-face gradients. We first compute initial Laplace coordinates $\delta_i = \Delta(\mathbf{p}_i)$, manipulate them to $\delta'_i = \mathbf{M}_i\,\delta_i$ as discussed in Section 9.4.3, and find new coordinates $\mathbf{p}'_i$ that match the target Laplacian coordinates. In the continuous setting this problem amounts to minimizing

$$
E(\mathbf{p}') = \iint_\Omega \left\| \Delta \mathbf{p}'(u,v) - \delta'(u,v) \right\|^2 \, du\, dv,
$$

which leads to the Euler-Lagrange equation

$$
\Delta^2 \mathbf{p}' = \Delta \delta'.
$$

For a discrete triangle mesh, this yields a bi-Laplacian system that has to be solved for the x-, y-, and z-coordinates of the deformed vertices $\mathbf{p}'_i$:

$$
\mathbf{L}^2 \cdot \begin{pmatrix} \mathbf{p}'_1{}^T \\ \vdots \\ \mathbf{p}'_n{}^T \end{pmatrix} = \begin{pmatrix} \Delta\delta'_1{}^T \\ \vdots \\ \Delta\delta'_n{}^T \end{pmatrix}.
$$

Again, suitable boundary constraints for $\mathcal{F}$ and $\mathcal{H}$ must be employed. Note that although the original works use the uniform Laplacian (3.10), the cotangent Laplacian (3.11) has been shown to yield better results for irregular meshes [Botsch and Sorkine 08].

There is an interesting connection of Laplacian-based deformation to the shell-based deformation of Section 9.2. Let us neglect for a moment the local transformations $\delta_i \mapsto \delta_i'$ and instead compute the new coordinates $\mathbf{p}_i'$ from the *original* Laplacians δ_i, i.e., by solving $\Delta^2 \mathbf{p}' = \Delta\delta$, again imposing constraints $\mathbf{p}_i' = \bar{\mathbf{p}}_i$ for $\mathbf{p}_i \in \mathcal{H} \cup \mathcal{F}$. Using the two identities $\mathbf{p}' = \mathbf{p} + \mathbf{d}$ and $\delta = \Delta\mathbf{p}$ reveals that the latter PDE is equivalent to the Euler-Lagrange equation $\Delta^2 \mathbf{d} = \mathbf{0}$ of the shell-based approach. As a consequence, the two methods are equivalent up to the way they model the local rotations of geometric details or differential coordinates, respectively, employing either a multi-scale technique (Section 9.3) or local transformations of Laplacians, as discussed next. Another consequence is that Laplacian editing yields C^1 continuous deformation, in contrast to the C^0 deformations of gradient-based editing.

9.4.3   Local Transformations

The missing component for gradient-based or Laplacian-based deformation is a technique for modifying the gradients $\mathbf{J}_T$ or Laplacians δ_i based on the handle transformation provided by the user. The methods discussed below derive local per-vertex or per-face transformations $\mathbf{M}_i$ or $\mathbf{M}_T$, respectively, in order to transform gradients or Laplacians, as discussed above:

$$\mathbf{J}_T' \;=\; \mathbf{M}_T\,\mathbf{J}_T \qquad \text{or} \qquad \delta_i' \;=\; \mathbf{M}_i\,\delta_i.$$

Propagation of deformation gradients. The first approach is to transform the differential coordinates by the gradient of the handle transformation, which is interpolated over the deformable region similar to Section 9.1 [Yu et al. 04, Zayer et al. 05a]. Typically, the user manipulates the handle by prescribing an affine transformation

$$\mathbf{T}(\mathbf{x}) \;=\; \mathbf{M}\mathbf{x} + \mathbf{t}.$$

The gradient of $\mathbf{T}(\mathbf{x})$ is the constant 3×3 matrix $\mathbf{M}$, which represents the rotation and scale/shear components of the handle transformation.

We would like to propagate this matrix over the deformable region and damp it using the smooth scalar field $s\colon \mathcal{S} \to [0,1]$ from Section 9.1 such that we smoothly blend from the full transformation $\mathbf{M}$ at the handle $\mathcal{H}$ to no transformation $\mathbf{Id}$ at the fixed region $\mathcal{F}$.

However, since rotations should be interpolated differently than scalings, these two components have to be separated first. The tool to decompose the matrix $\mathbf{M}$ into rotation $\mathbf{R}$ and scale/shear $\mathbf{S}$ is the so-called *polar decomposition* [Shoemake and Duff 92]. After computing the singular value decomposition $\mathbf{M} = \mathbf{U}\boldsymbol{\Sigma}\mathbf{V}^T$, we can find rotation and scale/shear as

$$\mathbf{R} \;=\; \mathbf{U}\mathbf{V}^T \qquad \text{and} \qquad \mathbf{S} \;=\; \mathbf{V}\boldsymbol{\Sigma}\mathbf{V}^T.$$

Since $\mathbf{U}$ and $\mathbf{V}$ are orthogonal matrices we get

$$\mathbf{R}\mathbf{S} \;=\; \mathbf{U}\mathbf{V}^T\mathbf{V}\boldsymbol{\Sigma}\mathbf{V}^T \;=\; \mathbf{U}\boldsymbol{\Sigma}\mathbf{V}^T \;=\; \mathbf{M}.$$

The rotation and scaling components are then interpolated separately over the deformable region, yielding the damped local transformation $\mathbf{M}_i$ at vertex v_i

$$\mathbf{M}_i \;=\; \mathrm{slerp}(\mathbf{R}, \mathbf{Id}, s_i) \cdot \left((1 - s_i)\,\mathbf{S} + s_i\,\mathbf{Id}\right),$$

where $\mathrm{slerp}(\cdot)$ denotes quaternion interpolation between the full rotation $\mathbf{R}$ and the identity matrix $\mathbf{Id}$, and $s_i = s(\mathbf{p}_i)$ is the vertex blending value. The local transformation $\mathbf{M}_T$ for a face $T = (\mathbf{p}_i, \mathbf{p}_j, \mathbf{p}_k)$ is computed using the blending value $s_T = (s_i + s_j + s_k)/3$.

By construction this method works very well for rotations (see Figure 9.11), but it unfortunately is insensitive to handle translations. Adding a translation $\mathbf{t}$ to a given handle deformation $\mathbf{T}(\mathbf{x})$ does *not* change its gradient $\mathbf{M}$ and thus has no influence on the resulting surface gradients $\mathbf{J}'_T$ or Laplacian coordinates $\boldsymbol{\delta}'_i$. But because there is a (nonlinear) connection between handle translations and local rotations of the surface, these methods will give counter-intuitive results for deformations containing large translations (see also Section 9.7).

Implicit optimization. Sorkine and colleagues simultaneously optimize for both the new vertex positions $\mathbf{p}'_i$ and the local rotations $\mathbf{M}_i$ by minimizing the energy functional [Sorkine et al. 04]

$$E(\mathbf{p}') \;=\; \sum_{i=1}^{n} A_i \,\|\mathbf{M}_i\,\boldsymbol{\delta}_i - \Delta\mathbf{p}'_i\|^2, \tag{9.11}$$

where $A_i = A(v_i)$ is the local vertex area. In this equation the transformations $\mathbf{M}_i = \mathbf{M}_i(\mathbf{p}')$ depend on the new vertex positions $\mathbf{p}'_j$. Note that boundary constraints for $\mathcal{H}$ and $\mathcal{F}$ again have to be prescribed.

To avoid a nonlinear optimization, which would be necessary for *rigid transformations* $\mathbf{M}_i$ (i.e., rotations), the local transformations are restricted to *linearized similarity transformations*. These can be represented by skew-symmetric matrices

$$\mathbf{M}_i \;=\; \begin{bmatrix} s_i & -h_{i,z} & h_{i,y} \\ h_{i,z} & s_i & -h_{i,x} \\ -h_{i,y} & h_{i,x} & s_i \end{bmatrix}.$$

The parameters $(s_i, \mathbf{h}_i)$ can be determined by writing down the desired transformation constraints

$$\mathbf{M}_i(\mathbf{p}_i - \mathbf{p}_j) = \mathbf{p}_i' - \mathbf{p}_j', \quad \forall\, \mathbf{p}_j \in \mathcal{N}_1(\mathbf{p}_i)$$

and extracting $(s_i, \mathbf{h}_i)$ as linear combinations of $\mathbf{p}_i'$. The precise derivation can be found in [Sorkine et al. 04]. Plugging the linear expression for $\mathbf{M}_i$ back into (9.11) leads to a linear least-squares problem, which can be solved efficiently. On the downside, however, the linearized transformations lead to artifacts in the case of large rotations (see Section 9.7).

9.5 Freeform Deformation

All deformation approaches described so far are *surface-based*: they compute a smooth deformation field *on* the surface $\mathcal{S}$ by minimizing some quadratic energy, which amounts to solving a linear system corresponding to the respective Euler-Lagrange equation.

An apparent drawback of such methods is that their computational effort and numerical robustness are strongly related to the complexity and quality of the surface tessellation. In the presence of degenerate triangles, the discrete cotangent weights (3.11) for the Laplacian operator are not well defined and thus the involved linear systems become singular. Similarly, topological artifacts like gaps or non-manifold configurations lead to problems, since local vertex neighborhoods become inconsistent. In such cases quite some effort has to be spent to still be able to compute smooth deformations, like eliminating degenerate triangles (Chapter 8) or even remeshing the complete surface (Chapter 6). But even if the mesh quality is sufficiently high, extremely complex meshes will result in linear systems that cannot be solved due to their sheer size.

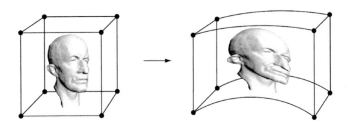

Figure 9.12.   Space deformations warp the embedding space around an object and thus implicitly deform the object. (Image taken from [Botsch et al. 06b]. ©2006 ACM, Inc. Included here by permission.)

These problems are avoided by *space deformations*, which deform the ambient space and thus implicitly deform the embedded objects (see Figure 9.12). In contrast to surface-based methods, space deformation approaches employ a trivariate deformation function $\mathbf{d} \colon \mathbb{R}^3 \to \mathbb{R}^3$ to transform all points of the original surface $\mathcal{S}$. Since the space deformation function $\mathbf{d}$ does not depend on a particular surface representation, it can be used to deform all kinds of explicit surface representations, e.g., by transforming all vertices of a triangle mesh or all points of a point-sampled model.

9.5.1   Lattice-Based Freeform Deformation

Classical freeform deformation (FFD) [Sederberg and Parry 86] represents the space deformation by a trivariate tensor-product spline function

$$\mathbf{d}(u, v, w) \;=\; \sum_i \sum_j \sum_k \boldsymbol{\delta}\mathbf{c}_{ijk}\, N_i(u)\, N_j(v)\, N_k(w)\,, \qquad (9.12)$$

where N_i are B-spline basis functions and $\boldsymbol{\delta}\mathbf{c}_{ijk} = (\mathbf{c}'_{ijk} - \mathbf{c}_{ijk})$ are the displacements of the control points $\mathbf{c}_{ijk}$ (compare this to tensor-product spline surfaces of Section 1.3.1). Let us for the sake of simpler notation order the grid points and basis functions in a linear manner:

$$\boldsymbol{\delta}\mathbf{c}_l := \boldsymbol{\delta}\mathbf{c}_{ijk} \quad \text{and} \quad N_l(\mathbf{u}) = N_l(u, v, w) := N_i(u)\, N_j(v)\, N_k(w)\,.$$

This allows us to re-write Equation (9.12) as

$$\mathbf{d}(\mathbf{u}) \;=\; \sum_{l=1}^{n} \boldsymbol{\delta}\mathbf{c}_l\, N_l(\mathbf{u})\,.$$

Each original vertex $\mathbf{p}_i \in \mathcal{S}$ has a corresponding parameter value $\mathbf{u}_i = (u_i, v_i, w_i)$ such that $\mathbf{p}_i = \sum_l \mathbf{c}_l N_l(\mathbf{u}_i)$. The vertex is then transformed by $\mathbf{p}'_i = \mathbf{p}_i + \mathbf{d}(\mathbf{u}_i)$, which can be computed efficiently since $N_l(\mathbf{u}_i)$ stays constant and can be precomputed.

The deformation can be controlled by manipulating the positions of control points, i.e., by prescribing the control point displacements $\boldsymbol{\delta}\mathbf{c}_l$ (see Figure 9.13 (left)). This, however, can become tedious for more complex control grids. Moreover, the support of the deformation is sometimes difficult to predict since it is determined as the intersection of a volumetric basis function's support with the surface $\mathcal{S}$.

A handle-based interface for direct manipulation, allowing the user to specify displacements of surface points $\mathbf{p}_i \in \mathcal{S}$ instead of control points $\mathbf{c}_l$, simplifies the deformation process [Hsu et al. 92]. Given a set of displacement constraints $\mathbf{d}(\mathbf{u}_i) = \bar{\mathbf{d}}_i$ for $\{\mathbf{p}_1, \ldots, \mathbf{p}_m\} = \mathcal{H} \cup \mathcal{F}$, one solves a linear

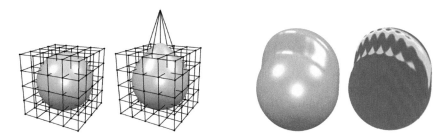

Figure 9.13. In the FFD approach a 3D control grid is used to specify a volumetric displacement function (left). The regular placement of grid basis functions can lead to alias artifacts in the deformed surface (right). (Image taken from [Botsch 05].)

system for the required movements $\delta\mathbf{c}_l$ of control points:

$$\begin{bmatrix} N_1(\mathbf{u}_1) & \cdots & N_n(\mathbf{u}_1) \\ \vdots & \ddots & \vdots \\ N_1(\mathbf{u}_m) & \cdots & N_n(\mathbf{u}_m) \end{bmatrix} \begin{pmatrix} \delta\mathbf{c}_1 \\ \vdots \\ \delta\mathbf{c}_n \end{pmatrix} = \begin{pmatrix} \bar{\mathbf{d}}_1 \\ \vdots \\ \bar{\mathbf{d}}_m \end{pmatrix}. \tag{9.13}$$

This $(m \times n)$ system can be over- as well as under-determined, and is therefore solved using the *pseudo-inverse* [Hsu et al. 92, Golub and Loan 89]. This yields a *least-squares* and *least-norm* solution, which minimizes the error in the constraints $\sum_i \left\| \mathbf{d}(\mathbf{u}_i) - \bar{\mathbf{d}}_i \right\|^2$ as well as the amount of control point movement $\sum_l \left\| \delta\mathbf{c}_l \right\|^2$.

While this yields a well-defined solution, it has two drawbacks: First, in an over-determined setting the displacement constraints cannot be satisfied exactly, but only in the least square sense. Second, in the under-determined setting the remaining degrees of freedom are determined by minimizing control point movements, instead of optimizing for an as-smooth-as-possible deformation, as was the case for the fair surface-based deformation of Section 9.2.

The placement of basis functions $N_l(\mathbf{u})$ on a regular grid is another potential problem. As shown in Figure 9.13 (right), a deformation that is not well-aligned with the grid axes can lead to aliasing artifacts. This problem can be addressed by using more flexible (pre-deformed) control lattices that better represent the desired deformation, but these can be difficult to set up for complex deformations [Coquillart 90, MacCracken and Joy 96].

9.5.2   Cage-Based Freeform Deformation

Cage-based techniques can be considered a generalization of the lattice-based freeform deformation. Instead of a regular control lattice, a so-called *control cage* is used to deform the object. This cage typically is a coarse, arbitrary triangle mesh enclosing the object to be modified, which allows the cage to better match the shape and structure of the embedded object than regular control lattices do (see Figure 9.14).

The vertices $\mathbf{p}_i$ of the original mesh $\mathcal{S}$ can be represented as linear combinations of the cage's control vertices $\mathbf{c}_l$ by

$$\mathbf{p}_i = \sum_{l=1}^{n} \mathbf{c}_l\, \varphi_l(\mathbf{p}_i), \qquad (9.14)$$

where the weights $\varphi_l(\mathbf{p}_i)$ are *generalized barycentric coordinates* [Floater et al. 05, Ju et al. 05, Ju et al. 07, Lipman et al. 08]. The coordinate functions φ_l in (9.14) therefore correspond to the spline basis functions N_l in Equation (9.12).

Once the per-vertex weights $\varphi_l(\mathbf{p}_i)$ have been pre-computed, the object can be deformed by manipulating the cage vertices $\mathbf{c}_l \mapsto \mathbf{c}_l + \delta\mathbf{c}_l$ and computing the per-vertex displacement as

$$\mathbf{d}(\mathbf{p}_i) = \sum_{l=1}^{n} \delta\mathbf{c}_l\, \varphi_l(\mathbf{p}_i).$$

Finding control vertex displacements $\delta\mathbf{c}_l$ resulting in a deformation that satisfies user-defined constraints $\mathbf{d}(\mathbf{p}_i) = \bar{\mathbf{d}}_i$ works equivalently to Equation (9.13), with $N_l(\mathbf{u}_i)$ replaced by $\varphi_l(\mathbf{p}_i)$. While being much more flexible

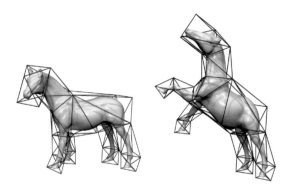

Figure 9.14. Manipulating a horse using a cage-based space deformation, where surface vertices are represented and deformed relative to the cage using generalized barycentric coordinates. (Model courtesy of [Ju et al. 05].)

in terms of the control grid, cage-based methods share the drawback of a least norm solution that does not necessarily correspond to a fair deformation.

9.6   Radial Basis Functions

In the case of surface-based deformations, high-quality results are achieved by interpolating the user's displacement constraints with a deformation function $\mathbf{d} \colon \mathcal{S} \to \mathbb{R}^3$ that minimizes some fairness energies (e.g., Section 9.2). Motivated by this, we derive in this section a smoothly interpolating trivariate *space deformation* function $\mathbf{d} \colon \mathbb{R}^3 \to \mathbb{R}^3$ that minimizes analogous fairness energies.

On a more abstract level, the problem is to find a function $\mathbf{d}$ that interpolates some prescribed values $\bar{\mathbf{d}}_i$ at position $\mathbf{p}_i$, while being smooth and fair in between these constraints. *Radial basis functions* (RBFs) are known to be very well suited for this kind of scattered data interpolation problem [Wendland 05].

A trivariate RBF deformation is defined as a superposition of radially symmetric kernels $\varphi_j(\mathbf{x})$, located at centers $\mathbf{c}_j \in \mathbb{R}^3$ and weighted by $\mathbf{w}_j \in \mathbb{R}^3$:

$$\mathbf{d}(\mathbf{x}) \;=\; \sum_{j=1}^{n} \mathbf{w}_j \, \varphi(\|\mathbf{c}_j - \mathbf{x}\|) \;+\; \boldsymbol{\pi}(\mathbf{x}),$$

where $\varphi_j(\mathbf{x}) = \varphi(\|\mathbf{c}_j - \mathbf{x}\|)$ is the basis function corresponding to the jth center $\mathbf{c}_j$, and $\boldsymbol{\pi}(\mathbf{x})$ is a polynomial of low degree used to guarantee polynomial precision. To simplify explanation and notation, we omit the polynomial term in the following.

In order to find an RBF function that interpolates the displacement constraints $\mathbf{d}(\mathbf{p}_i) = \bar{\mathbf{d}}_i$ for $\{\mathbf{p}_1, \ldots, \mathbf{p}_n\} = \mathcal{H} \cup \mathcal{F}$, we use as many RBF kernels as we have constraints and place them on the constraints, i.e., $\mathbf{c}_j = \mathbf{p}_j$. The weights $\mathbf{w}_j$ are then found as the solution of the symmetric linear system

$$\begin{bmatrix} \varphi(\|\mathbf{p}_1 - \mathbf{p}_1\|) & \cdots & \varphi(\|\mathbf{p}_n - \mathbf{p}_1\|) \\ \vdots & \ddots & \vdots \\ \varphi(\|\mathbf{p}_1 - \mathbf{p}_n\|) & \cdots & \varphi(\|\mathbf{p}_n - \mathbf{p}_n\|) \end{bmatrix} \begin{pmatrix} \mathbf{w}_1 \\ \vdots \\ \mathbf{w}_n \end{pmatrix} = \begin{pmatrix} \bar{\mathbf{d}}_1 \\ \vdots \\ \bar{\mathbf{d}}_n \end{pmatrix}. \qquad (9.15)$$

Once the weights have been computed, i.e., the RBF function $\mathbf{d}$ has been fit to the constraints, the mesh vertices can be displaced as $\mathbf{p}_i' = \mathbf{p}_i + \mathbf{d}(\mathbf{p}_i)$.

The choice of the kernel function φ has a strong influence on the computational complexity and the resulting surface's fairness. While compactly supported radial basis functions lead to sparse linear systems and hence can

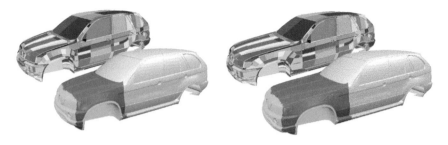

Figure 9.15. Using three independent handles allows one to stretch the car's hood while rigidly preserving the shape of the wheel houses. This 3M triangle model consists of 10k individual connected components, which are neither 2-manifold nor consistently oriented. (Model courtesy of BMW AG. Image taken from [Botsch et al. 06b]. ©2006 ACM, Inc. Included here by permission.)

be used to interpolate a large number of constraints [Morse et al. 01,Ohtake et al. 04], they do not provide the same degree of fairness as basis functions of global support [Carr et al. 01]. It was shown by Duchon [Duchon 77] that the globally supported basis function $\varphi(r) = r^3$ yields a tri-harmonic function $\mathbf{d}$, i.e., $\Delta^3 \mathbf{d} = 0$. From variational calculus we know that it therefore minimizes the fairness energy

$$\int_{\mathbb{R}^3} \|\mathbf{d}_{xxx}(\mathbf{x})\|^2 + \|\mathbf{d}_{xxy}(\mathbf{x})\|^2 + \ldots + \|\mathbf{d}_{zzz}(\mathbf{x})\|^2 \, d\mathbf{x}.$$

Notice that these functions are *conceptually* equivalent to the minimum variation surfaces of [Moreton and Séquin 92] and the tri-harmonic surfaces used in [Botsch and Kobbelt 04a], and therefore provide the same degree of fairness. The difference is that for tri-harmonic RBFs the energy minimization is "built in," whereas for surface-based approaches we explicitly optimized for it (see Section 9.2). The major drawback is that the global support of $\varphi(r) = r^3$ leads to a *dense* linear system (9.15), which is numerically harder to solve (see [Botsch and Kobbelt 05]).

Note that as soon as the constraints change, e.g., by interactively manipulating the handle, the linear system (9.15) has to be solved again for the new right-hand side. For efficiency reasons one can factorize the matrix once, and only compute a back-substitution for each new right-hand side [Golub and Loan 89]. As shown in [Botsch and Kobbelt 05], when restricting to *affine* handle transformations one can precompute special basis functions, which can efficiently be evaluated instead of solving (9.15). Moreover, evaluating these basis functions on the graphics card further accelerates this approach and provides real-time space deformations of several million points per second. As shown in Figure 9.15, even complex surfaces consisting of disconnected patches can be handled by this technique, whereas all surface-based techniques would fail in this situation.

For the two space deformation approaches described in Sections 9.5 and 9.6, the deformed surface $\mathcal{S}'$ depends *linearly* on the displacement constraints $\mathbf{d}(\mathbf{p}_i) = \bar{\mathbf{d}}_i$. As a consequence, nonlinear effects such as local detail rotation cannot be achieved, similar to the linear surface-based methods discussed in Sections 9.2–9.4. Although space deformations can be enhanced by multi-scale techniques as well (see, e.g., [Marinov et al. 07]), they generally suffer from the same limitations as surface-based methods when it comes to large-scale deformation, as discussed next.

9.7 Limitations of Linear Methods

The methods we described so far provide high quality results and can be computed robustly and efficiently. However, it is equally important to understand their limitations as it is to understand their strengths. In this section we therefore compare some of the discussed methods and point out their limitations. To this end, the goal is *not* to show the best-possible results each method can produce (those can be found in the original papers) but rather to show under which circumstances each individual method fails. Figure 9.16 shows deformation examples that were particularly chosen to identify the respective limitations of the different techniques. For comparison we show the results of the nonlinear surface deformation PriMo [Botsch et al. 06a], which does not suffer from linearization artifacts.

▶ The shell-based deformation (Section 9.2), in combination with a multi-scale technique (Section 9.3), works fine for pure translations and yields fair and detail-preserving deformations. However, due to the linearization of the shell energy, this approach fails for large rotations.

▶ Gradient-based editing (Section 9.4.1) updates the face gradients using the gradient of the handle transformation (its rotation and scale/shear components) and therefore works very well for rotational deformation. However, the explicit propagation of local rotations is translation insensitive, such that the plane example is neither smooth nor detail preserving.

▶ Laplacian surface editing (Section 9.4.2) implicitly optimizes for local rotations and hence works comparatively well for translations and rotations. However, the required linearization of rotations yields artifacts for large deformations.

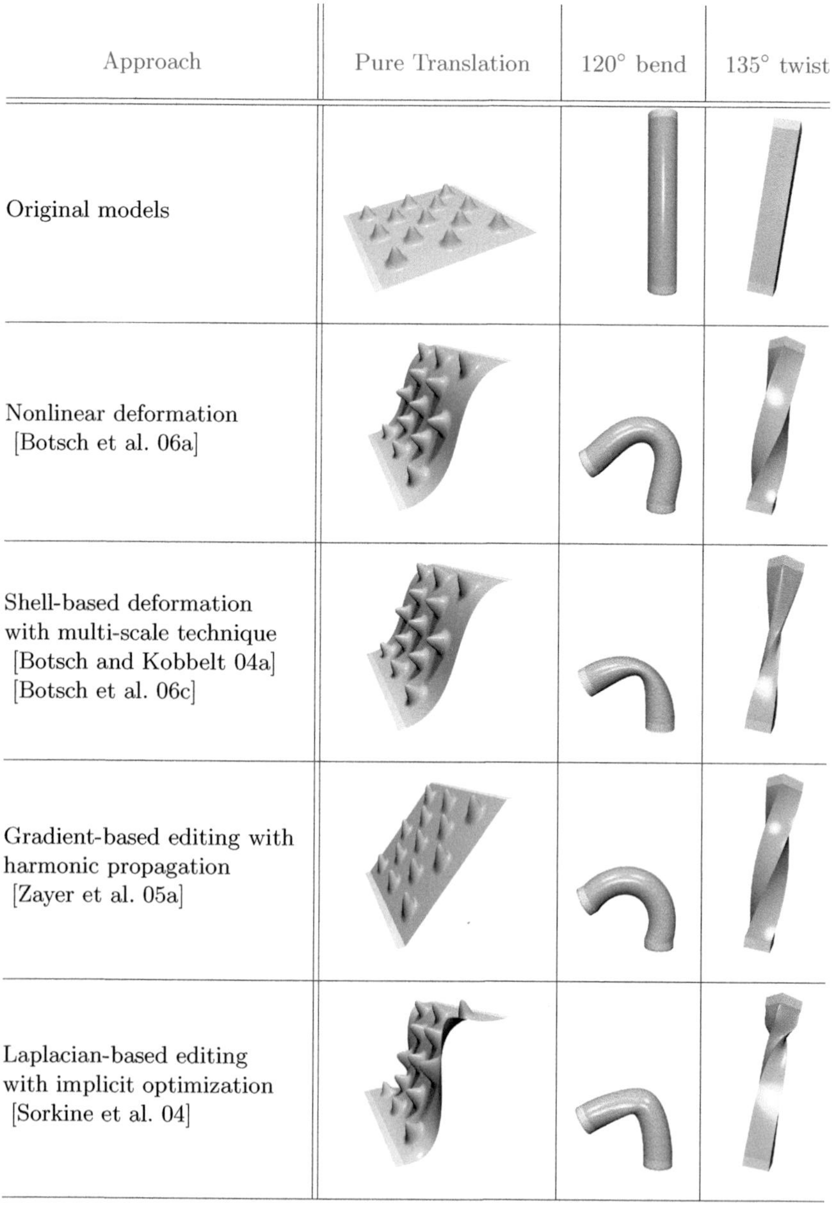

Approach	Pure Translation	120° bend	135° twist
Original models			
Nonlinear deformation [Botsch et al. 06a]			
Shell-based deformation with multi-scale technique [Botsch and Kobbelt 04a] [Botsch et al. 06c]			
Gradient-based editing with harmonic propagation [Zayer et al. 05a]			
Laplacian-based editing with implicit optimization [Sorkine et al. 04]			

Figure 9.16. The extreme examples shown in this comparison matrix were particularly chosen to reveal the limitations of the respective deformation approaches. (Image taken from [Botsch and Sorkine 08]. ©2008 IEEE.)

9.8   Summary and Further Reading

In this chapter we introduced several methods of deforming a given surface and showed that accurate and high-quality deformations can be obtained by minimizing suitable energies, which in the end involve solving a linear system for the deformed vertex positions. With the linear system solvers described in the appendix, this can be computed robustly and at interactive rates. The interested reader can find more details on linear surface deformation methods in [Botsch and Sorkine 08].

However, the accurate physical equations governing the surface deformation process are inherently nonlinear, which requires simplifying or linearizing the involved energies at some point. We have seen the consequence of this in Section 9.7: all linear techniques fail under certain circumstances. The shell-based approach typically works well for translations, but has problems with large rotations, whereas it is the other way around for methods based on differential coordinates. From those examples one can derive the following guidelines for picking the "right" deformation technique for a specific application scenario:

▶ In technical, CAD-like engineering applications, the required shape deformations are typically rather small, since in many cases an existing prototype has to be adjusted only slightly, but they have high requirements for surface fairness, boundary continuity, and the precise control thereof. For such problems a linearized shell model is typically the best suited.

▶ In contrast, applications like character animation mostly involve (possibly large) rotations of limbs around bends and joints. Here, methods based on differential coordinates clearly are the better choice. Moreover, the required rotations might be available from, e.g., a sketching interface [Zhou et al. 05, Nealen et al. 05] or a motion capture system [Shi et al. 06].

▶ Applications that require both large-scale translations and rotations are problematic for all linear approaches. In this case one can either employ a more complex nonlinear technique or split up large deformations into a sequence of smaller ones. While the nonlinear techniques are computationally and implementation-wise more involved, splitting up deformations or providing a denser set of constraints complicates the user interaction.

Thanks to the rapid increase in both computational power and available memory of today's workstations, nonlinear deformation methods have become more and more tractable, which in the last few years has already led to a first set of nonlinear yet interactive surface deformation approaches.

Below we briefly mention some nonlinear approaches for surface-based and space deformation and refer the reader to the original papers. While a nonlinear implementation of the previously discussed approaches seems to be straightforward ("simply do not use any linearization"), in the nonlinear case special attention has to be paid to computational efficiency and numerical robustness of the involved energy minimizations.

Nonlinear surface deformation. Pyramid coordinates (see [Sheffer and Kraevoy 04, Kraevoy and Sheffer 06]) can be considered nonlinear versions of Laplacian coordinates, leading to differential coordinates invariant under rigid motions, which can be used for deformation as well as for morphing.

Huang et al. employ a nonlinear version of the volumetric graph Laplacian, which also features nonlinear volume preservation constraints [Huang et al. 06]. In order to increase the performance and efficiency of their optimization, they use a subspace approach: the original mesh is embedded in a coarse control cage (see Section 9.5.2), and the optimization is performed on the cage vertices $\mathbf{c}_j$ while considering the constraints from the original mesh vertices $\mathbf{p}_i$ in a least-squares manner.

An alternative approach to subspace methods is the handle-aware iso-line technique of [Au et al. 07]. In a preprocessing step one constructs a set of iso-lines of the geodesic distance from either the fixed regions or the handle regions, similar in spirit to [Zayer et al. 05a]. For each of these iso-lines, a local transformation $\mathbf{M}_i$ for a Laplacian-based deformation is found by a nonlinear optimization. The number of required iso-lines is relatively small, which guarantees an efficient numerical optimization and thereby allows for interactive editing.

Shi et al. combine Laplacian-based deformation with skeleton-based inverse kinematics [Shi et al. 07]. Their approach allows for easy and intuitive character posing, featuring control of lengths, rigidity, and joint limits, but it in turn requires a complex cascading optimization for the involved nonlinear energy minimization.

PriMo [Botsch et al. 06a] is a nonlinear version of the shell-based minimization of bending and stretching energies. The surface is modeled as a thin layer of triangular prisms, which are coupled by a nonlinear elastic energy. During deformation the prisms are kept rigid, which allows for a robust geometric optimization. A hierarchical optimization is used to increase the computational efficiency.

The as-rigid-as-possible surface deformation of [Sorkine and Alexa 07] models local rotations in terms of each vertex's one-ring. An easy-to-implement alternating optimization solves for the local rotations and the new vertex positions.

Eigensatz and Pauly introduce a surface deformation method that allows directly prescribing positional, metric, and curvature constraints anywhere on the surface. A global nonlinear optimization solves for a deformed surface that satisfies these user constraints as best as possible, while minimizing the overall metric and curvature distortion [Eigensatz and Pauly 09].

Nonlinear space deformation. Sumner et al. compute detail-preserving space deformations by formulating an energy functional that explicitly penalizes deviation from local rigidity by optimizing the local deformation gradients to be rotations [Sumner et al. 07]. In addition to static geometries, their method can also be applied to hand-crafted animations and precomputed simulations.

Botsch et al. extend the PriMo framework [Botsch et al. 06a] to deformations of solid objects [Botsch et al. 07]. The input model is voxelized in an adaptive manner, and the resulting hexahedral cells are kept rigid under deformations to ensure numerical robustness. The deformation is governed by a nonlinear elastic energy coupling neighboring rigid cells.

Another class of approaches uses divergence-free vector fields to deform shapes [Angelidis et al. 06, von Funck et al. 06]. The advantage of those techniques is that by construction they yield volume-preserving and intersection-free deformations. As a drawback, it is harder to construct vector fields that exactly satisfy user-defined deformation constraints.

NUMERICS

In this appendix we describe different types of solvers for dense and sparse linear systems. Within this class of systems, we further concentrate on *symmetric positive definite* (spd) matrices, since exploiting their special structure allows for the most efficient and most robust implementations. Examples of such matrices are Laplacian systems (to be analyzed in Section A.1) and least-squares systems. The general case of a non-symmetric indefinite system is outlined afterwards in Section A.5.

Following [Botsch et al. 05], we propose the use of direct solvers for sparse spd systems. After reviewing frequently used data structures and standard linear solvers, we introduce the sparse direct solvers and point out their advantages.

For the following discussion we restrict ourselves to sparse spd problems $\mathbf{Ax} = \mathbf{b}$, i.e., square, symmetric, positive definite matrices $\mathbf{A} \in \mathbb{R}^{n \times n}$ and $\mathbf{x}, \mathbf{b} \in \mathbb{R}^n$. We furthermore denote by $\mathbf{x}^*$ the exact solution $\mathbf{A}^{-1}\mathbf{b}$, and by $a_{i,j}$ and x_i the individual entries of a matrix $\mathbf{A}$ and a vector $\mathbf{x}$, respectively.

A.1 Discretizing Poisson and Laplace Equations

Since Poisson and Laplace equations play a major role in several geometry processing applications, including smoothing (Chapter 4), conformal parameterization (Chapter 5), and shape deformation (Chapter 9), we first briefly describe the matrices obtained by discretizing these equations.

Let us consider the discretization and solution of a Poisson PDE $\Delta f = b$ or a higher-order PDE $\Delta^k f = b$ on a triangle mesh. The scalar-valued function $f \colon S \to \mathbb{R}$ is defined by piecewise linear interpolation of its function values $f_i = f(v_i)$ at the mesh vertices v_i. As discussed in Chapter 3, the continuous Laplace or Laplace-Beltrami Δf can be discretized at a mesh vertex v_i by a linear combination of the function values at the center vertex v_i and its one-ring neighbors v_j:

$$\Delta f(v_i) \;=\; w_i \sum_{v_j \in \mathcal{N}_1(v_i)} w_{ij}\left(f(v_j) - f(v_i)\right).$$

Using, for instance, the cotangent discretization of Equation (3.11), the weights are $w_i = \frac{1}{2A_i}$ and $w_{ij} = (\cot \alpha_{i,j} + \cot \beta_{i,j})$.

If we stack the function values $f(v_i)$ and Laplacians $\Delta f(v_i)$ of all n vertices into two vectors, the discretized Laplacian of all mesh vertices can be written in matrix notation:

$$\begin{pmatrix} \Delta f(v_1) \\ \vdots \\ \Delta f(v_n) \end{pmatrix} = \underbrace{\mathbf{D\,M}}_{\mathbf{L}} \begin{pmatrix} f(v_1) \\ \vdots \\ f(v_n) \end{pmatrix}.$$

Here, $\mathbf{D} = \operatorname{diag}(w_1, \ldots, w_n)$ is a diagonal matrix of the vertex weights w_i, and $\mathbf{M}$ is a symmetric matrix of edge weights w_{ij}:

$$m_{i,j} \;=\; \begin{cases} -\sum_{v_k \in \mathcal{N}_1(v_i)} w_{ik}, & i = j, \\ w_{ij}, & v_j \in \mathcal{N}_1(v_i), \\ 0, & \text{otherwise.} \end{cases}$$

Discretizations of higher-order Laplacians can be obtained recursively by

$$\Delta^k f(v_i) \;=\; w_i \sum_{v_j \in \mathcal{N}_1(v_i)} w_{ij}\left(\Delta^{k-1} f(v_j) - \Delta^{k-1} f(v_i)\right).$$

Their matrix representation simply corresponds to the k-th power $\mathbf{L}^k = (\mathbf{DM})^k$ of the Laplacian matrix $\mathbf{L}$.

The discretization of a higher-order Laplace PDE $\Delta^k f = b$ on a mesh of n vertices therefore leads to the $(n \times n)$ linear system

$$\mathbf{L}^k \mathbf{x} \;=\; \mathbf{b}, \tag{A.1}$$

with $\mathbf{x} = (f(v_1), \ldots, f(v_n))^T$ and $\mathbf{b} = (b(v_1), \ldots, b(v_n))^T$. In order to pick the most efficient linear solver for this problem, we have to analyze the properties of the system matrix $\mathbf{L}$, or $\mathbf{L}^k$, respectively.

Sparsity. Since the Laplacian $\Delta f(v_i)$ of a vertex v_i is defined *locally* in terms of its one-ring neighbors, the matrix $\mathbf{M}$—and hence the Laplacian matrix $\mathbf{L}$—is highly sparse. In the ith row it has non-zeros on the diagonal and in the columns corresponding to v_i's one-ring neighbors $v_j \in \mathcal{N}_1(v_i)$ only. Since in a triangle mesh each vertex has six neighbors on average (see Section 1.3.3), $\mathbf{L}$ has about seven non-zero entries per row. As an example, for a (small) mesh with 10,000 vertices there will only be about 0.07% non-zero entries. For more complex meshes the sparsity will be even higher. A bi-Laplacian matrix $\mathbf{L}^2$ has an increased density of about 19 non-zeros per row, which is still very sparse.

Symmetry. Due to the diagonal matrix $\mathbf{D}$, which scales each row of $\mathbf{M}$ by w_i, the Laplacian matrix $\mathbf{L} = \mathbf{DM}$ is not symmetric in general. However, Laplacian systems $\mathbf{L}^k \mathbf{x} = \mathbf{b}$ of any order k can easily be turned into symmetric systems by moving the left-most factor $\mathbf{D}$ to the right-hand side:

$$\mathbf{M}\,(\mathbf{DM})^{k-1}\,\mathbf{x} \;=\; \mathbf{D}^{-1}\mathbf{b}. \tag{A.2}$$

Definiteness. For the PDE to have a well-defined solution, and for the matrix to be non-singular, suitable boundary constraints have to be employed. Typically the values $f(v_i)$ of a set of constrained vertices $v_i \in \mathcal{C}$ are prescribed (so-called *Dirichlet constraints*). When we solve a linear system $\mathbf{Ax} = \mathbf{b}$ with certain values x_i for $v_i \in \mathcal{C}$ being constrained, these values are no longer unknown variables. Hence, their corresponding columns $\mathbf{a}_i$ are moved to the right-hand side ($\mathbf{b} \leftarrow \mathbf{b} - x_i \mathbf{a}_i$) and their corresponding rows i are removed from the system. Note that symmetrically eliminating both column i and row i from the system keeps the matrix symmetric. After incorporating constraints into a Laplacian system, the resulting matrix $\mathbf{L}$ can be shown to be negative definite [Pinkall and Polthier 93]. As a consequence, we multiply the system by -1 to get a positive definite system.

Combining these three observations we see that higher-order Laplacian systems $\mathbf{L}^k \mathbf{x} = \mathbf{b}$ can be rewritten as

$$(-1)^k\,\mathbf{M}\,(\mathbf{DM})^{k-1}\,\mathbf{x} \;=\; (-1)^k\,\mathbf{D}^{-1}\mathbf{b},$$

which is a sparse, symmetric, and positive definite (spd) linear system. These beneficial properties allow us to apply the efficient linear solvers presented in the remainder of this appendix.

However, note that most other matrices used in mesh processing have very similar properties. For instance, solving overdetermined systems $\mathbf{Ax} = \mathbf{b}$ in a least squares manner through the normal equations $\mathbf{A}^T \mathbf{Ax} = \mathbf{A}^T \mathbf{b}$ also leads to spd systems. Moreover, discretizing PDEs typically leads to very sparse matrices, since the required partial derivatives depend on local vertex neighborhoods only.

A.2   Data Structures for Sparse Matrices

An apparent practical requirement for an efficient implementation are data structures that are able to exploit the sparsity of the matrices. We therefore review some popular data structures for sparse matrices first, before we discuss different algorithms for solving sparse spd linear systems in the next sections.

The design of data structures for sparse matrices follows two major goals: the compact storage of the matrix $\mathbf{A}$ and the efficient computation of matrix-vector products $\mathbf{y} = \mathbf{Ax}$. In the following we will use the simple example matrix

$$\mathbf{A} = \begin{bmatrix} 0.0 & 1.1 & 0.0 & 0.0 \\ 2.2 & 0.0 & 3.3 & 4.4 \\ 0.0 & 5.5 & 0.0 & 6.6 \\ 0.0 & 7.7 & 8.8 & 9.9 \end{bmatrix} \tag{A.3}$$

to explain the different sparse matrix formats.

A.2.1   Triplet Format

A first approach is to store only the non-zero coefficients $a_{i,j} = v \neq 0$ of the matrix $\mathbf{A}$ as triplets (i, j, v). In an actual implementation one stores three arrays: row indices i[], column indices j[], and matrix values v[], respectively. Each array has NNZ (number of non-zeros) elements, which is much more compact that a naive storage of all n^2 matrix entries.

This data structure is referred to as the *Triplet format* or *TRIAD format*. The example matrix of Equation (A.3) would be represented as

i[]:	0	1	1	1	2	2	3	3	3
j[]:	1	0	2	3	1	3	1	2	3
v[]:	1.1	2.2	3.3	4.4	5.5	6.6	7.7	8.8	9.9

The code below shows an example implementation of the Triplet format in C or C++, together with a function for computing the product of a Triplet matrix and a vector. This function may be used to implement a solver based on the conjugate gradients method (see Section A.3.2).

```
// Triplet format for sparse matrices
struct TripletMatrix
{
  int n;        // matrix dimension
  int nnz;      // number of non-zero coefficients
  int i[];      // row indices (array of size nnz)
  int j[];      // column indices (array of size nnz)
  double v[];   // non-zero coefficients (array of size nnz)
};
```

```
// sparse matrix vector product y=A*x
void mult(Vector& y, const TripletMatrix& A, const Vector& x)
{
  for(int i=0; i<A.n; i++)
    y[i] = 0.0;

  for (int k=0; k<A.nnz; k++)
    y[A.i[k]] += A.v[k] * x[A.j[k]];
}
```

Despite the gain realized by the Triplet format as compared to a naive dense regular 2D array, this representation still contains redundancy for the indices i[], which store the row associated to each entry. For this reason, this format is seldom used in numerical libraries except for reading input file formats or initially setting up the system matrices.

A.2.2 Compressed Row Storage

The *compressed row storage* (CRS) data structure provides a higher memory compactness and allows for a more efficient matrix vector product. It is therefore one of the most frequently used sparse matrix data structures in numerical libraries. Its transposed variant, the *compressed column storage* (CCS) format, is also used depending on the underlying algorithms and implementation choices.

The CRS data structure uses three arrays to represent non-zero coefficients and their associated row and column indices: as in the Triplet format, the array v[] stores all the non-zero matrix entries; the array colind[] indicates for each entry the corresponding column index. The rows are encoded in a compact manner through the rowptr[] array. This array indicates for each row its start index and end index in the arrays v[] and colind[].

To facilitate an easier implementation of algorithms, a common practice consists of completing the array rowptr[] by an additional entry that points one entry past the last entry of the matrix, i.e., rowptr[A.n]=A.nnz. This additional entry, called *sentry*, avoids resorting to a special case for the last row in the matrix-vector product.

The CRS representation of the matrix (A.3) is depicted below.

rowptr[]:	0	1	4	6	9				
colind[]:	1	0	2	3	1	3	1	2	3
v[]:	1.1	2.2	3.3	4.4	5.5	6.6	7.7	8.8	9.9

Below is a C++ example implementation of the CRS data structure.

```
// CRS format for sparse matrices
struct CRSMatrix
{
   int n;           // matrix dimension
   int nnz;         // number of non-zero coefficients
   int rowptr[];    // row pointers (array of size n+1)
   int colind[];    // column indices (array of size nnz)
   double v[];      // non-zero coefficients (array of size nnz)
};

// sparse matrix vector product y=A*x
void mult(Vector& y, const CRSMatrix& A, const Vector& x)
{
   for(int i=0; i<A.n; i++)
     y[i] = 0.0;

   for (int i=0; i<A.n; i++)
     for (int k=A.rowptr[i]; k<A.rowptr[i+1]; k++)
       y[i] += A.v[k] * x[A.colind[k]];
}
```

There are several variants of the CRS data structure [Barrett et al. 94]. If the matrix is symmetric, it is possible to store the lower triangular part of the matrix only. Other variants store the diagonal coefficients in a separate array to facilitate the implementation of a diagonal Jacobi preconditioner. Alternatively, the block compressed row storage (BCRS) format partitions the matrix into fixed-size blocks and stores these (instead of scalars) in the array v[]. This both optimizes memory access and is amenable to the use of extended instruction sets, such as SSE on Intel processors. It is also well suited for efficient GPU implementations [Buatois et al. 09].

The CRS data structure and its variants are both compact and efficient, at the price of an increased rigidity compared to, e.g., the Triplet data structure. This rigidity translates into either the need to generate the matrix one row after the other (i.e., each row must be completed before starting a new one) or into two mesh traversals required to first count the number of non-zero entries before filling the matrix. Practical implementations therefore typically create a Triplet matrix first, which can then be converted into a CRS matrix using efficient conversion routines [Davis 06]. An alternative is a CRS-like data structure based on dynamic arrays per row, which is slightly less efficient but more flexible than the static CRS format; an example implementation is available in the OpenNL library.[1]

---

[1] http://alice.loria.fr/index.php/software/4-library/23-opennl.html

A.3   Iterative Solvers

Iterative solvers are designed to exploit the sparsity of the matrix $\mathbf{A}$ and allow for simple implementations [Golub and Loan 89, Press et al. 92]. A detailed overview of iterative methods with valuable implementation hints can be found in [Barrett et al. 94].

Iterative methods have in common that they compute a converging sequence $\mathbf{x}^{(0)}, \mathbf{x}^{(1)}, \ldots, \mathbf{x}^{(k)}$ of approximations to the solution $\mathbf{x}^*$ of the linear system, i.e., $\lim_{k \to \infty} \mathbf{x}^{(k)} = \mathbf{x}^*$. In practice one has to find a suitable criterion to stop the iteration as soon as the current approximation $\mathbf{x}^{(k)}$ is accurate enough, i.e., if the norm of the *error*

$$\mathbf{e}^{(k)} := \mathbf{x}^* - \mathbf{x}^{(k)}$$

is less than some ε. Since the solution $\mathbf{x}^*$ is not known beforehand, the error must be estimated by considering the *residual*

$$\mathbf{r}^{(k)} := \mathbf{b} - \mathbf{A}\mathbf{x}^{(k)}.$$

Error and residual are related by the *residual equations*

$$\mathbf{A}\mathbf{e}^{(k)} = \mathbf{r}^{(k)}.$$

This leads to an upper bound of the error

$$\|\mathbf{e}^{(k)}\| \leq \|\mathbf{A}^{-1}\| \, \|\mathbf{r}^{(k)}\|,$$

which, however, requires the norm of the inverse matrix to be estimated or approximated in some way [Barrett et al. 94]. In practice, the vector $\mathbf{x}^{(k)}$ is often updated until the residual $\|\mathbf{A}\mathbf{x}^{(k)} - \mathbf{b}\| < \epsilon$ for some user-defined tolerance ϵ. It is also common practice to specify a maximum number of iterations such that the algorithm stops even if it does not converge due to numerical inaccuracies. We now review the most frequently used iterative methods for sparse spd systems.

A.3.1   Jabobi and Gauss-Seidel

The Jacobi and Gauss-Seidel methods are the simplest approaches, both from the conceptual and from the implementation point of view. However, they are rather inefficient and hence should not be used for meshes larger than a few thousand vertices.

The two approaches are derived by writing the linear system $\mathbf{A}\mathbf{x} = \mathbf{b}$ line by line:

$$
\begin{array}{ccccccccc}
a_{1,1}x_1 & + & a_{1,2}x_2 & + & \ldots & + & a_{1,n}x_n & = & b_1, \\
a_{2,1}x_1 & + & a_{2,2}x_2 & + & \ldots & + & a_{2,n}x_n & = & b_2, \\
\vdots & & \vdots & & \ldots & & \vdots & & \vdots \\
a_{n,1}x_1 & + & a_{n,2}x_2 & + & \ldots & + & a_{n,n}x_n & = & b_n.
\end{array}
$$

The Jacobi method traverses these equations one by one and updates the value x_i by rearranging equation i and assuming all the other variables x_j for $j \neq i$ to be known. This leads to the following simple update rule:

$$x_i^{(k+1)} = \frac{1}{a_{i,i}} \left(b_i - \sum_{j \neq i} a_{i,j} x_j^{(k)} \right).$$

The complete algorithm for a simple Jacobi solver can be summarized by the following pseudocode:

```
while  (‖Ax(k) − b‖ < ϵ)  and  (k < kmax)
    for i from 1 to n
        x_i^(k+1) = (b_i − Σ_{j≠i} a_{i,j} x_j^(k)) / a_{i,i}
    end
    k = k + 1
end
```

Here, ϵ denotes the precision specified by the user and k_{max} the maximum number of iterations. Note that the computation of $x_i^{(k+1)}$ does not make use of the already available new values $x_1^{(k+1)}, \ldots, x_{i-1}^{(k+1)}$. Taking them into account leads to the update rule of the Gauss-Seidel method:

$$x_i^{(k+1)} = \frac{1}{a_{i,i}} \left(b_i - \sum_{j=1}^{i-1} a_{i,j} x_j^{(k+1)} - \sum_{j=i+1}^{n} a_{i,j} x_j^{(k)} \right).$$

It is easy to see that the Gauss-Seidel method needs one copy of the solution vector $\mathbf{x}$ only, which is successively overwritten, whereas the Jacobi method has to store the current state (k) and the next state $(k+1)$. However, the Gauss-Seidel method depends on the order to variables x_i and is inherently serial, whereas a Jacobi solver is order-independent and can trivially be parallelized.

As can be seen from the pseudocode, both algorithms are not applicable to matrices with zero values on the diagonal. More specifically, it is possible to prove a sufficient condition for convergence. If the matrix is *diagonal dominant*, i.e.,

$$|a_{i,i}| > \sum_{j \neq i} |a_{i,j}| \quad \forall\, i = 1, \ldots, n,$$

then the algorithm converges.

The main advantage of the Jacobi and Gauss-Seidel methods is their extreme simplicity from the implementation point of view, as they do not even require a sparse matrix data structure (see [Taubin 95, Floater and Hormann 05]). Their main disadvantage, however, is the slow convergence for the many cases where the matrix is not strongly diagonal dominant. Both methods rapidly remove the high frequencies of the error, but the iteration stalls as soon as the error becomes a smooth function. As a consequence, the convergence to the exact solution $\mathbf{x}^*$ is usually too slow in practice. We review next the conjugate gradients method, which can be several orders of magnitude faster in such cases.

A.3.2   Conjugate Gradients

In this section we provide a short introduction to the conjugate gradients algorithm and refer the interested reader to the book [Golub and Loan 89] and the comprehensive tutorial [Shewchuk 94] for more details.

The conjugate gradients (CG) algorithm is based on the equivalence of solving the linear system $\mathbf{A}\mathbf{x} = \mathbf{b}$ and minimizing the quadratic form

$$\Phi(\mathbf{x}) \;=\; \frac{1}{2}\mathbf{x}^T\mathbf{A}\mathbf{x} - \mathbf{b}^T\mathbf{x}.$$

Straightforwardly minimizing $\Phi(\mathbf{x})$ by gradient descent results in inefficient zig-zag paths in steep valleys of $\Phi(\mathbf{x})$, which correspond to strongly differing eigenvalues of $\mathbf{A}$ (see [Shewchuk 94]). The speed of convergence is influenced by the ratio

$$\kappa(\mathbf{A}) \;=\; \lambda_{\max}(\mathbf{A})\,/\lambda_{\min}(\mathbf{A}) \tag{A.4}$$

of the largest to the smallest eigenvalue, called the *condition number* of $\mathbf{A}$. Problems with low or high condition numbers are said to be well-conditioned or ill-conditioned, respectively.

In order to reduce the effect of $\mathbf{A}$'s eigenvalues, the CG method successively minimizes $\Phi(\mathbf{x})$ along a set of *linearly independent* search directions $\mathbf{p}^{(k)}$ that define the so-called *Krylov spaces* $\mathcal{K}^{(k)}$:

$$\mathbf{x}^{(k)} \;=\; \operatorname*{argmin}_{\mathbf{x}\in\mathcal{K}^{(k)}} \Phi(\mathbf{x}) \quad \text{with} \quad \mathcal{K}^{(k)} \;=\; \operatorname{span}\left\{\mathbf{p}^{(0)},\ldots,\mathbf{p}^{(k-1)}\right\}. \tag{A.5}$$

The search directions are chosen to be $\mathbf{A}$-*conjugate*, i.e., orthogonal with respect to the scalar product induced by $\mathbf{A}$: $\mathbf{p}^{(j)^T}\mathbf{A}\mathbf{p}^{(i)} = 0$ for $i \neq j$. Fortunate simplifications in the computations make it possible to obtain the vectors $\mathbf{p}^{(k)}$ one by one, by only keeping one vector in memory. The next one is then obtained as a linear combination of the previous one and the gradient $\nabla\Phi = \mathbf{A}\mathbf{x}^{(k)} - \mathbf{b} = -\mathbf{r}^{(k)}$ at the current point $\mathbf{x}^{(k)}$. The complete algorithm can be summarized as follows:

```
Initialize k = 0, r⁽⁰⁾ = p⁽⁰⁾ = Ax⁽⁰⁾ − b
while  (‖Ax⁽ᵏ⁾ − b‖ < ε)  and  (k < kₘₐₓ)
```

$$\alpha = \left(\mathbf{r}^{(k)} \cdot \mathbf{r}^{(k)}\right) / \left(\mathbf{p}^{(k)} \cdot \mathbf{A}\mathbf{p}^{(k)}\right)$$
$$\mathbf{x}^{(k+1)} = \mathbf{x}^{(k)} + \alpha\,\mathbf{p}^{(k)}$$
$$\mathbf{r}^{(k+1)} = \mathbf{r}^{(k)} - \alpha\,\mathbf{A}\mathbf{p}^{(k)}$$
$$\beta = \left(\mathbf{r}^{(k+1)} \cdot \mathbf{r}^{(k+1)}\right) / \left(\mathbf{r}^{(k)} \cdot \mathbf{r}^{(k)}\right)$$
$$\mathbf{p}^{(k+1)} = \mathbf{r}^{(k+1)} + \beta\,\mathbf{p}^{(k)}$$
$$k = k+1$$

```
end
```

Due to the nestedness of the spaces $\mathcal{K}^{(k)}$, the error decreases monotonically, and the exact solution $\mathbf{x}^* \in \mathbb{R}^n$ is found after at most n steps (neglecting rounding errors), since $\mathcal{K}^{(n)} = \mathbb{R}^n$. The complexity of each CG iteration is dominated by the matrix-vector product $\mathbf{A}\mathbf{p}$, which is of the order $O(n)$ if the matrix is sparse. Given the maximum number of n iterations, the total complexity is $O(n^2)$ in the worst case, but it is usually better in practice.

As the convergence rate mainly depends on the spectral properties of the matrix $\mathbf{A}$, a proper pre-conditioning scheme should be used to increase the efficiency and robustness of the CG method [Golub and Loan 89, Barrett et al. 94]. While very sophisticated preconditioners exist (SSOR, incomplete Cholesky, etc.), our experiments with Laplacian systems have shown that a simple diagonal Jacobi preconditioner is often satisfactory.

Although the conjugate gradients method decreases the computational complexity from $O(n^3)$ to $O(n^2)$, it is still too slow to compute exact (or sufficiently accurate) solutions of large and possibly ill-conditioned systems. This motivates the use of multigrid iterative solvers.

A.3.3   Multigrid Iterative Solvers

One drawback of most iterative solvers is that they attenuate the high frequencies of the error $\mathbf{e}^{(k)}$ very fast, but their convergence stalls in the case where the error is a fairly smooth function (which is typically the case of Laplacian systems). These solvers are therefore often called *smoothers* or *relaxation methods*.

Multigrid methods overcome the problem of slow convergence by building a fine-to-coarse hierarchy of meshes

$$\mathcal{M} = \mathcal{M}_0 \supset \mathcal{M}_1 \supset \cdots \supset \mathcal{M}_k$$

of the computational domain $\mathcal{M}$ and solving the linear system hierarchically from coarse to fine [Hackbusch 86, Briggs et al. 00]. After a few smoothing iterations (e.g., Jacobi, Gauss-Seidel) on the finest level $\mathcal{M}_0$ (so-called *pre-smoothing*), the high frequencies of the error are removed and the smoothing iterations become inefficient. However, the remaining low frequency error $\mathbf{e}_0 = \mathbf{x}^* - \mathbf{x}_0$ on $\mathcal{M}_0$ corresponds to higher frequencies when restricted to the coarser level mesh $\mathcal{M}_1$ and therefore can be removed efficiently on $\mathcal{M}_1$.

Hence, the error is solved for using the residual equations $\mathbf{A}\mathbf{e}_1 = \mathbf{r}_1$ on $\mathcal{M}_1$, where $\mathbf{r}_1 = \mathbf{R}_1\mathbf{r}_0$ is the residual on $\mathcal{M}_0$ transferred to $\mathcal{M}_1$ by a restriction operator $\mathbf{R}_1$. The result $\mathbf{e}_1$ is prolongated back to $\mathcal{M}_0$ by $\mathbf{e}_0 \leftarrow \mathbf{P}_1\mathbf{e}_1$ and used to correct the current approximation: $\mathbf{x}_0 \leftarrow \mathbf{x}_0 + \mathbf{e}_0$. Small high-frequency errors due to the prolongation are finally removed by a few Jacobi iterations (so-called *post-smoothing*) on $\mathcal{M}_0$.

The recursive application of this two-level approach to the whole hierarchy can be summarized as follows:

$$\begin{aligned} \Phi_i &= \mathbf{S}_\mu\mathbf{P}_{i+1}\Phi_{i+1}\mathbf{R}_{i+1}\mathbf{S}_\lambda, \quad i = 0,\ldots,k-1, \\ \Phi_k &= \mathbf{A}_k^{-1}\mathbf{b}, \end{aligned}$$

where $\mathbf{S}_\lambda$ and $\mathbf{S}_\mu$ denote λ pre-smoothing and μ post-smoothing iterations, respectively. The recursion stops on the coarsest level $\mathcal{M}_k$, where the (small) linear system $\mathbf{A}_k\mathbf{e}_k = \mathbf{r}_k$ is solved using any linear solver, denoted by the operator Φ_k. One recursive run is referred to as a *V-cycle* iteration.

Another concept is the method of *nested iterations*, which exploits the fact that iterative solvers are very efficient if the starting value is sufficiently close to the actual solution. One thus starts by computing the exact solution on the coarsest level $\mathcal{M}_k$, which can be done efficiently since the system $\mathbf{A}_k\mathbf{x}_k = \mathbf{b}_k$ corresponding to the restriction to $\mathcal{M}_k$ is small. The prolongated solution $\mathbf{P}_k\mathbf{x}_k^*$ is then used as the starting value for an iterative solver on level $\mathcal{M}_{k-1}$, and this process is repeated until the finest level $\mathcal{M}_0$ is reached and the solution $\mathbf{x}_0^* = \mathbf{x}^*$ is computed.

The remaining question is what kind of iterative solver to choose for the solution on each level $\mathcal{M}_i$ in a nested iterations approach? The typical method is to perform one or two V-cycle iterations (from $\mathcal{M}_i$ to $\mathcal{M}_k$ an back to $\mathcal{M}_i$). This results in the so-called *full multigrid* method. However, one can also use an iterative smoothing solver (e.g., Jacobi or CG) at each level and completely avoid V-cycles. In the latter case the number of iterations m_i at level i should not be constant but instead should be chosen as $m_i = m\gamma^i$ to decrease exponentially from coarse to fine [Bornemann and Deuflhard 96]. Besides easier implementation, the advantage of this *cascading multigrid* approach is that once a level is computed, it is not involved in further computations and can thus be discarded. A comparison of the three methods in terms of visited multigrid levels is given in Figure A.1.

$\mathcal{M}_0$
$\mathcal{M}_1$
$\mathcal{M}_2$
$\mathcal{M}_3$

Figure A.1. A schematic comparison in terms of visited multigrid levels for V-cycle (left), full multigrid with one V-cycle per level (center), and cascading multigrid (right). (Image taken from [Botsch et al. 05].)

Since in our case the discrete computational domain $\mathcal{M}$ is an irregular triangle mesh instead of a regular 2D or 3D grid, the coarsening operator for building the hierarchy is based on mesh decimation techniques (Chapter 7). The shape of the resulting triangles is important for numerical robustness, and the edge lengths on the different levels should mimic the case of regular grids. Therefore, the decimation usually removes edges in the order of increasing lengths, such that the hierarchy levels have uniform edge lengths and triangles of bounded aspect ratio. The simplification from one hierarchy level $\mathcal{M}_i$ to the next coarser one $\mathcal{M}_{i+1}$ should additionally be restricted to remove a *maximally independent set* of vertices, i.e., no two removed vertices $v_j, v_l \in \mathcal{M}_i \setminus \mathcal{M}_{i+1}$ are connected by an edge $e_{jl} \in \mathcal{M}_i$. In [Aksoylu et al. 05] some more efficient alternatives for building the hierarchy are described.

Due to the logarithmic number of hierarchy levels $O(\log n)$, the full multigrid method and the cascading multigrid method can both be shown to have $O(n)$ asymptotic complexity, as opposed to $O(n^2)$ complexity for non-hierarchical iterative methods. This linear complexity allows for highly efficient implementations even for very complex systems. Successful applications of multigrid methods in computer graphics are, for instance, [Ray and Lévy 03, Bolz et al. 03, Shi et al. 06, Georgii and Westermann 06, Kazhdan and Hoppe 08, Zhu et al. 10].

However, the main problem of multigrid solvers is their involved implementation, since special care must be taken for building the hierarchy, for specialized preconditioners, and for the inter-level conversion by restriction and prolongation operators. In addition, appropriate numbers of iterations per hierarchy level are chosen either empirically or from experience, since they depend not only on the nature of the problem (here the structure of $\mathbf{A}$) but also on its specific instance (the values of $\mathbf{A}$). A detailed overview of these techniques is given in [Aksoylu et al. 05].

For these reasons, sparse direct solvers, as described in the following, are easier to use since they do not require complicated parameter tuning and furthermore can exploit synergies when the linear system has to be solved several times for multiple right-hand sides.

A.4   Sparse Direct Cholesky Solver

Direct solvers for linear systems are based on the factorization of the matrix $\mathbf{A}$ into matrices of simpler structure, e.g., triangular or orthogonal matrices. Once the factorization has been computed, this special structure allows for an efficient solution of the linear system. It can therefore also be used to efficiently solve the linear system for multiple right-hand sides.

For symmetric and positive definite linear systems the *Cholesky factorization* is the most efficient choice [Golub and Loan 89, Trefethen and Bau 97]: it factorizes the matrix $\mathbf{A}$ into the product $\mathbf{LL}^T$ of a lower triangular matrix $\mathbf{L}$ and its transpose. Once the Cholesky factorization is obtained, it is a trivial matter to solve the linear system $\mathbf{Ax} = \mathbf{b}$:

$$\mathbf{Ax} = \mathbf{b} \quad \Leftrightarrow \quad \mathbf{LL}^T\mathbf{x} = \mathbf{b} \quad \Leftrightarrow \quad \begin{cases} \mathbf{Ly} & = \quad \mathbf{b}, \\ \mathbf{L}^T\mathbf{x} & = \quad \mathbf{y}. \end{cases}$$

A Cholesky solver thus solves the linear system by solving two triangular systems, which can be performed efficiently through trivial forward and backward substitutions. The Cholesky solver, in comparison to the more general LU-factorization, exploits the symmetry of $\mathbf{A}$ and is numerically very robust due to the positive definiteness of $\mathbf{A}$.

On the downside, we have to consider that the asymptotic time complexity of a standard Cholesky solver is $O(n^3)$ for computing the factorization and $O(n^2)$ for solving the two triangular systems. Since, for the problems we are targeting, n can be of the order of 10^6, this cubic complexity is prohibitive. In practice, on a recent computer, it takes 0.01 seconds to solve a (tiny) linear system of size $n = 100$, but the cubic complexity makes this timing become 10 centuries if $n = 10^6$! Even if the matrix $\mathbf{A}$ is highly sparse, a naive Cholesky solver does not exploit this structure, such that the matrix factor $\mathbf{L}$ is dense in general (see Figure A.2, top row). Note that this is true for all dense matrix factorizations (LU, QR, SVD), which all have cubic time complexity.

However, an analysis of the Cholesky factorization reveals that the *bandwidth* of the matrix $\mathbf{A}$ is preserved. The bandwidth of $\mathbf{A}$ is defined as

$$\beta(\mathbf{A}) \; = \; \max_{i,j} \left\{ |i - j| : a_{i,j} \neq 0 \right\},$$

and intuitively describes the maximum distance of a non-zero entry from the diagonal. If $\mathbf{A}$ has a certain bandwidth, then so does its factor $\mathbf{L}$, i.e., $\beta(\mathbf{L}) \leq \beta(\mathbf{A})$. Hence, additional non-zeros (so-called *fill-in* elements

$l_{i,j} \neq 0 = a_{i,j}$) can only appear *within* the band around the diagonal. This additional structure can be exploited in both the factorization and the solution processes, such that their complexities reduce from $O(n^3)$ to $O(n\beta^2)$ and from $O(n^2)$ to $O(n\beta)$, respectively [George and Liu 81].

An even stricter bound is that the Cholesky factorization also preserves the so-called *envelope*, i.e., all leading zeros of each row. The time complexity of factorization and solution generally depend linearly on the number of non-zeros of the factor **L**. If the number of non-zeros is in turn of the order $O(n)$—for instance, if the width of the band or the envelope is a small constant—then we get the same $O(n)$ time complexity as for multigrid solvers!

However, if the matrix **A** is sparse but does not have a special band- or envelope-structure, this result does not apply: the Cholesky factor **L** will be a dense matrix and the complexity stays cubic (see Figure A.2, top row). We can, however, minimize the matrix envelope in a first step, which can be achieved by symmetric row and column permutations. This simply corresponds to a reordering of the mesh vertices. Although finding the optimal reordering is an NP-complete problem, several good heuristics exist, of which we outline the most frequently used in the following. All of these methods work on the undirected *adjacency graph* Adj(**A**), where two nodes $i, j \in \{1, \ldots, n\}$ are connected by an edge if and only if $a_{i,j} \neq 0$.

The standard method for envelope minimization is the *Cuthill-McKee* algorithm [Cuthill and McKee 69], which picks a start node and renumbers all its neighbors by traversing the adjacency graph in a greedy breadth-first manner. Reverting this permutation further improves the reordering, leading to the *reverse Cuthill-McKee* method [Liu and Sherman 76]. The result of this reordering is shown in the second row of Figure A.2.

The *minimum degree* algorithm [George and Liu 89, Liu 85] builds on the fact that the non-zero structure of **L** can symbolically be derived from the non-zero structure of the matrix **A**, or, equivalently, from its adjacency graph Adj(**A**). By analyzing the graph interpretation of the Cholesky factorization it tries to minimize fill-in elements. This reordering does not yield a band structure (which implicitly limits fill-in), but instead explicitly minimizes fill-in, which usually yields fewer non-zeros and thus higher performance (see Figure A.2, third row).

The last class of reordering approaches is based on graph partitioning. A matrix **A** whose adjacency graph has m separate connected components can be restructured to a block-diagonal matrix of m blocks, such that the factorization can be performed on each block individually. If the adjacency graph is connected, a small subset S of separating nodes, whose elimination would separate the graph into two components of roughly equal size, is found by one of several heuristics [Karypis and Kumar 98]. This graph partitioning results in a matrix consisting of two large diagonal

Ordering	Matrix $\mathbf{A} = \mathbf{L}\mathbf{L}^T$	Factor $\mathbf{L}$	NNZ($\mathbf{L}$)

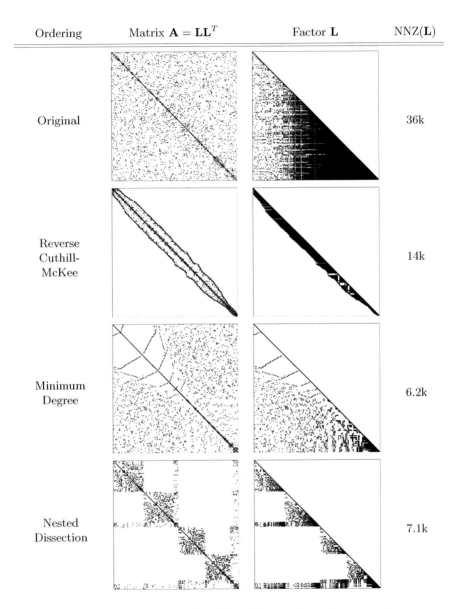

Original			36k
Reverse Cuthill-McKee			14k
Minimum Degree			6.2k
Nested Dissection			7.1k

Figure A.2. Nonzero pattern of a 500×500 matrix $\mathbf{A}$ (corresponding to a Laplacian system on an irregular triangle mesh) and of its Cholesky factor $\mathbf{L}$, and the numbers of non-zeros of the matrices $\mathbf{L}$, for different matrix reordering schemes. (Image taken from [Botsch et al. 05].)

blocks (two connected components) and $|\mathcal{S}|$ rows representing the separator $\mathcal{S}$. Recursively repeating this process leads to the method of *nested dissection*, which yields matrices of the block structure shown in the bottom row of Figure A.2. Besides the obvious fill-in reduction, the block structure also allows for parallelization of the factorization and the solution.

Analogously to the dense direct solvers, the factorization can be exploited to solve for different right-hand sides in a very efficient manner since only the forward and backward substitutions have to be performed again. Furthermore, no additional parameters have to be chosen in a problem-dependent manner (such as iteration numbers for iterative solvers). The only degree of freedom is the matrix reordering, which depends on the symbolic structure of the matrix only and therefore can be chosen quite easily. Highly efficient implementations are publicly available in the libraries TAUCS [Toledo et al. 03] and CHOLMOD [Chen et al. 08].

A.5   Non-Symmetric Indefinite Systems

When the assumptions about the symmetry and positive definiteness of matrix $\mathbf{A}$ are not satisfied, optimal methods like the Cholesky factorization or conjugate gradients cannot be used. In this section we shortly outline which techniques are applicable instead.

For a non-symmetric matrix, it is possible to apply the conjugate gradients method to the normal equation $\mathbf{A}^T \mathbf{A} \mathbf{x} = \mathbf{A}^T \mathbf{b}$. The resulting method is called *conjugate gradients squared* (CGSQ). However, since this squares the condition number (see Equation (A.4)), the loss of numerical stability makes this method unsuitable in general.

Another idea consists of deriving from the system $\mathbf{A}\mathbf{x} = \mathbf{b}$ an equivalent symmetric system:

$$\begin{bmatrix} \mathbf{Id} & \mathbf{A} \\ \mathbf{A}^T & \mathbf{0} \end{bmatrix} \begin{pmatrix} \mathbf{0} \\ \mathbf{x} \end{pmatrix} = \begin{pmatrix} \mathbf{b} \\ \mathbf{0} \end{pmatrix}.$$

It is then possible to apply the conjugate gradients method to this system. This defines the *bi-conjugate gradient* (BiCG) algorithm [Press et al. 92]. Although it works well in most cases, BiCG does not provide any theoretical convergence guarantees and has a very irregular non-monotonically decreasing residual error for ill-conditioned systems.

On the other hand, the generalized minimal residual (GMRES) method converges monotonically with guarantees, but its computational cost and memory consumption increase in each iteration [Golub and Loan 89]. As a good trade-off, the stabilized bi-conjugate gradients (BiCGStab) [Barrett et al. 94] represent a mixture between the efficient BiCG and the smoothly converging GMRES; it provides a much smoother convergence and is reasonably efficient and easy to implement. For this reason, BiCGStab was used in early parameterization methods [Floater 97].

When considering dense direct solvers, the Cholesky factorization cannot be used for general matrices. Therefore, the LU factorization is typically employed since it is similarly efficient and also extends well to sparse direct methods. After factorizing the matrix $\mathbf{A}$ into the product of a lower triangular matrix $\mathbf{L}$ and an upper triangular matrix $\mathbf{U}$, it solves two triangular systems by forward and backward substitution:

$$\mathbf{A}\mathbf{x} = \mathbf{b} \quad \Leftrightarrow \quad \mathbf{L}\mathbf{U}\mathbf{x} = \mathbf{b} \quad \Leftrightarrow \quad \left\{ \begin{array}{rcl} \mathbf{L}\mathbf{y} & = & \mathbf{b}, \\ \mathbf{U}\mathbf{x} & = & \mathbf{y}. \end{array} \right.$$

In contrast to the Cholesky factorization, (partial) row and column pivoting is essential for the numerical robustness of the LU factorization.

Similarly to the Cholesky factorization, the LU factorization also preserves the bandwidth and envelope of the matrix $\mathbf{A}$. Techniques like the minimum degree algorithm generalize to non-symmetric matrices as well. However, as for dense matrices, the sparse LU factorization relies on pivoting in order to guarantee numerical stability. This means that two competing types of permutations are involved: permutations for matrix reordering and pivoting permutations for numerical robustness. Because these permutations cannot be handled separately, a trade-off between stability and fill-in minimization has to be found, resulting in a more complex factorization. Efficient implementations of sparse LU factorization are provided by the libraries SuperLU [Demmel et al. 99] and UMFPACK [Davis 04].

A.6   Comparison

In the following we compare four different linear system solvers on Laplacian and bi-Laplacian systems of varying size:

▶ CG. The iterative conjugate gradients solver from the gmm++ library [Renard and Pommier 05], using incomplete $\mathbf{LDL}^T$ factorization as preconditioner.

▶ MG. The cascading multigrid solver of [Botsch and Kobbelt 04a], which exploits SSE instructions in order to solve for up to four right-hand sides simultaneously.

▶ LL^T. The sparse Cholesky solver of the TAUCS library [Toledo et al. 03], using nested dissection matrix reordering.

▶ LU. Although our linear systems are spd, we also compare to the popular SuperLU solver [Demmel et al. 99], which is based on a sparse LU factorization.

All timings were taken on a 3.0 GHz Pentium4 running Linux.

Iterative solvers (CG, MG) have the advantage that the computation can be stopped as soon as a sufficiently small error is reached, which—in typical computer graphics applications—does not have to be the highest possible precision. In contrast, direct methods (LL^T, LU) always compute the exact solution up to numerical round-off errors, which in our application examples was more precise than required. The stopping criteria of the iterative methods were therefore chosen to yield results comparable to that achieved by direct solvers. Their residual errors were allowed to be about one order of magnitude higher than those of the direct solvers.

Table A.1 shows timings for the different solvers on Laplacian systems $\Delta \mathbf{x} = \mathbf{b}$ for 10k–50k and 100k–500k unknowns. For each solver three columns of timings are given:

▶ Setup. Computing the cotangent weights for the Laplace discretization and building the matrix structure (done per-level for MG).

▶ Precomputation. Preconditioning (CG), computing the hierarchy by mesh decimation (MG), matrix reordering and factorization (LL^T, LU).

▶ Solution. Solving the linear system for three different right-hand sides corresponding to the x, y, and z components of the free vertices $\mathbf{x}$.

Due to its effective preconditioner, which computes a sparse incomplete factorization, the iterative solver scales almost linearly with the system complexity. However, for large and thus ill-conditioned systems, it breaks down. Notice that without preconditioning the solver would not converge for the larger systems.

The experiments clearly verify the linear complexity of multigrid and sparse direct solvers. Once their sparse factorizations are pre-computed, the computational costs for actually solving the system are about the same for the LU and Cholesky solver. However, they differ significantly in the factorization performance because the numerically more robust Cholesky factorization allows for more optimizations, whereas pivoting is required for the LU factorization to guarantee robustness.

Interactive applications often require the solution of the same linear system for multiple right-hand sides (e.g., once per frame), which typically reflects the change of boundary constraints due to user interaction. For

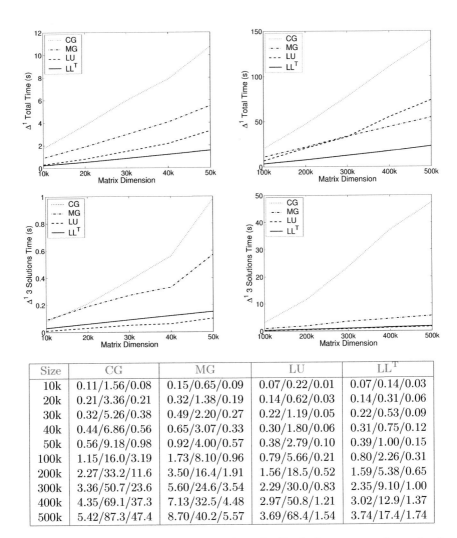

Table A.1. Comparison of different solvers for Laplacian systems $\Delta \mathbf{x} = \mathbf{b}$ of 10k–50k (left) and 100k–500k (right) free vertices $\mathbf{x}$. The three timings for each solver represent matrix setup, pre-computation, and three solutions for the x, y, and z components of $\mathbf{x}$. The graphs in the upper row show the total computation times (sum of all three timing columns). The second row plots the solution times only (third column of timings), as those typically determine the per-frame cost in interactive applications. (Image taken from [Botsch et al. 05].)

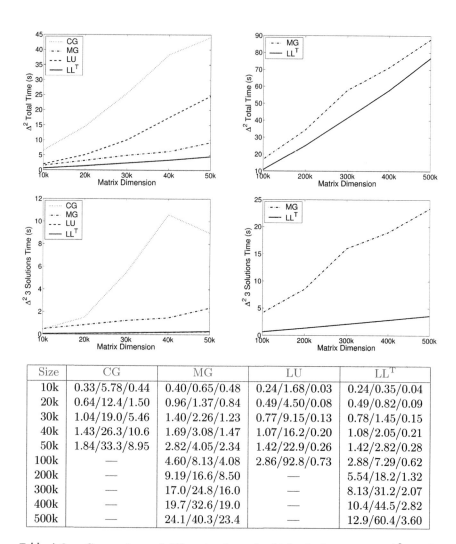

Size	CG	MG	LU	LL$^\mathrm{T}$
10k	0.33/5.78/0.44	0.40/0.65/0.48	0.24/1.68/0.03	0.24/0.35/0.04
20k	0.64/12.4/1.50	0.96/1.37/0.84	0.49/4.50/0.08	0.49/0.82/0.09
30k	1.04/19.0/5.46	1.40/2.26/1.23	0.77/9.15/0.13	0.78/1.45/0.15
40k	1.43/26.3/10.6	1.69/3.08/1.47	1.07/16.2/0.20	1.08/2.05/0.21
50k	1.84/33.3/8.95	2.82/4.05/2.34	1.42/22.9/0.26	1.42/2.82/0.28
100k	—	4.60/8.13/4.08	2.86/92.8/0.73	2.88/7.29/0.62
200k	—	9.19/16.6/8.50	—	5.54/18.2/1.32
300k	—	17.0/24.8/16.0	—	8.13/31.2/2.07
400k	—	19.7/32.6/19.0	—	10.4/44.5/2.82
500k	—	24.1/40.3/23.4	—	12.9/60.4/3.60

Table A.2. Comparison of different solvers for bi-Laplacian systems $\Delta^2 \mathbf{x} = \mathbf{b}$ of 10k–50k (left) and 100k–500k (right) free vertices $\mathbf{P}$. The three timings for each solver represent matrix setup, pre-computation, and three solutions for the components of $\mathbf{x}$. The graphs in the upper row again show the total computation times, while the second row depicts the solution times only. For the larger systems, the iterative solver and the sparse LU factorization fail to compute a solution. (Image taken from [Botsch et al. 05].)

such problems the solution times, i.e., the third columns of the timings, are more relevant, as they correspond to the per-frame computational costs. Here, the pre-computation of a sparse factorization clearly pays off and the direct solvers are superior to the multigrid method.

Table A.2 shows the same timings for bi-Laplacian systems $\Delta^2 \mathbf{x} = \mathbf{b}$. In this case, the matrix setup is more complex, the condition number is squared, and the sparsity decreases from about 7 to about 19 non-zeros per row. Due to the higher condition number, the iterative solver takes much longer and even fails to converge on large systems.

In contrast, the multigrid solver converges robustly without numerical problems. The computational costs required for the sparse factorization are proportional to the increased number of non-zeros per row. The LU factorization additionally has to incorporate pivoting for numerical stability, and it failed for larger systems. In contrast, the Cholesky factorization worked robustly in all experiments.

Besides computational cost, memory consumption is also a very important property of a linear system solver. The memory consumption of the multigrid method is mainly determined by the meshes representing the different hierarchy levels. In contrast, the memory required for the Cholesky factorization depends significantly on the sparsity of the matrix, too. On the largest example (500k unknowns) the multigrid method consumes about 1 GB memory for the Laplacian system and about 1.1 GB for the bi-Laplacian system, whereas the Cholesky solver needs about 600 MB and 1.2 GB, respectively. Hence, the direct solver would not be able to factorize large higher-order Laplacian systems on standard PCs, while the multigrid method would still succeed.

These comparisons show that direct solvers are a valuable and efficient alternative to multigrid methods, even for complex linear systems. In all experiments the sparse Cholesky solver was faster than the multigrid method, and if the system has to be solved for multiple right-hand sides, the

Method	Pros	Cons
Jacobi	easy to implement low memory cost	inefficient
conjugate gradients	easy to implement low memory cost	low performance
multigrid	highly efficient low memory cost	difficult to implement difficult to tune
sparse Cholesky	highly efficient public codes available	high memory cost implementations are complex

Table A.3. Advantages and disadvantages of different classes of linear system solvers.

Name	Location
SuperLU	http://crd.lbl.gov/~xiaoye/SuperLU/
TAUCS	http://www.tau.ac.il/~stoledo/taucs/
MUMPS	http://graal.ens-lyon.fr/MUMPS/
UMFPAK	http://www.cise.ufl.edu/research/sparse/umfpack/
OpenNL	http://alice.loria.fr/software

Table A.4. Some publicly available sparse direct solvers and APIs.

precomputation of a sparse factorization is even more beneficial. Table A.3 summarizes the conclusions of these comparisons. Finally, we mention that direct solvers with out-of-core storage [Meshar et al. 06] let the user benefit from the high efficiency of sparse direct solvers while keeping the control of the used amount of RAM. References to publicly available sparse direct solvers are given in Table A.4. The OpenNL library can be used as a convenient front end for these sparse solvers.

BIBLIOGRAPHY

[Aksoylu et al. 05] B. Aksoylu, A. Khodakovsky, and P. Schröder. "Multilevel Solvers for Unstructured Surface Meshes." *SIAM Journal on Scientific Computing* 26:4 (2005), 1146–65.

[Aleardi et al. 08] L. C. Aleardi, O. Devillers, and G. Schaeffer. "Succinct Representations of Planar Maps." *Theoretical Computer Science* 408:2–3 (2008), 174–87.

[Alliez and Desbrun 01] P. Alliez and M. Desbrun. "Valence-Driven Connectivity Encoding for 3D Meshes." *Computer Graphics Forum (Proc. Eurographics)* 20:3 (2001), 480–89.

[Alliez et al. 99] Pierre Alliez, Nathalie Laurent, Henri Sanson, and Francis Schmitt. "Mesh Approximation Using a Volume-Based Metric." In *Proc. of Pacific Graphics*, pp. 292–301. Washington, DC: IEEE Computer Society, 1999.

[Alliez et al. 02] P. Alliez, M. Meyer, and M. Desbrun. "Interactive Geometry Remeshing." *ACM Transactions on Graphics (Proc. SIGGRAPH)* 21:3 (2002), 347–54.

[Alliez et al. 03a] P. Alliez, D. Cohen-Steiner, O. Devillers, B. Lévy, and M. Desbrun. "Anisotropic Polygonal Remeshing." *ACM Transactions on Graphics (Proc. SIGGRAPH)* 22:3 (2003), 485–93.

[Alliez et al. 03b] P. Alliez, É. Colin de Verdière, O. Devillers, and M. Isenburg. "Isotropic Surface Remeshing." In *Proc. of Shape Modeling International*, pp. 49–58. Washington, DC: IEEE Computer Society, 2003.

[Alliez et al. 07] P. Alliez, G. Ucelli, C. Gotsman, and M. Attene. "Recent Advances in Remeshing of Surfaces." In *Shape Analysis and Structuring*, edited by Leila de Floriani and Michela Spagnuolo, pp. 53–82. Heidelberg: Springer-Verlag, 2007.

[Amenta et al. 99] N. Amenta, M. Bern, and D. Eppstein. "Optimal Point Placement for Mesh Smoothing." *Journal of Algorithms* 30:2 (1999), 302–22.

[Angelidis et al. 06] A. Angelidis, M.-P. Cani, G. Wyvill, and S. King. "Swirling-Sweepers: Constant Volume Modeling." *Graphical Models* 68:4 (2006), 324–32.

[Attene 10] M. Attene. "A Lightweight Approach to Repairing Digitized Polygon Meshes." *The Visual Computer* 26 (2010), To appear.

[Au et al. 07] Oscar Kin-Chung Au, Hongbo Fu, Chiew-Lan Tai, and Daniel Cohen-Or. "Handle-Aware Isolines for Scalable Shape Editing." *ACM Transactions on Graphics (Proc. SIGGRAPH)* 26:3 (2007), 83.

[Bærentzen and Aanæs 05] J. Bærentzen and H. Aanæs. "Signed Distance Computation Using the Angle Weighted Pseudo-normal." *IEEE Transactions on Visualization and Computer Graphics* 11:3 (2005), 243–53.

[Bajaj and Xu 03] C. L. Bajaj and G. Xu. "Anisotropic Diffusion of Surfaces and Functions on Surfaces." *ACM Transaction on Graphics* 22:1 (2003), 4–32.

[Barequet and Kumar 97] G. Barequet and S. Kumar. "Repairing CAD Models." In *VIS '97: Proceedings of the Conference on Visualization '97*, pp. 363–70. Washington, DC: IEEE Computer Society, 1997.

[Barequet and Sharir 95] G. Barequet and M. Sharir. "Filling Gaps in the Boundary of a Polyhedron." *Computer Aided Geometric Design* 12:2 (1995), 207–29.

[Barrett et al. 94] R. Barrett, M. Berry, T. F. Chan, J. Demmel, J. Donato, J. Dongarra, V. Eijkhout, R. Pozo, C. Romine, and H. Van der Vorst. *Templates for the Solution of Linear Systems: Building Blocks for Iterative Methods*, Second edition. Philadelphia: SIAM, 1994.

[Baumgart 72] B. G. Baumgart. "Winged-Edge Polyhedron Representation." Technical Report STAN-CS320, Computer Science Department, Stanford University, 1972.

[Ben-Chen et al. 08] M. Ben-Chen, C. Gotsman, and G. Bunin. "Conformal Flattening by Curvature Prescription and Metric Scaling." *Computer Graphics Forum (Proc. Eurographics)* 27 (2008), 449–58.

[Bendels and Klein 03] G. H. Bendels and R. Klein. "Mesh Forging: Editing of 3D-Meshes Using Implicitly Defined Occluders." In *Proc. of Eurographics Symposium on Geometry Processing*, pp. 207–17. Aire-la-Ville, Switzerland: Eurographics Association, 2003.

[Berger 07] Marcel Berger. *A Panoramic View of Riemannian Geometry.* Berlin: Springer, 2007.

[Bern and Eppstein 00] M. W. Bern and D. Eppstein. "Quadrilateral Meshing by Circle Packing." *International Journal of Computational Geometry and Applications* 10:4 (2000), 347–60.

[Bischoff and Kobbelt 03] S. Bischoff and L. Kobbelt. "Sub-Voxel Topology Control for Level-Set Surfaces." *Computer Graphics Forum (Proc. Eurographics)* 22:3 (2003), 273–80.

[Bischoff and Kobbelt 05] S. Bischoff and L. Kobbelt. "Structure Preserving CAD Model Repair." *Computer Graphics Forum (Proc. Eurographics)* 24:3 (2005), 527–36.

[Bischoff et al. 05] S. Bischoff, D. Pavic, and L. Kobbelt. "Automatic Restoration of Polygon Models." *ACM Transaction on Graphics* 24:4 (2005), 1332–52.

[Bobenko and Hoffmann 01] A. I. Bobenko and T. Hoffmann. "Conformally Symmetric Circle Packings: A Generalization of Doyle Spirals." *Experimental Mathematics* 10:1 (2001), 141–50.

[Bobenko and Schröder 05] A. I. Bobenko and P. Schröder. "Discrete Willmore Flow." In *Proc. of Eurographics Symposium on Geometry Processing*, pp. 101–110. Aire-la-Ville, Switzerland: Eurographics Association, 2005.

[Bobenko and Springborn 07] A. I. Bobenko and B. A. Springborn. "A Discrete Laplace-Beltrami Operator for Simplicial Surfaces." *Discrete and Computational Geometry* 38:4 (2007), 740–56.

[Bobenko et al. 06] A.I. Bobenko, T. Hoffmann, and B.A. Springborn. "Minimal Surfaces from Circle Patterns: Geometry from Combinatorics." *Annals of Mathematics* 164:1 (2006), 1–24.

[Boier-Martin et al. 04] I. Boier-Martin, H. Rushmeier, and J. Jin. "Parameterization of Triangle Meshes over Quadrilateral Domains." In *Proc. of Eurographics Symposium on Geometry Processing*, pp. 193–203. Aire-la-Ville, Switzerland: Eurographics Association, 2004.

[Boissonnat and Oudot 05] J.-D. Boissonnat and S. Oudot. "Provably Good Sampling and Meshing of Surfaces." *Graphical Models* 67 (2005), 405–51.

[Boissonnat and Yvinec 98] J.-D. Boissonnat and M. Yvinec. *Algorithmic Geometry*. Cambridge, UK: Cambridge University Press, 1998.

[Bolz et al. 03] J. Bolz, I. Farmer, E. Grinspun, and P. Schröder. "Sparse Matrix Solvers on the GPU: Conjugate Gradients and Multigrid." *ACM Transactions on Graphics (Proc. SIGGRAPH)* 22:3 (2003), 917–24.

[Bommes and Kobbelt 07] D. Bommes and L. Kobbelt. "Accurate Computation of Geodesic Distance Fields for Polygonal Curves on Triangle Meshes." In *Proc. of Vision, Modeling, Visualization*, pp. 151–60. Berlin: Akademische Verlagsgesellschaft, 2007.

[Bommes et al. 09] D. Bommes, H. Zimmer, and L. Kobbelt. "Mixed-Integer Quadrangulation." *ACM Transactions on Graphics (Proc. SIGGRAPH)* 28:3 (2009), 77:1–77:10.

[Bornemann and Deuflhard 96] F. A. Bornemann and P. Deuflhard. "The Cascading Multigrid Method for Elliptic Problems." *Num. Math.* 75:2 (1996), 135–52.

[Borodin et al. 02] P. Borodin, M. Novotni, and R. Klein. "Progressive Gap Closing for Mesh Repairing." In *Advances in Modelling, Animation and Rendering*, edited by J. Vince and R. Earnshaw, pp. 201–13. London: Springer Verlag, 2002.

[Borodin et al. 04] P. Borodin, G. Zachmann, and R. Klein. "Consistent Normal Orientation for Polygonal Meshes." In *Proc. of Computer Graphics International*, pp. 18–25. Washington, DC: IEEE Computer Society, 2004.

[Borouchaki and Frey 05] H. Borouchaki and P. Frey. "Simplification of Surface Mesh Using Hausdorff Envelope." *Computer Methods in Applied Mechanics and Engineering* 194:48-49 (2005), 4864–84.

[Bossen and Heckbert 96] F. J. Bossen and P. S. Heckbert. "A Pliant Method for Anisotropic Mesh Generation." In *Proc. of International Meshing Roundtable*, pp. 63–74. New York: Springer, 1996.

[Botsch and Kobbelt 03] M. Botsch and L. Kobbelt. "Multiresolution Surface Representation Based on Displacement Volumes." *Computer Graphics Forum (Proc. Eurographics)* 22:3 (2003), 483–91.

[Botsch and Kobbelt 04a] M. Botsch and L. Kobbelt. "An Intuitive Framework for Real-Time Freeform Modeling." *ACM Transactions on Graphics (Proc. SIGGRAPH)* 23:3 (2004), 630–34.

[Botsch and Kobbelt 04b] M. Botsch and L. Kobbelt. "A Remeshing Approach to Multiresolution Modeling." In *Proc. of Eurographics Symposium on Geometry Processing*, pp. 189–96. Aire-la-Ville, Switzerland: Eurographics Association, 2004.

[Botsch and Kobbelt 05] M. Botsch and L. Kobbelt. "Real-Time Shape Editing Using Radial Basis Functions." *Computer Graphics Forum (Proc. Eurographics)* 24:3 (2005), 611–21.

[Botsch and Sorkine 08] M. Botsch and O. Sorkine. "On Linear Variational Surface Deformation Methods." *IEEE Transactions on Visualization and Computer Graphics* 14:1 (2008), 213–30.

[Botsch et al. 02] M. Botsch, S. Steinberg, S. Bischoff, and L. Kobbelt. Paper presented at the OpenSG Symposium 02, 2002.

[Botsch et al. 04] M. Botsch, D. Bommes, C. Vogel, and L. Kobbelt. "GPU-Based Tolerance Volumes for Mesh Processing." In *Proc. of Pacific Graphics*. Washington, DC: IEEE Computer Society, 2004.

[Botsch et al. 05] M. Botsch, D. Bommes, and L. Kobbelt. "Efficient Linear System Solvers for Mesh Processing." *Lecture Notes in Computer Science (Proc. Mathematics of Surfaces)* 3604 (2005), 62–83.

[Botsch et al. 06a] Mario Botsch, Mark Pauly, Markus Gross, and Leif Kobbelt. "PriMo: Coupled Prisms for Intuitive Surface Modeling." In *Proc. of Eurographics Symposium on Geometry Processing*, pp. 11–20. Aire-la-Ville, Switzerland: Eurographics Association, 2006.

[Botsch et al. 06b] Mario Botsch, Mark Pauly, Christian Rössl, Stephan Bischoff, and Leif Kobbelt, 2006. Course presented at ACM SIGGRAPH 2006.

[Botsch et al. 06c] Mario Botsch, Robert Sumner, Mark Pauly, and Markus Gross. "Deformation Transfer for Detail-Preserving Surface Editing." In *Proc. of Vision, Modeling, Visualization*, pp. 357–64. Berlin: Akademische Verlagsgesellschaft, 2006.

[Botsch et al. 07] M. Botsch, M. Pauly, M. Wicke, and M. Gross. "Adaptive Space Deformations Based on Rigid Cells." *Computer Graphics Forum (Proc. Eurographics)* 26:3 (2007), 339–47.

[Botsch 05] M. Botsch. *High Quality Surface Generation and Efficient Multiresolution Editing Based on Triangle Meshes*. Aachen: Shaker Verlag, 2005.

[Bremner et al. 01] David Bremner, Ferran Hurtado, Suneeta Ramaswami, and Vera Sacristan. "Small Convex Quadrangulations of Point Sets." In *Algorithms and Computation, 12th International Symposium, ISAAC*, 2223, pp. 623–35. Berlin: Springer, 2001.

[Briggs et al. 00] W. L. Briggs, V. E. Henson, and S. F. McCormick. *A Multigrid Tutorial*, Second edition. Philadelphia: SIAM, 2000.

[Buatois et al. 09] Luc Buatois, Guillaume Caumon, and Bruno Lévy. "Concurrent Number Cruncher: A GPU Implementation of a General Sparse Linear Solver." *International Journal of Parallel, Emergent and Distributed Systems* 24:3 (2009), 205–23.

[Campagna et al. 98] S. Campagna, L. Kobbelt, and H.-P. Seidel. "Directed Edges: A Scalable Representation for Triangle Meshes." *Journal of Graphics, GPU, and Game Tools* 3:4 (1998), 1–12.

[Campen and Kobbelt 10] Marcel Campen and Leif Kobbelt. "Exact and Robust (Self-)Intersections for Polygonal Meshes." *Computer Graphics Forum (Proc. Eurographics)* 29:2 (2010), 397–406.

[Carr et al. 01] J. C. Carr, R. K. Beatson, J. B. Cherrie, T. J. Mitchell, W. R. Fright, B. C. McCallum, and T. R. Evans. "Reconstruction and Representation of 3D Objects with Radial Basis Functions." In *Proc. of ACM SIGGRAPH*, pp. 67–76. New York: ACM, 2001.

[Cazals and Pouget 03] F. Cazals and M. Pouget. "Estimating Differential Quantities Using Polynomial Fitting of Osculating Jets." In *Proc. of Eurographics Symposium on Geometry Processing*, pp. 177–87. Aire-la-Ville, Switzerland: Eurographics Association, 2003.

[Celniker and Gossard 91] G. Celniker and D. Gossard. "Deformable Curve and Surface Finite-Elements for Free-Form Shape Design." In *Proc. of ACM SIGGRAPH*, pp. 257–66. New York: ACM, 1991.

[CGAL 09] CGAL. "CGAL, Computational Geometry Algorithms Library." http://www.cgal.org, 2009.

[Chen et al. 08] Yanqing Chen, Timothy A. Davis, William W. Hager, and Sivasankaran Rajamanickam. "Algorithm 887: CHOLMOD, Supernodal Sparse Cholesky Factorization and Update/Downdate." *ACM Transactions on Mathematical Software* 35:3 (2008), 1–14.

[Chen 04] Long Chen. "Mesh Smoothing Schemes Based on Optimal Delaunay Triangulations." In *Proc. of International Meshing Roundtable*, pp. 109–20. New York: Springer, 2004.

[Chew 93] P. Chew. "Guaranteed-Quality Mesh Generation for Curved Surfaces." In *Proc. of Symposium on Computational Geometry*, pp. 274–80. New York: ACM, 1993.

[Cignoni et al. 98a] P. Cignoni, C. Montani, and R. Scopigno. "A Comparison of Mesh Simplification Algorithms." In *Computers & Graphics*, pp. 37–54. Amsterdam: Elsevier Science, 1998.

[Cignoni et al. 98b] P. Cignoni, C. Rocchini, and R. Scopigno. "Metro: Measuring Error on Simplified Surfaces." *Computer Graphics Forum* 17:2 (1998), 167–74.

[Cignoni et al. 99] P. Cignoni, C. Montani, C. Rocchini, R. Scopigno, and M. Tarini. "Preserving Attribute Values on Simplified Meshes by Resampling Detail Textures." *The Visual Computer* 15:10 (1999), 519–39.

[Cignoni et al. 04] Paolo Cignoni, Fabio Ganovelli, Enrico Gobbetti, Fabio Marton, Federico Ponchio, and Roberto Scopigno. "Adaptive Tetrapuzzles: Efficient Out-Of-Core Construction and Visualization of Gigantic Multiresolution Polygonal Models." *ACM Transactions on Graphics (Proc. SIGGRAPH)* 23:3 (2004), 796–803.

[Clarenz et al. 00] U. Clarenz, U. Diewald, and M. Rumpf. "Anisotropic Geometric Diffusion in Surface Processing." In *Proc. of IEEE Visualization*, pp. 397–406. Washington, DC: IEEE Computer Society, 2000.

[Cohen et al. 96] J. Cohen, A. Varshney, D. Manocha, G. Turk, H. Weber, P. Agarwal, F. P. Brooks, Jr., and W. Wright. "Simplification Envelopes." In *Proc. of ACM SIGGRAPH*, pp. 119–28. New York: ACM, 1996.

[Cohen et al. 98] J. Cohen, M. Olano, and D. Manocha. "Appearance-Preserving Simplification." In *Proc. of ACM SIGGRAPH*, pp. 115–22. New York: ACM, 1998.

[Cohen-Steiner and Morvan 03] D. Cohen-Steiner and J.-M. Morvan. "Restricted Delaunay Triangulations and Normal Cycle." In *Proc. of Symposium on Computational Geometry*, pp. 237–46. New York: ACM, 2003.

[Cohen-Steiner et al. 04] D. Cohen-Steiner, P. Alliez, and M. Desbrun. "Variational Shape Approximation." *ACM Transactions on Graphics (Proc. SIGGRAPH)* 23:3 (2004), 905–14.

[Coquillart 90] S. Coquillart. "Extended Free-Form Deformation: A Sculpturing Tool for 3D Geometric Modeling." In *Proc. of ACM SIGGRAPH*, pp. 187–96. New York: ACM, 1990.

[Courant 50] R. Courant. *Dirichlet's Principle, Conformal Mapping and Minimal Surfaces.* New York: Interscience, 1950.

[Coxeter 89] H. Coxeter. *Introduction to Geometry.* New York: John Wiley & Sons, 1989.

[Curless and Levoy 96] B. Curless and M. Levoy. "A Volumetric Method for Building Complex Models from Range Images." In *Proc. of ACM SIGGRAPH*, pp. 303–12. New York: ACM, 1996.

[Cuthill and McKee 69] E. Cuthill and J. McKee. "Reducing the Bandwidth of Sparse Symmetric Matrices." In *ACM '69: Proc. of the 24th ACM National Conference*, pp. 157–72. New York: ACM, 1969.

[Davis et al. 02] J. Davis, S. Marschner, M. Garr, and M. Levoy. "Filling Holes in Complex Surfaces Using Volumetric Diffusion." In *Proc. International Symposium on 3D Data Processing, Visualization, Transmission*, pp. 428–38. Washington, DC: IEEE Computer Society, 2002.

[Davis 04] T. A. Davis. "Algorithm 832: UMFPACK, An Unsymmetric-Pattern Multifrontal Method." *ACM Transactions on Mathematical Software* 30:2 (2004), 196–99.

[Davis 06] Timothy A. Davis. *Direct Methods for Sparse Linear Systems.* Philadelphia: SIAM, 2006.

[de Verdiere 90] Y. Colin de Verdiere. "Sur un nouvel invariant des graphes et un critere de planarite." *Journal of Combinatorial Theory* 50 (1990), 11–21.

[Degener et al. 03] P. Degener, J. Meseth, and R. Klein. "An Adaptable Surface Parameterization Method." In *Proc. of International Meshing Roundtable*, pp. 201–13. New York: Springer, 2003.

[Demmel et al. 99] J. W. Demmel, S. C. Eisenstat, J. R. Gilbert, X. S. Li, and J. W. H. Liu. "A Supernodal Approach to Sparse Partial Pivoting." *SIAM Journal on Matrix Analysis and Applications* 20:3 (1999), 720–55.

[Desbrun et al. 99] M. Desbrun, M. Meyer, P. Schröder, and A. H. Barr. "Implicit Fairing of Irregular Meshes Using Diffusion and Curvature Flow." In *Proc. of ACM SIGGRAPH*, pp. 317–24. New York: ACM, 1999.

[Desbrun et al. 00] M. Desbrun, M. Meyer, P. Schröder, and A. H. Barr. "Anisotropic Feature-Preserving Denoising of Height Fields and Images." In *Proc. of Graphics Interface*, pp. 145–52. Toronto: Canadian Information Processing Society, 2000.

[Desbrun et al. 02] M. Desbrun, M. Meyer, and P. Alliez. "Intrinsic Parameterizations of Surface Meshes." *Computer Graphics Forum (Proc. Eurographics)* 21:3 (2002), 209–18.

[Dey et al. 99] T. K. Dey, H. Edelsbrunner, S. Guha, and D. V. Nekhayev. "Topology Preserving Edge Contraction." *Publ. Inst. Math. (Beograd)* 66 (1999), 23–45.

[Dey et al. 05] T. K. Dey, G. Li, and T. Ray. "Polygonal Surface Remeshing with Delaunay Refinement." In *Proc. of International Meshing Roundtable*, pp. 343–61. New York: Springer, 2005.

[Dey 06] T. K. Dey. *Curve and Surface Reconstruction: Algorithms with Mathematical Analysis.* Cambridge, UK: Cambridge University Press, 2006.

[do Carmo 76] M. P. do Carmo. *Differential Geometry of Curves and Surfaces.* Englewood Cliffs, NJ: Prentice Hall, 1976.

[Douglas 31] J. Douglas. "Solution of the Problem of Plateau." *Transactions of the American Mathematical Society* 33:1 (1931), 263–321.

[Du et al. 99] Qiang Du, Vance Faber, and Max Gunzburger. "Centroidal Voronoi Tesselations: Applications and Algorithms." *SIAM Review* 41:4 (1999), 637–76.

[Duchon 77] J. Duchon. "Spline Minimizing Rotation-Invariant Semi-Norms in Sobolev Spaces." In *Constructive Theory of Functions of Several Variables*, number 571 in Lecture Notes in Mathematics, edited by W. Schempp and K. Zeller, pp. 85–100. Berlin: Springer Verlag, 1977.

[Eck et al. 95] M. Eck, T. DeRose, T. Duchamp, H. Hoppe, M. Lounsbery, and W. Stuetzle. "Multiresolution Analysis of Arbitrary Meshes." In *Proc. of ACM SIGGRAPH*, pp. 173–82. New York: ACM, 1995.

[Edelsbrunner and Shah 94] H. Edelsbrunner and N. R. Shah. "Triangulating Topological Spaces." In *Proc. of Symposium on Computational Geometry*, pp. 285–92. New York: ACM, 1994.

[Edelsbrunner 06] Herbert Edelsbrunner. *Geometry and Topology for Mesh Generation*. Cambridge, UK: Cambridge University Press, 2006.

[Eigensatz and Pauly 09] Michael Eigensatz and Mark Pauly. "Positional, Metric, and Curvature Control for Constraint-Based Surface Deformation." *Computer Graphics Forum (Proc. Eurographics)* 28:2 (2009), 551–558.

[Eigensatz et al. 08] M. Eigensatz, R. Sumner, and M. Pauly. "Curvature-Domain Shape Processing." *Computer Graphics Forum (Proc. Eurographics)* 27:2 (2008), 241–250.

[Eppstein 01] D. Eppstein. *Global Optimization of Mesh Quality*. Tutorial at the 10th International Meshing Roundtable, New York: Springer, 2001.

[Farin 97] G. Farin. *Curves and Surfaces for Computer Aided Geometric Design*, Fourth edition. San Diego: Academic Press, 1997.

[Fleishman et al. 03] S. Fleishman, I. Drori, and D. Cohen-Or. "Bilateral Mesh Denoising." *ACM Transactions on Graphics (Proc. SIGGRAPH)* 22:3 (2003), 950–53.

[Floater and Hormann 05] M. S. Floater and K. Hormann. "Surface Parameterization: A Tutorial and Survey." In *Advances in Multiresolution for Geometric Modelling, Mathematics and Visualization*, edited by N. A. Dodgson, M. S. Floater, and M. A. Sabin, pp. 157–186. Berlin: Springer, 2005.

[Floater et al. 05] Michael S. Floater, G. Kos, and M. Reimers. "Mean Value Coordinates in 3D." *Computer Aided Geometric Design* 22 (2005), 623–31.

[Floater 97] M. S. Floater. "Parametrization and Smooth Approximation of Surface Triangulations." *Computer Aided Geometric Design* 14:3 (1997), 231–50.

[Floater 03] M. S. Floater. "Mean Value Coordinates." *Computer Aided Geometric Design* 20:1 (2003), 19–27.

[Floriani and Hui 03] L. De Floriani and A. Hui. "A Scalable Data Structure for Three-Dimensional Non-Manifold Objects." In *Proc. of Eurographics Symposium on Geometry Processing*, pp. 72–82. Aire-la-Ville, Switzerland: Eurographics Association, 2003.

[Floriani and Hui 05] L. De Floriani and A. Hui. "Data Structures for Simplicial Complexes: An Analysis and a Comparison." In *Proc. of Eurographics Symposium on Geometry Processing*, pp. 119–28. Berlin: Eurographics Association, 2005.

[Foley et al. 90] James D. Foley, Andries van Dam, Steven K. Feiner, and John F. Hughes. *Computer Graphics: Principles and Practice*, Second edition. Boston, MA: Addison Welsey, 1990.

[Forsey and Bartels 88] D. Forsey and R. H. Bartels. "Hierarchical B-spline Refinement." In *Proc. of ACM SIGGRAPH*, pp. 205–12. New York: ACM, 1988.

[Forsey and Bartels 95] D. Forsey and R. H. Bartels. "Surface Fitting with Hierarchical Splines." *ACM Transaction on Graphics* 14:2 (1995), 134–61.

[Frisken et al. 00] S. Frisken, R. Perry, A. Rockwood, and T. Jones. "Adaptively Sampled Distance Fields: A General Representation of Shape for Computer Graphics." In *Proc. of ACM SIGGRAPH*, pp. 249–54. New York: ACM, 2000.

[Garland and Heckbert 97] M. Garland and P. Heckbert. "Surface Simplification Using Quadric Error Metrics." In *Proc. of ACM SIGGRAPH*, pp. 209–16. New York: ACM, 1997.

[Garland and Heckbert 98] M. Garland and P. Heckbert. "Simplifying Surfaces with Color and Texture Using Quadric Error Metrics." In *Proc. of IEEE Visualization*. Washington, DC: IEEE Computer Society, 1998.

[Gelfand and Fomin 00] I. M. Gelfand and S. V. Fomin. *Calculus of Variations*. New York: Dover Publications, 2000.

[George and Liu 81] A. George and J. W. H. Liu. *Computer Solution of Large Sparse Positive Definite Matrices*. Englewood Cliffs, NJ: Prentice Hall, 1981.

[George and Liu 89] A. George and J. W. H. Liu. "The Evolution of the Minimum Degree Ordering Algorithm." *SIAM Review* 31:1 (1989), 1–19.

[Georgii and Westermann 06] Joachim Georgii and Rüdiger Westermann. "A Multigrid Framework for Real-Time Simulation of Deformable Bodies." *Computers & Graphics* 30:3 (2006), 408–15.

[Goldfeather and Interrante 04] J. Goldfeather and V. Interrante. "A Novel Cubic-Order Algorithm for Approximating Principal Directions Vectors." *ACM Transaction on Graphics* 23:1 (2004), 45–63.

[Golub and Loan 89] G. H. Golub and C. F. Van Loan. *Matrix Computations*. Baltimore: Johns Hopkins University Press, 1989.

[Gortler et al. 06] S. J. Gortler, C. Gotsman, and D. Thurston. "Discrete One-Forms on Meshes and Applications to 3D Mesh Parameterization." *Computer Aided Geometric Design* 23:2 (2006), 83–112.

[Gotsman et al. 02] C. Gotsman, S. Gumhold, and L. Kobbelt. "Simplification and Compression of 3D Meshes." In *Tutorials on Multiresolution in Geometric Modeling*, edited by M. Floater A. Iske, E. Quak. Berlin: Springer, 2002.

[Greß and Klein 03] A. Greß and R. Klein. "Efficient Representation and Extraction of 2-Manifold IsoSurfaces Using kd-Trees." In *Proc. of Pacific Graphics*, pp. 364–376. Washington, DC: IEEE Computer Society, 2003.

[Grinspun et al. 08] E. Grinspun, M. Desbrun, P. Schröder, and M. Wardetzky, 2008. Course presented at SIGGRAPH Asia 2008.

[Gu and Yau 03] X. Gu and S.-T. Yau. "Global Conformal Surface Parameterization." In *Proc. of Eurographics Symposium on Geometry Processing*, pp. 127–37. Aire-la-Ville, Switzerland: Eurographics Association, 2003.

[Gu and Yau 04] X. Gu and S.-T. Yau. "Optimal Global Conformal Surface Parameterization for Visualization." In *Proc. of IEEE Visualization*, pp. 267–274. Washington, DC: IEEE Computer Society, 2004.

[Gu et al. 02] X. Gu, S. J. Gortler, and H. Hoppe. "Geometry Images." *ACM Transactions on Graphics (Proc. SIGGRAPH)* 21:3 (2002), 355–361.

[Guéziec et al. 01] A. Guéziec, G. Taubin, F. Lazarus, and B. Horn. "Cutting and Stitching: Converting Sets of Polygons to Manifold Surfaces." *IEEE Transactions on Visualization and Computer Graphics* 7:2 (2001), 136–51.

[Guibas and Stolfi 85] L. Guibas and J. Stolfi. "Primitives for the Manipulation of General Subdivisions and Computation of Voronoi Diagrams." *ACM Transaction on Graphics* 4:2 (1985), 74–123.

[Gumhold et al. 03] Stephan Gumhold, Pavel Borodin, and Reinhard Klein. "Intersection-Free Simplification." *International Journal of Shape Modeling* 9:2 (2003), 155–76.

[Guskov and Wood 01] I. Guskov and Z. J. Wood. "Topological Noise Removal." In *Proc. of Graphics Interface*, pp. 19–26. Toronto: Canadian Information Processing Society, 2001.

[Guskov et al. 99] I. Guskov, W. Sweldens, and P. Schröder. "Multiresolution Signal Processing for Meshes." In *Proc. of ACM SIGGRAPH*, pp. 325–34. New York: ACM, 1999.

[Guskov et al. 00] I. Guskov, K. Vidimce, W. Sweldens, and P. Schröder. "Normal Meshes." In *Proc. of ACM SIGGRAPH*, pp. 95–102. New York: ACM, 2000.

[Hackbusch 86] W. Hackbusch. *Multi-Grid Methods and Applications*. Berlin: Springer Verlag, 1986.

[Haralick et al. 87] R. M. Haralick, S. R. Sternberg, and X. Zhuang. "Image Analysis Using Mathematical Morphology." *IEEE Transactions on Pattern Analysis and Machine Intelligence* 9:4 (1987), 532–50.

[Hétroy et al. 08] F. Hétroy, S. Rey, C. Andújar, P. Brunet, and À. Vinacua. "Mesh Repair with Topology Control." Technical Report 6535, INRIA, 2008.

[Hildebrandt and Polthier 04] K. Hildebrandt and K. Polthier. "Anisotropic Filtering of Non-Linear Surface Features." *Computer Graphics Forum (Proc. Eurographics)* 23:3 (2004), 391–400.

[Hildebrandt et al. 06] K. Hildebrandt, K. Polthier, and M. Wardetzky. "On the Convergence of Metric and Geometric Properties of Polyhedral Surfaces." In *Geometriae Dedicata*, pp. 89–112. Aire-la-Ville, Switzerland: Eurographics Association, 2006.

[Ho et al. 05] C.-C. Ho, F.-C. Wu, B.-Y. Chen, Y.-Y. Chuang, and M. Ouhyoung. "Cubical Marching Squares: Adaptive Feature Preserving Surface Extraction from Volume Data." *Computer Graphics Forum (Proc. Eurographics)* 24:3 (2005), 537–545.

[Hoppe et al. 92] H. Hoppe, T. DeRose, T. Duchamp, J. McDonald, and W. Stuetzle. "Surface Reconstruction from Unorganized Points." In *Proc. of ACM SIGGRAPH*, pp. 71–78. New York: ACM, 1992.

[Hoppe et al. 93] H. Hoppe, T. DeRose, T. Duchamp, J. McDonald, and W. Stuetzle. "Mesh Optimization." In *Proc. of ACM SIGGRAPH*, pp. 19–26. New York: ACM, 1993.

[Hoppe 96] H. Hoppe. "Progressive Meshes." In *Proc. of ACM SIGGRAPH*, pp. 99–108. New York: ACM, 1996.

[Hormann and Greiner 00] K. Hormann and G. Greiner. "MIPS: An Efficient Global Parametrization Method." In *Curve and Surface Design: Saint-Malo 1999*, edited by P.-J. Laurent, P. Sablonniere, and L. Schumaker, pp. 153–62. Nashville, TN: Vanderbilt University Press, 2000.

[Hormann et al. 07] Kai Hormann, Bruno Lévy, and Alla Sheffer, 2007. Course presented at ACM SIGGRAPH 2007.

[Hsu et al. 92] W. M. Hsu, J. F. Hughes, and H. Kaufman. "Direct Manipulation of Free-Form Deformations." In *Proc. of ACM SIGGRAPH*, pp. 177–84. New York: ACM, 1992.

[Hu et al.] L. Hu, P. Sander, and H. Hoppe. In *Proc. of the Symposium on Interactive 3D Graphics and Games*. New York: ACM.

[Huang et al. 06] Jin Huang, Xiaohan Shi, Xinguo Liu, Kun Zhou, Li-Yi Wei, Shanghua Teng, Hujun Bao, Baining Guo, and Heung-Yeung Shum. "Subspace Gradient Domain Mesh Deformation." *ACM Transactions on Graphics (Proc. SIGGRAPH)* 25:3 (2006), 1126–34.

[Isenburg and Lindstrom 05] M. Isenburg and P. Lindstrom. "Streaming Meshes." In *Proc. of IEEE Visualization*, pp. 231–38. Washington, DC: IEEE Computer Society, 2005.

[Isenburg et al. 03] M. Isenburg, P. Lindstrom, S. Gumhold, and J. Snoeyink. "Large Mesh Simplification Using Processing Sequences." In *Proc. of IEEE Visualization*, pp. 465–72. Washington, DC: IEEE Computer Society, 2003.

[Jin et al. 05] Shuangshuang Jin, Robert R. Lewis, and David West. "A Comparison of Algorithms for Vertex-Normal Computation." *The Visual Computer* 21:1–2 (2005), 71–82.

[Jones et al. 03] T. R. Jones, F. Durand, and M. Desbrun. "Non-Iterative, Feature-Preserving Mesh Smoothing." *ACM Transactions on Graphics (Proc. SIGGRAPH)* 22:3 (2003), 943–49.

[Ju et al. 02] T. Ju, F. Lasasso, S. Schaefer, and J. Warren. "Dual Contouring of Hermite Data." *ACM Transactions on Graphics (Proc. SIGGRAPH)* 21:3 (2002), 339–46.

[Ju et al. 05] Tao Ju, Scott Schaefer, and Joe Warren. "Mean Value Coordinates for Closed Triangular Meshes." *ACM Transactions on Graphics (Proc. SIGGRAPH)* 24:3 (2005), 561–66.

[Ju et al. 07] Tao Ju, P. Liepa, and Joe Warren. "A General Geometric Construction of Coordinates in a Convex Simplicial Polytope." *Computer Aided Geometric Design* 24:3 (2007), 161–78.

[Ju 04] T. Ju. "Robust Repair of Polygonal Models." *ACM Transactions on Graphics (Proc. SIGGRAPH)* 23:3 (2004), 888–95.

[Ju 09] Tao Ju. "Fixing Geometric Errors on Polygonal Models: A Survey." *Journal of Computer Science and Technology* 1:24 (2009), 19–29.

[Julius et al. 05] D. Julius, V. Kraevoy, and A. Sheffer. "D-Charts: Quasi-Developable Mesh Segmentation." *Computer Graphics Forum (Proc. Eurographics)* 24:3 (2005), 581–90.

[Kälberer et al. 05] F. Kälberer, K. Polthier, U. Reitebuch, and M. Wardetzky. "FreeLence: Coding with Free Valences." *Computer Graphics Forum (Proc. Eurographics)* 24:3 (2005), 469–78.

[Kallmann and Thalmann 01] Marcelo Kallmann and Daniel Thalmann. "Star-Vertices: A Compact Representation for Planar Meshes with Adjacency Information." *Journal of Graphics, GPU, and Game Tools* 6:1 (2001), 7–18.

[Karypis and Kumar 98] G. Karypis and V. Kumar. "A Fast and High Quality Multilevel Scheme for Partitioning Irregular Graphs." *SIAM Journal on Scientific Computing* 20:1 (1998), 359–92.

[Kaufman 87] A. Kaufman. "Efficient Algorithms for 3D Scan-Conversion of Parametric Curves, Surfaces, and Volumes." In *Proc. of ACM SIGGRAPH*, pp. 171–79. New York: ACM, 1987.

[Kazhdan and Hoppe 08] Michael Kazhdan and Hugues Hoppe. "Streaming Multigrid for Gradient-Domain Operations on Large Images." *ACM Transactions on Graphics (Proc. SIGGRAPH)* 27:3 (2008), 21:1–21:10.

[Kettner 99] L. Kettner. "Using Generic Programming for Designing a Data Structure for Polyhedral Surfaces." *Computational Geometry: Theory and Applications* 13:1 (1999), 65–90.

[Kimmel and Sethian 98] R. Kimmel and J. A. Sethian. "Computing Geodesic Paths on Manifolds." *Proc. Natl. Acad. Sci. USA* 95 (1998), 8431–35.

[Klein et al. 96] R. Klein, G. Liebich, and W. Straßer. "Mesh Reduction with Error Control." In *Proc. of IEEE Visualization*, pp. 311–18. Los Alamitos, CA: IEEE Computer Society Press, 1996.

[Klincsek 80] G. Klincsek. "Minimal Triangulation of Polygonal Domains." *Annals of Discrete Mathemathics* 9 (1980), 121–23.

[Kobbelt and Botsch 04] L. Kobbelt and M. Botsch. "A Survey of Point-Based Techniques in Computer Graphics." *Computers & Graphics* 28:6 (2004), 801–14.

[Kobbelt et al. 98a] L. Kobbelt, S. Campagna, and H.-P. Seidel. "A General Framework for Mesh Decimation." In *Proc. of Graphics Interface*, pp. 43–50. Toronto: Canadian Information Processing Society, 1998.

[Kobbelt et al. 98b] L. Kobbelt, S. Campagna, J. Vorsatz, and H.-P. Seidel. "Interactive Multi-Resolution Modeling on Arbitrary Meshes." In *Proc. of ACM SIGGRAPH*, pp. 105–14. New York: ACM, 1998.

[Kobbelt et al. 99a] L. Kobbelt, J. Vorsatz, U. Labsik, and H.-P. Seidel. "A Shrink Wrapping Approach to Remeshing Polygonal Surfaces." *Computer Graphics Forum (Proc. Eurographics)* 18:3 (1999), 119–30.

[Kobbelt et al. 99b] L. Kobbelt, J. Vorsatz, and H.-P. Seidel. "Multiresolution Hierarchies on Unstructured Triangle Meshes." *Computational Geometry: Theory and Applications* 14:1–3 (1999), 5–24.

[Kobbelt et al. 00] L. Kobbelt, T. Bareuther, and H.-P. Seidel. "Multiresolution Shape Deformations for Meshes with Dynamic Vertex Connectivity." *Computer Graphics Forum (Proc. Eurographics)* 19:3 (2000), 249–60.

[Kobbelt et al. 01] L. Kobbelt, M. Botsch, U. Schwanecke, and H.-P. Seidel. "Feature Sensitive Surface Extraction from Volume Data." In *Proc. of ACM SIGGRAPH*, pp. 57–66. New York: ACM, 2001.

[Kobbelt et al. 05] L. Kobbelt, M. Botsch, U. Schwanecke, and H.-P. Seidel. "Extended Marching Cubes Implementation." http://www-i8.informatik.rwth-aachen.de/software/software.html, 2002–2005.

[Kobbelt 97] L. Kobbelt. "Discrete Fairing." In *Proc. of 7th IMA Conference on the Mathematics of Surfaces*, pp. 101–31. Berlin: Springer, 1997.

[Kobbelt 03] L. Kobbelt. "Freeform Shape Representations for Efficient Geometry Processing." Presentation at Eurographics, 2003.

[Lee et al. 98] A. W. F. Lee, W. Sweldens, P. Schröder, L. Cowsar, and D. Dobkin. "MAPS: Multiresolution Adaptive Parameterization of Surfaces." In *Proc. of ACM SIGGRAPH*, pp. 95–104. New York: ACM, 1998.

[Lee et al. 00] A. Lee, H. Moreton, and H. Hoppe. "Displaced Subdivision Surfaces." In *Proc. of ACM SIGGRAPH*, pp. 85–94. New York: ACM, 2000.

[Lévy et al. 02] Bruno Lévy, Sylvain Petitjean, Nicolas Ray, and Jérome Maillot. "Least Squares Conformal Maps for Automatic Texture Atlas Generation." *ACM Trans. Graph.* 21 (2002), 362–71.

[Liepa 03] P. Liepa. "Filling Holes in Meshes." In *Proc. of Eurographics Symposium on Geometry Processing*, pp. 200–205. Aire-la-Ville, Switzerland: Eurographics Association, 2003.

[Light 92] W. Light. *Advances in Numerical Analysis: Wavelets, Subdivision Algorithms, and Radial Basis Functions*, 2. Oxford: Clarendon Press, 1992.

[Lindstrom and Silva 01] P. Lindstrom and C. Silva. "A Memory-Insensitive Technique for Large Model Simplification." In *Proc. of IEEE Visualization*, pp. 121–6. Washington, DC: IEEE Computer Society, 2001.

[Lindstrom 00] P. Lindstrom. "Out-Of-Core Simplification of Large Polygonal Models." In *Proc. of ACM SIGGRAPH*, pp. 259–62. New York: ACM, 2000.

[Lipman et al. 04] Y. Lipman, O. Sorkine, D. Cohen-Or, D. Levin, C. Rössl, and H.-P. Seidel. "Differential Coordinates for Interactive Mesh Editing." In *Proc. of Shape Modeling International*, pp. 181–90. Washington, DC: IEEE Computer Society, 2004.

[Lipman et al. 08] Yaron Lipman, David Levin, and Daniel Cohen-Or. "Green Coordinates." *ACM Transactions on Graphics (Proc. SIGGRAPH)* 27:3 (2008), 1–10.

[Liu and Sherman 76] J. W. H. Liu and A. H. Sherman. "Comparative Analysis of the Cuthill-McKee and the Reverse Cuthill-McKee Ordering Algorithms for Sparse Matrices." *SIAM Journal on Numerical Analysis* 2:13 (1976), 198–213.

[Liu 85] J. W. H. Liu. "Modification of the Minimum-Degree Algorithm by Multiple Elimination." *ACM Trans. Math. Softw.* 11:2 (1985), 141–53.

[Lloyd 82] S. Lloyd. "Least Square Quantization in PCM." *IEEE Trans. Inform. Theory* 28 (1982), 129–37.

[Lorensen and Cline 87] W. E. Lorensen and H. E. Cline. "Marching Cubes: A High Resolution 3D Surface Construction Algorithm." In *Proc. of ACM SIGGRAPH*, pp. 163–70. New York: ACM, 1987.

[Losasso et al. 03] F. Losasso, H. Hoppe, S. Schaefer, and J. Warren. "Smooth Geometry Images." In *Proc. of Eurographics Symposium on Geometry Processing*, pp. 138–45. Aire-la-Ville, Switzerland: Eurographics Association, 2003.

[Luebke et al. 03] David Luebke, Martin Reddy, Jonathan D. Cohen, Amitabh Varshney, Benjamin Watson, and Robert Huebner. *Level of Detail for 3D Graphics*. San Francisco: Morgan Kaufmann, 2003.

[MacCracken and Joy 96] R. MacCracken and K. I. Joy. "Free-Form Deformations with Lattices of Arbitrary Topology." In *Proc. of ACM SIGGRAPH*, pp. 181–88. New York: ACM, 1996.

[Maillot et al. 93] J. Maillot, H. Yahia, and A. Verroust. "Interactive Texture Mapping." In *Proc. of ACM SIGGRAPH*, pp. 27–34. New York: ACM, 1993.

[Mantyla 88] M. Mantyla. *An Introduction to Solid Modeling*. New York: Computer Science Press, 1988.

[Marinov and Kobbelt 04] M. Marinov and L. Kobbelt. "Direct Anisotropic Quad-Dominant Remeshing." In *Proc. of Pacific Graphics*, pp. 207–16. Washington, DC: IEEE Computer Society, 2004.

[Marinov and Kobbelt 05] M. Marinov and L. Kobbelt. "Automatic Generation of Structure Preserving Multiresolution Models." *Computer Graphics Forum (Proc. Eurographics)* 24:3 (2005), 479–86.

[Marinov and Kobbelt 06] M. Marinov and L. Kobbelt. "A Robust Two-Step Procedure for Quad-Dominant Remeshing." *Computer Graphics Forum (Proc. Eurographics)* 25:3 (2006), 537–46.

[Marinov et al. 07] M. Marinov, M. Botsch, and L. Kobbelt. "GPU-Based Multiresolution Deformation Using Approximate Normal Field Reconstruction." *Journal of Graphics, GPU, and Game Tools* 12:1 (2007), 27–46.

[Max 99] Nelson Max. "Weights for Computing Vertex Normals from Facet Normals." *Journal of Graphics, GPU, and Game Tools* 4:2 (1999), 1–6.

[Meeks 81] W. H. Meeks. "A Survey of the Geometric Results in the Classical Theory of Minimal Surfaces." *Bulletin of the Brazilian Mathematical Society* 12:1 (1981), 29–86.

[Meshar et al. 06] O. Meshar, D. Irony, and S. Toledo. "An Out-Of-Core Sparse Symmetric Indefinite Factorization Method." *ACM Transactions on Mathematical Software* 32 (2006), 445–71.

[Meyer et al. 03] M. Meyer, M. Desbrun, P. Schröder, and A. H. Barr. "Discrete Differential-Geometry Operators for Triangulated 2-Manifolds." In *Visualization and Mathematics III*, edited by Hans-Christian Hege and Konrad Polthier, pp. 35–57. Heidelberg: Springer-Verlag, 2003.

[Montani et al. 94] C. Montani, R. Scateni, and R. Scopigno. "A Modified Lookup Table for Implicit Disambiguation of Marching Cubes." *The Visual Computer* 10:6 (1994), 353–55.

[Moreton and Séquin 92] H. P. Moreton and C. H. Séquin. "Functional Optimization for Fair Surface Design." In *Proc. of ACM SIGGRAPH*, pp. 167–76. New York: ACM, 1992.

[Morse et al. 01] B. S. Morse, T. S. Yoo, D. T. Chen, P. Rheingans, and K. R. Subramanian. "Interpolating Implicit Surfaces from Scattered Surface Data Using Compactly Supported Radial Basis Functions." In *Proc. of Shape Modeling International*, pp. 89–98. Washington, DC: IEEE Computer Society, 2001.

[Murali and Funkhouser 97] T. M. Murali and T. A. Funkhouser. "Consistent Solid and Boundary Representations from Arbitrary Polygonal Data." In *Proc. of the Symposium on Interactive 3D Graphics*, pp. 155–62. New York: ACM, 1997.

[Nadler 86] Edmond Nadler. "Piecewise-Linear Best L2 Approximation on Triangulations." In *Approximation Theory V*, edited by C. K. Chui, L. L. Schumaker, and J. D. Ward, pp. 499–502. New York: Academic Press, 1986.

[Nealen et al. 05] A. Nealen, O. Sorkine, M. Alexa, and D. Cohen-Or. "A Sketch-Based Interface for Detail-Preserving Mesh Editing." *ACM Transactions on Graphics (Proc. SIGGRAPH)* 24:3 (2005), 1142–47.

[Needham 94] Tristan Needham. *Visual Complex Analysis.* Oxford, UK: Oxford Press, 1994. http://www.usfca.edu/vca/.

[Nooruddin and Turk 03] F.S. Nooruddin and G. Turk. "Simplification and Repair of Polygonal Models Using Volumetric Techniques." *IEEE Transactions on Visualization and Computer Graphics* 9:2 (2003), 191–205.

[Ohtake et al. 03] Y. Ohtake, A. Belyaev, M. Alexa, G. Turk, and H.-P. Seidel. "Multi-Level Partition of Unity Implicits." *ACM Transactions on Graphics (Proc. SIGGRAPH)* 22:3 (2003), 463–70.

[Ohtake et al. 04] Y. Ohtake, A. Belyaev, and H.-P. Seidel. "3D Scattered Data Approximation with Adaptive Compactly Supported Radial Basis Functions." In *Proc. of Shape Modeling International,* pp. 31–9. Washington, DC: IEEE Computer Society, 2004.

[Okabe et al. 92] A. Okabe, B. Boots, and K. Sugihara. *Spatial Tessellations: Concepts and Applications of Voronoi Diagrams.* Chichester, UK: Wiley, 1992.

[O'Rourke 94] J. O'Rourke. *Computational Geometry in C.* Cambridge, UK: Cambridge University Press, 1994.

[Pauly et al. 00] Mark Pauly, Thomas Kollig, and Alexander Keller. "Metropolis Light Transport for Participating Media." In *Proc. of Eurographics Workshop on Rendering Techniques,* pp. 11–22. Aire-la-Ville, Switzerland: Eurographics Association, 2000.

[Pauly et al. 03] M. Pauly, R. Keiser, L. Kobbelt, and M. Gross. "Shape Modeling with Point-Sampled Geometry." *ACM Transactions on Graphics (Proc. SIGGRAPH)* 22:3 (2003), 641–50.

[Pauly et al. 05] M. Pauly, N. Mitra, J. Giesen, M. Gross, and L. J. Guibas. "Example-Based 3D Scan Completion." In *Proc. of Eurographics Symposium on Geometry Processing,* pp. 23–32. Aire-la-Ville, Switzerland: Eurographics Association, 2005.

[Pauly et al. 06] M. Pauly, L. Kobbelt, and M. Gross. "Point-Based Multi-Scale Surface Representation." *ACM Transaction on Graphics* 25:2 (2006), 177–93.

[Pauly 03] Mark Pauly. *Point Primitives for Interactive Modeling and Processing of 3D Geometry.* PhD Thesis, ETH Zurich, Konstanz, Germany: Hartung Gorre, 2003.

[Perona and Malik 90] P. Perona and J. Malik. "Scale-Space and Edge Detection Using Anisotropic Diffusion." *IEEE Transactions on Pattern Analysis and Machine Intelligence* 12:7 (1990), 629–39.

[Peters and Reif 08] J. Peters and U. Reif. *Subdivision Surfaces,* Geometry and Computing edition. Berlin: Springer Verlag, 2008.

[Petitjean 02] S. Petitjean. "A Survey of Methods for Recovering Quadrics in Triangle Meshes." *ACM Computing Surveys* 34:2 (2002), 211–62.

[Peyré and Cohen 04] G. Peyré and L. Cohen. "Surface Segmentation Using Geodesic Centroidal Tesselation." In *3DPVT '04: Proceedings of the 3D Data Processing, Visualization, and Transmission*, pp. 995–1002. Washington, DC: IEEE Computer Society, 2004.

[Piegl and Tiller 97] L. A. Piegl and W. Tiller. *The NURBS Book*, Second edition. Berlin: Springer, 1997.

[Pinkall and Polthier 93] U. Pinkall and K. Polthier. "Computing Discrete Minimal Surfaces and Their Conjugates." *Experimental Mathematics* 2:1 (1993), 15–36.

[Plateau 73] J. A. F. Plateau. *Statistique Experimentale et Theorie des Liquides Soumis aux Seules Forces Moleculaires.* Paris: Gauthier-Villars, 1873.

[Podolak and Rusinkiewicz 05] J. Podolak and S. Rusinkiewicz. "Atomic Volumes for Mesh Completion." In *Proc. of Eurographics Symposium on Geometry Processing*, pp. 33–41. Aire-la-Ville, Switzerland: Eurographics Association, 2005.

[Prautzsch et al. 02] H. Prautzsch, W. Boehm, and M. Paluszny. *Bézier and B-Spline Techniques.* Berlin: Springer Verlag, 2002.

[Press et al. 92] W. H. Press, B. P. Flannery, S. A. Teukolsky, and W. T. Vetterling. *Numerical Recipes: The Art of Scientific Computing*, Second edition. Cambrdige, UK: Cambridge University Press, 1992.

[Rado 30] T. Rado. "The Problem of Least Area and the Problem of Plateau." In *Mathematische Zeitschrift*, 32, pp. 763–96. Berlin: Springer, 1930.

[Ray and Lévy 03] Nicolas Ray and Bruno Lévy. "Hierarchical Least Squares Conformal Maps." In *Proc. of Pacific Graphics*, pp. 263–70. Washington, DC: IEEE Computer Society, 2003.

[Ray et al. 06] Nicolas Ray, Wan Chiu Li, Bruno Lévy, Alla Sheffer, and Pierre Alliez. "Periodic Global Parameterization." *ACM Transaction on Graphics* 25:4 (2006), 1460–85.

[Renard and Pommier 05] Y. Renard and J. Pommier. "Gmm++: A Generic Template Matrix C++ Library." http://www-gmm.insa-toulouse.fr/getfem/gmm_intro, 2005.

[Rivara 84] Ceciliar Rivara. "Mesh Refinement Processes Based on the Generalized Bisection of Simplices." *SIAM Journal on Numerical Analysis* 21 (1984), 604–13.

[Ross 80] K. Ross. *Elementary Analysis: The Theory of Calculus.* Berlin: Springer Verlag, 1980.

[Rossignac and Borrel 93] J. Rossignac and P. Borrel. "Multi-resolution 3D Approximations for Rendering Complex Scenes." In *Modeling in Computer Graphics*, edited by B. Falcidieno and T. L. Kunii, pp. 455–65. Berlin: Springer Verlag, 1993.

[Rudin 02] W. Rudin. *Principles of Mathematical Analysis*, Third edition. New York: McGraw-Hill, 2002.

[Rusinkiewicz 04] S. Rusinkiewicz. "Estimating Curvatures and Their Derivatives on Triangle Meshes." In *3DPVT '04: Proceedings of the 3D Data Processing, Visualization, and Transmission*, pp. 486–93. Washington, DC: IEEE Computer Society, 2004.

[Samet 94] H. Samet. *The Design and Analysis of Spatial Data Structures*. Reading, MA: Addison Wesley, 1994.

[Sander et al. 01] P. V. Sander, J. Snyder, S. J. Gortler, and H. Hoppe. "Texture Mapping Progressive Meshes." In *Proc. of ACM SIGGRAPH*, pp. 409–16. New York: ACM, 2001.

[Sander et al. 02] P. Sander, S. Gortler, J. Snyder, and H. Hoppe. "Signal-Specialized Parametrization." In *Proc. of Eurographics Workshop on Rendering Techniques*. Aire-la-Ville, Switzerland: Eurographics Association, 2002.

[Sander et al. 03] P. Sander, Z. Wood, S. Gortler, J. Snyder, and H. Hoppe. "Multi-Chart Geometry Images." In *Proc. of Eurographics Symposium on Geometry Processing*, pp. 146–55. Aire-la-Ville, Switzerland: Eurographics Association, 2003.

[Schneider and Kobbelt 00] R. Schneider and L. Kobbelt. "Generating Fair Meshes with G^1 Boundary Conditions." In *Proc. of Geometric Modeling and Processing*, pp. 251–61. Washington, DC: IEEE Computer Society, 2000.

[Schneider and Kobbelt 01] R. Schneider and L. Kobbelt. "Geometric Fairing of Irregular Meshes for Free-Form Surface Design." *Computer Aided Geometric Design* 18:4 (2001), 359–79.

[Schroeder et al. 92] W. Schroeder, J. Zarge, and W. Lorensen. "Decimation of Triangle Meshes." In *Proc. of ACM SIGGRAPH*, pp. 65–70. New York: ACM, 1992.

[Schroeder 97] W. Schroeder. "A Topology Modifying Progressive Decimation Algorithm." In *Proc. of IEEE Visualization*, pp. 205–12. Washington, DC: IEEE Computer Society, 1997.

[Sederberg and Parry 86] T. W. Sederberg and S. R. Parry. "Free-Form Deformation of Solid Geometric Models." In *Proc. of ACM SIGGRAPH*, pp. 151–59. New York: ACM, 1986.

[Sederberg et al. 03] T. Sederberg, J. Zheng, A. Bakenov, and A. Nasri. "T-splines and T-NURCCs." *ACM Transactions on Graphics (Proc. SIGGRAPH)* 22:3 (2003), 477–84.

[Sethian 96] J. Sethian. "A Fast Marching Level Set Method for Monotonically Advancing Fronts." *Proc. of the National Academy of Science* 93 (1996), 1591–95.

[Shaffer and Garland 01] E. Shaffer and M. Garland. "Efficient Adaptive Simplification of Massive Meshes." In *Proc. of IEEE Visualization*, pp. 127–34. Washington, DC: IEEE Computer Society, 2001.

[Sharf et al. 04] Andrei Sharf, Marc Alexa, and Daniel Cohen-Or. "Context-Based Surface Completion." *ACM Transactions on Graphics (Proc. SIG-GRAPH)* 23:3 (2004), 878–87.

[Sheffer and de Sturler 01] Alla Sheffer and Eric de Sturler. "Parameterization of Faceted Surfaces for Meshing Using Angle Based Flattening." *Engineering with Computers* 17:3 (2001), 326–37.

[Sheffer and Hart 02] A. Sheffer and J. C. Hart. "Seamster: Inconspicuous Low-Distortion Texture Seam Layout." In *Proc. of IEEE Visualization*, pp. 291–98. Washington, DC: IEEE Computer Society, 2002.

[Sheffer et al. 05] Alla Sheffer, Bruno Lévy, Maxim Mogilnitsky, and Alexander Bogomyakov. "ABF++: Fast and Robust Angle Based Flattening." *ACM Transaction on Graphics* 24:2 (2005), 311–30.

[Shen et al. 04] C. Shen, J. F. O'Brien, and J. R. Shewchuk. "Interpolating and Approximating Implicit Surfaces from Polygon Soup." *ACM Transactions on Graphics (Proc. SIGGRAPH)* 23:3 (2004), 896–904.

[Shewchuk 94] J. R. Shewchuk. "An Introduction to the Conjugate Gradient Method without the Agonizing Pain." Technical report, Carnegie Mellon University, 1994.

[Shewchuk 97] J. R. Shewchuk. "Delaunay Refinement Mesh Generation." Ph.D. thesis, Carnegie Mellon University, Pittsburg, 1997.

[Shewchuk 02] J. R. Shewchuk. "What Is a Good Linear Element? Interpolation, Conditioning, and Quality Measures." In *Proc. of International Meshing Roundtable*, pp. 115–26. New York: Springer, 2002.

[Shi et al. 06] Lin Shi, Yizhou Yu, Nathan Bell, and Wei-Wen Feng. "A Fast Multigrid Algorithm for Mesh Deformation." *ACM Transactions on Graphics (Proc. SIGGRAPH)* 25:3 (2006), 1108–17.

[Shi et al. 07] Xiaohan Shi, Kun Zhou, Yiying Tong, Mathieu Desbrun, Hujun Bao, and Baining Guo. "Mesh Puppetry: Cascading Optimization of Mesh Deformation with Inverse Kinematics." *ACM Transactions on Graphics (Proc. SIGGRAPH)* 26:3 (2007), 81:1–81:10.

[Shoemake and Duff 92] K. Shoemake and T. Duff. "Matrix Animation and Polar Decomposition." In *Proc. of Graphics Interface*, pp. 258–64. Toronto: Canadian Information Processing Society, 1992.

[Shreiner and Khronos OpenGL ARB Working Group 09] Dave Shreiner and Khronos OpenGL ARB Working Group. *OpenGL Programming Guide: The Official Guide to Learning OpenGL*, 7th edition. Reading, MA: Addison-Wesley Professional, 2009.

[Sorkine and Alexa 07] O. Sorkine and M. Alexa. "As-Rigid-As-Possible Surface Modeling." In *Proc. of Eurographics Symposium on Geometry Processing*. Aire-la-Ville, Switzerland: Eurographics Association, 2007.

[Sorkine et al. 04] O. Sorkine, D. Cohen-Or, Y. Lipman, M. Alexa, C. Rössl, and H.-P. Seidel. "Laplacian Surface Editing." In *Proc. of Eurographics Symposium on Geometry Processing*, pp. 179–88. Aire-la-Ville, Switzerland: Eurographics Association, 2004.

[Springborn et al. 08] Boris Springborn, Peter Schröder, and Ulrich Pinkall. "Conformal Equivalence of Triangle Meshes." *ACM Transactions on Graphics (Proc. SIGGRAPH)* 27:3 (2008), 1–11.

[Steiner and Fischer 05] D. Steiner and A. Fischer. "Planar Parameterization for Closed Manifold Genus-g Meshes Using Any Type of Positive Weights." *JCISE* 5:2 (2005), 118–26.

[Sumner and Popović 04] R. W. Sumner and J. Popović. "Deformation Transfer for Triangle Meshes." *ACM Transactions on Graphics (Proc. SIGGRAPH)* 23:3 (2004), 399–405.

[Sumner et al. 07] R. Sumner, J. Schmid, and M. Pauly. "Embedded Deformation for Shape Manipulation." *ACM Transactions on Graphics (Proc. SIGGRAPH)* 26:3 (2007), 80:1–80:7.

[Surazhsky and Gotsman 03] V. Surazhsky and C. Gotsman. "Explicit Surface Remeshing." In *Proc. of Eurographics Symposium on Geometry Processing,* pp. 20–30. Aire-la-Ville, Switzerland: Eurographics Association, 2003.

[Surazhsky et al. 03] V. Surazhsky, P. Alliez, and C. Gotsman. "Isotropic Remeshing of Surfaces: A Local Parameterization Approach." In *Proc. of International Meshing Roundtable,* pp. 215–24. New York: Springer, 2003.

[Surazhsky et al. 05] Vitaly Surazhsky, Tatiana Surazhsky, Danil Kirsanov, Steven J. Gortler, and Hugues Hoppe. "Fast Exact and Approximate Geodesics on Meshes." *ACM Transactions on Graphics (Proc. SIGGRAPH)* 24:3 (2005), 553–60.

[Szymczak et al. 02] A. Szymczak, D. King, and J. Rossignac. "Piecewise Regular Meshes: Construction and Compression." *Graphical Models* 64:3–4 (2002), 183–98.

[Taubin 95] G. Taubin. "A Signal Processing Approach to Fair Surface Design." In *Proc. of ACM SIGGRAPH,* pp. 351–58. New York: ACM, 1995.

[Taubin 00] G. Taubin. "Geometric Signal Processing on Polygonal Meshes." In *Eurographics 2000 State of the Art Report.* Aire-la-Ville, Switzerland: Eurographics Association, 2000.

[Terzopoulos et al. 87] D. Terzopoulos, J. Platt, A. Barr, and K. Fleischer. "Elastically Deformable Models." In *Proc. of ACM SIGGRAPH,* pp. 205–14. New York: ACM, 1987.

[Theisel et al. 04] H. Theisel, C. Rössl, R. Zayer, and H.-P. Seidel. "Normal Based Estimation of the Curvature Tensor for Triangular Meshes." In *Proc. of Pacific Graphics,* pp. 288–97. Washington, DC: IEEE Computer Society, 2004.

[Toledo et al. 03] S. Toledo, D. Chen, and V. Rotkin. "TAUCS: A Library of Sparse Linear Solvers." http://www.tau.ac.il/~stoledo/taucs, 2003.

[Tomasi and Manduchi 98] C. Tomasi and R. Manduchi. "Bilateral Filtering for Gray and Color Images." In *ICCV '98: Proc. of the 6th International Conference on Computer Vision,* pp. 839–46. Washington, DC: IEEE Computer Society, 1998.

[Tong et al. 03] Y. Tong, S. Lombeyda, A. N. Hirani, and M. Desbrun. "Discrete Multiscale Vector Field Decomposition." *ACM Transactions on Graphics (Proc. SIGGRAPH)* 22:3 (2003), 445–52.

[Tong et al. 06] Y. Tong, P. Alliez, D. Cohen-Steiner, and M. Desbrun. "Designing Quadrangulations with Discrete Harmonic Forms." In *Proc. of Eurographics Symposium on Geometry Processing*, pp. 201–10. Aire-la-Ville, Switzerland: Eurographics Association, 2006.

[Touma and Gotsman 98] C. Touma and C. Gotsman. "Triangle Mesh Compression." In *Proc. of Graphics Interface*, pp. 26–34. Toronto: Canadian Information Processing Society, 1998.

[Trefethen and Bau 97] L. N. Trefethen and D. Bau. *Numerical Linear Algebra*. Philadelphia: SIAM, 1997.

[Turk and Levoy 94] G. Turk and M. Levoy. "Zippered Polygon Meshes from Range Images." In *Proc. of ACM SIGGRAPH*, pp. 311–18. New York: ACM, 1994.

[Tutte 60] W. Tutte. "Convex Representation of Graphs." *Proc. London Math. Soc.* 10 (1960), 304–20.

[Valette and Chassery 04] S. Valette and J.-M. Chassery. "Approximated Centroidal Voronoi Diagrams for Uniform Polygonal Mesh Coarsening." *Computer Graphics Forum (Proc. Eurographics)* 23:3 (2004), 381–89.

[Vallet and Lévy 08] Bruno Vallet and Bruno Lévy. "Spectral Geometry Processing with Manifold Harmonics." *Computer Graphics Forum (Proc. Eurographics)* 27:2 (2008), 251–60.

[von Funck et al. 06] Wolfram von Funck, Holger Theisel, and Hans-Peter Seidel. "Vector Field-Based Shape Deformations." *ACM Transactions on Graphics (Proc. SIGGRAPH)* 25:3 (2006), 1118–25.

[Vorsatz et al. 03] J. Vorsatz, C. Rössl, and H.-P. Seidel. "Dynamic Remeshing and Applications." In *Proc. of Symposium on Solid Modeling and Applications*, pp. 167–75. New York: ACM, 2003.

[Wardetzky et al. 07] M. Wardetzky, S. Mathur, F. Kälberer, and E. Grinspun. "Discrete Laplace Operators: No Free Lunch." In *Proc. of Eurographics Symposium on Geometry Processing*, pp. 33–37. Aire-la-Ville, Switzerland: Eurographics Association, 2007.

[Welch and Witkin 92] W. Welch and A. Witkin. "Variational Surface Modeling." In *Proc. of ACM SIGGRAPH*, pp. 157–66. New York: ACM, 1992.

[Welch and Witkin 94] W. Welch and A. Witkin. "Free-Form Shape Design Using Triangulated Surfaces." In *Proc. of ACM SIGGRAPH*, pp. 247–56. New York: ACM, 1994.

[Wendland 05] H. Wendland. *Scattered Data Approximation*. Cambridge, UK: Cambridge University Press, 2005.

[Westermann et al. 99] R. Westermann, L. Kobbelt, and T. Ertl. "Real-Time Exploration of Regular Volume Data by Adaptive Reconstruction of Iso-Surfaces." *The Visual Computer* 15 (1999), 100–111.

[Wood et al. 04] Z. Wood, H. Hoppe, M. Desbrun, and P. Schröder. "Removing Excess Topology from Isosurfaces." *ACM Transaction on Graphics* 23:2 (2004), 190–208.

[Wu and Kobbelt 03] J. Wu and L. Kobbelt. "Piecewise Linear Approximation of Signed Distance Fields." In *Proc. of Vision, Modeling, Visualization*, pp. 513–20. Berlin: Akademische Verlagsgesellschaft, 2003.

[Wu and Kobbelt 04] J. Wu and L. Kobbelt. "A Stream Algorithm for the Decimation of Massive Meshes." In *Proc. of Graphics Interface*, pp. 185–92. Toronto: Canadian Information Processing Society, 2004.

[Wu and Kobbelt 05] J. Wu and L. Kobbelt. "Structure Recovery via Hybrid Variational Surface Approximation." *Computer Graphics Forum (Proc. Eurographics)* 24:3 (2005), 277–84.

[Yan et al. 06] Dong-Ming Yan, Yang Liu, and Wenping Wang. "Quadric Surface Extraction by Variational Shape Approximation." In *Proceedings of Geometric Modeling and Processing 2006*, pp. 73–86. Berlin: Springer, 2006.

[Yan et al. 09] Dong-Ming Yan, Bruno Lévy, Yang Liu, Feng Sun, and Wenping Wang. "Isotropic Remeshing with Fast and Exact Computation of Restricted Voronoi Diagram." *Computer Graphics Forum (Proc. Symp. Geometry Processing)* 28:5 (2009), 1445–54.

[Yang et al. 08] Yong-Liang Yang, Junho Kim, Feng Luo, and Shi-Min Hu. "Optimal Surface Parameterization Using Inverse Curvature Map." *IEEE Transactions on Visualization and Computer Graphics* 14:4 (2008), 1054–66.

[Yu et al. 04] Y. Yu, K. Zhou, D. Xu, X. Shi, H. Bao, B. Guo, and H.-Y. Shum. "Mesh Editing with Poisson-Based Gradient Field Manipulation." *ACM Transactions on Graphics (Proc. SIGGRAPH)* 23:3 (2004), 644–51.

[Zayer et al. 05a] R. Zayer, C. Rössl, Z. Karni, and H.-P. Seidel. "Harmonic Guidance for Surface Deformation." *Computer Graphics Forum (Proc. Eurographics)* 24:3 (2005), 601–10.

[Zayer et al. 05b] R. Zayer, C. Rössl, and H.-P. Seidel. "Discrete Tensorial Quasi-Harmonic Maps." In *Proc. of Shape Modeling International*, pp. 276–85. Washington, DC: IEEE Computer Society, 2005.

[Zayer et al. 05c] Rhaleb Zayer, Christian Rössl, and Hans-Peter Seidel. "Setting the Boundary Free: A Composite Approach to Surface Parameterization." In *SGP '05: Proceedings of the Symposium on Geometry Processing*. Aire-la-Ville, Switzerland: Eurographics Association, 2005. Article no. 91.

[Zayer et al. 07] Rhaleb Zayer, Bruno Lévy, and Hans-Peter Seidel. "Linear Angle Based Parameterization." In *Proc. of Eurographics Symposium on Geometry Processing*, pp. 135–142. Aire-la-Ville, Switzerland: Eurographics Association, 2007.

[Zhou et al. 05] K. Zhou, J. Huang, J. Snyder, X. Liu, H. Bao, B. Guo, and H.-Y. Shum. "Large Mesh Deformation Using the Volumetric Graph Laplacian." *ACM Transactions on Graphics (Proc. SIGGRAPH)* 24:3 (2005), 496–503.

[Zhu et al. 10] Yongning Zhu, Eftychios Sifakis, Joseph Teran, and Achi Brandt. "An Efficient Multigrid Method for the Simulation of High-Resolution Elastic Solids." *ACM Transaction on Graphics* 29:2 (2010), 16:1–16:18.

[Zorin et al. 97] D. Zorin, P. Schröder, and W. Sweldens. "Interactive Multiresolution Mesh Editing." In *Proc. of ACM SIGGRAPH*, pp. 259–68. New York: ACM, 1997.

[Zorin et al. 00] D. Zorin, P. Schröder, T. DeRose, L. Kobbelt, A. Levin, and W. Sweldens. "Subdivision for Modeling and Animation." In *ACM SIGGRAPH 2000 Courses*. New York: ACM, 2000.

INDEX

2-manifold surface, 4, 11

adaptive octree, 15, 149
angle-based flattening (ABF), 77
anisotropic diffusion flow, 62
anisotropic element, 86
anisotropy ellipse, 36, 80
approximation, 111, 122
approximation power, 5
arc length, 30
artifact, 131, 132
    cap, 139
    complex edge, 132, 142, 148
    disconnected component, 138
    gap, 132, 142
    handle, 134, 143, 145
    hole, 132, 135, 143, 145
    inconsistent normal orientation, 134
    intersecting patch, 137
    island, 135, 141
    needle, 139
    non manifold, 142
    overlap, 132, 134, 135, 142
    self-intersection, 132, 136
    singular vertex, 134, 142, 148
    thin bridge, 145
    triangle flip, 139
    zero area, 139

bandwidth of a matrix, 193
barycentric cell, 41
barycentric coordinates, 10
    generalized, 172
barycentric interpolation, 161
barycentric mapping, 67
bending, 155
bending energy, 135
bi-conjugate gradient, 196
Bi-Laplacian, 156
bilateral filtering, 62
binary grid, 137
boundary loop, 143, 149
BSP-tree, 134, 137, 144, 147, 148

calculus of variations, 58, 156, 165, 174
cap triangles, 139
Cartesian grid, 134, 138, 148
Cauchy-Riemann equations, 74
centroidal Voronoi tessellation, 96, 97
Cholesky factorization, 193

clustering, 113
complex edge, 12, 21, 133
complex vertex, 12, 133
compressed column storage format, 185
compressed row storage format, 185
condition number, 189
conformal energy, 74, 75
conformal mapping, 71, 79
conjugate gradients solver, 189
conjugate gradients squared, 196
consistent normal orientation, 139
constructive solid geometry, 13
control cage, 172
control grid, 170
control mesh, 8, 9
curvature, 30, 37, 46
    discrete curvature tensor, 47
    discrete Gaussian curvature, 47
    discrete mean curvature, 47
    discrete principal curvatures, 47
    Gaussian, 38
    lines of curvature, 105
    maximum and minimum, 38
    mean curvature, 38
    mean curvature normal, 40, 56
    of a curve, 30
    principal curvatures, 38, 60, 105
curvature tensor, 37, 38, 47, 105
Cuthill-McKee reordering, 194

decimation, 115
deformation
    cage-based, 172
    differential coordinates, 164
    freeform deformation (FFD), 169
    gradient-based, 164
    Laplacian-based, 166
    multi-scale, 157
    nonlinear, 178
    radial basis function, 173
    shell-based, 155, 167
    space deformation, 152, 170
    surface-based, 152
deformation gradient, 167
deformation transfer, 163
Delaunay refinement, 92
Delaunay triangulation, 89, 90, 134

denoising, 49
developable surface, 79
differential coordinates, 164
diffusion equation, 55
dihedral angle, 140
dilation operator, 145
directed-edge data structure, 27
Dirichlet energy, 58, 74, 75
discrete differential operator, 40, 69, 79
displacement function, 151
displacement vectors, 160
displacement volumes, 163
distortion analysis, 78
divergence operator, discrete, 46
dual contouring, 18, 138, 146
dynamic programming, 140

edge collapse, 101, 117, 120, 121, 128, 130
edge flip, 101
edge split, 101
eigenfunction, of an operator, 52
eigenvector, of a matrix, 52
element shape
    isotropic, anisotropic, 86
elliptical point, 39
empty sphere property, 91
envelope of a matrix, 193
equiareal mapping, 79
erosion operator, 145
error quadric, 115, 120
error tolerance, 145
Euler characteristic, 12, 117
Euler formula, 12
Euler operator, 117
Euler theorem, 38
Euler-Lagrange equation, 59, 156
excess interior geometry, 136
explicit Euler integration, 55
extended Marching Cubes, 18
extraordinary vertex, 87

face degree, 25
face set, 22
fairing, 49, 57, 140
feature preservation, remeshing, 102
feature-sensitive, 145

file format, 23
Fourier transform, 50
frequency decomposition, 158
frequency domain, 51
fundamental form
    first, 35, 79, 80
    second, 37

gap, 137
Gauss-Seidel solver, 187
Gaussian curvature, 38
generalized barycentric coordinates, 172
genus, 138
geometric hashing, 142
gradient, 33, 43, 72
gradient-based deformation, 164
Green-Lagrange strain, 81

halfedge collapse, 117
halfedge data structure, 25
harmonic function, 75, 153
harmonic map, 74
Hausdorff distance, 121
heat equation, 55
hinge map, 110
hole filling, 136, 140, 141, 149
hyperbolic point, 39

illegal edge collapse, 118
implicit Euler integration, 55
implicit surface representation, 1, 13
indexed face set, 22
integration
    explicit Euler, 55
    implicit Euler, 55
irregular mesh, 87
irregular vertex, 87
isometric mapping, 79
isometry, 30
isosurface extraction
    dual contouring, 18
    extended Marching Cubes, 18
    Marching Cubes, 16
isotropic element, 86

Jacobi solver, 187
Jacobian matrix, 34, 35, 79

KD-tree, 134
Krylov space, 189

Laplace
    continuous, 40
    coordinates, 166
    cotangent weights, 44
    discrete, 44
    discrete operator, 182
    discretizations, 61
    for parameterization, 69
    higher-order, 57
    higher-order operator, 182
    higher-order PDE, 182
    linear system, 181
    matrix, 182
    matrix representation, 182
    operator, 39, 69
    uniform weights, 44
Laplacian smoothing, 56
Laplacian surface editing, 166
least squares conformal maps, 73
least-norm solution, 171
length of a curve, 35
linear solvers
    BiCG, GMRES, BiCGStab, 196
    conjugate gradients, 189
    Jacobi, Gauss-Seidel, 187
    LU factorization, 197
    multigrid, 190
    sparse Cholesky, 193
lines of curvatures, 106
link condition, 118
Lloyd relaxation, clustering, 97, 123
local frame encoding, 160
low-pass filter, 51, 53
LU factorization, 197

manifold, 23, 138, 147
manifold harmonics, 51
manifold surface, 4, 11
Marching Cubes, 16, 138, 145
matrix format
    block compressed row storage, 186
    compressed column storage, 185
    compressed row storage, 185
    Triplet, TRIAD, 184

matrix reordering, 194
mean curvature, 38
mean curvature flow, 56
mean curvature normal, 40, 56
mean value coordinates, 48, 69, 70
medial axis, 93
membrane energy, 58
membrane surface, 58
mesh
    2-manifold, 21
    connectivity, 23
    edge, 21
    face, 21
    irregular, 21
    local neighborhood, 21
    regular, 21
    semi-regular, 21
    traversal, 23
    vertex, 21, 23
mesh data structures
    directed edges, 27
    edge-based, 24
    face-based, 22
    halfedge-based, 25
mesh traversal, 23
metric tensor, 35, 36, 79
minimal surface, 58
minimum degree reordering, 194
minimum spanning tree, 139
minimum variation surfaces, 60
mixed Voronoi cell, 41
morphological operator, 134, 145
most isometric parameterization, 81
multi-scale decomposition, 159
multi-scale deformation, 157
multigrid solver, 190
multiple-right-hand-side problem, 157

natural frequencies, vibrations, 53
needle triangles, 139
nested dissection reordering, 196
non-manifold vertex, edge, 12, 133
nonlinear smoothing, 62
normal consistency, 140
normal curvature, 37
normal mapping, 64
normal orientation, 136

normal vector
    of a curve, 30
    of a surface, 34
    of a triangle, 42
    of a vertex, 42
NURBS, 8, 137

octree, 134, 145
one-ring neighborhood, 23
osculating circle, 31
out-of-core decimation, 127
overlap, 137

parabolic point, 39
parametric surface, 7, 31, 63
parametric surface representation, 1, 7
Phong shading, 161
polar decomposition, 168
polar map, 110
polygon soup, 22, 136
principal curvatures, 38, 60, 105
principle of simplest shape, 57

quad-edge data structure, 24
quadric error metric, 115, 120, 128, 147

radial basis function, 173
range scans, 135
ray-casting, 137
reach, 93
region growing, 144
regular, 14
regular curve, 30
regular mesh, 88
regular parameterization, 34
relaxation solvers, 187
repair, 131
residual equation, 187
restricted Delaunay triangulation, 91

second fundamental form, 37
self-intersection, 133
semiregular mesh, 87
shared-vertex data structure, 22
shell-based deformation, 155
shell-energy, 155
signal-specialized parameterization, 82

signed distance function, 14, 136
similarity transform, 72, 168
simplicial complex, 10
simplification, 111, 115
singular value decomposition, 168
singular vertex, 21, 133
skew-symmetric matrix, 168
smooth triangulation, 140
smoothing, 49
sparse Cholesky solver, 193
sparse matrix, 184
spectral analysis, 50
spline function, 8, 137, 170
STL, 22
stretching, 155
subdivision surface, 9
supporting plane, 146
surface area, 36, 75
surface Delaunay ball, 93

tangent vector
    of a curve, 29
    of a surface, 34
texture mapping, 64
theorema egregium, 39
thin-plate energy, 60
thin-shell energy, 155

three-color octree, 15
tolerance, 113, 115, 119
topology simplification, 143
triad data structure, 184
triangle soup, 22, 136, 145
triangle strip, 132, 142
Triplet/TRIAD matrix format, 184
Tutte's theorem, 67

umbilical point, 38, 105
umbilics, 105

variational calculus, 58, 156, 165, 174
variational shape approximation, 122
vertex clustering, 113
vertex contraction, 119
vertex insertion, 117
vertex removal, 117
vertex split, 117
Voronoi cell, 41
Voronoi diagram, 89
voxel, 138, 145, 149

watertight, 134, 138, 139
winged-edge data structure, 24

zippering, 135

9781568814261